# HUMAN ADAPTATION
# AND ITS FAILURES

# PERSONALITY AND PSYCHOPATHOLOGY:

*A Series of Texts, Monographs, and Treatises*

# HUMAN ADAPTATION
# AND ITS FAILURES

Leslie Phillips

INSTITUTE OF HUMAN SCIENCES AND
DEPARTMENT OF PSYCHOLOGY
BOSTON COLLEGE
CHESTNUT HILL, MASSACHUSETTS

1968

 ACADEMIC PRESS   New York and London

ACADEMIC PRESS INC.
111 Fifth Avenue, New York, New York 10003

*United Kingdom Edition published by*
ACADEMIC PRESS INC. (LONDON) LTD.
Berkeley Square House, London W.1

LIBRARY OF CONGRESS CATALOG CARD NUMBER: 68–14646

PRINTED IN THE UNITED STATES OF AMERICA

To Dit, Dave, and Ken

# PREFACE

This book is the product of a decade and a half of research and writing concerned with the nature of psychopathology and its relation to normal behavior. It brings together a body of work on a variety of theoretical issues undertaken with a number of co-workers. Yet, it is more than a review of individual studies. It attempts to place this research within the context of what is known in the broad field of psychological normality and mental disorder. In writing this book, however, I soon found that more was required than a synthesis of our own data with an established body of knowledge. A coherent and generally accepted conceptual framework simply does not exist in psychopathology, for the field is divided among a set of competing ideologies. There is a disease model of psychiatric disorder, but there are also psychodynamic as well as socio-cultural models of deviant behavior. The subject matter in this field is even further fragmented. The literature that relates social class factors to the prevalence and form of psychiatric disorder is, for example, almost totally dissociated from that concerned with the influence of culture on disorder.

The attempt to relate our findings to the general literature has involved, therefore, more than a search for a relevant body of knowledge. It has required that the literature itself be organized within a coherent conceptual framework. The framework adopted is a psychosocial or interactionist one which proposes that appropriate as well as nonconstructive patterns of adaptation in society are based on both psychological and environmental factors.

Many people have said that psychiatric disorder is best understood in terms of the social context in which it arises. The position adopted here is that we must also consider the individual's coping resources if we are to make some reasonable estimate of his potential for a normal or deviant way of life. How coping potential is to be measured has been a particular concern of mine for a long time. As a consequence, a good deal of space in this book is devoted to this topic. How the individual's coping resources and the conditions of community life affect his pattern of participation in society are the main themes around which this book is written.

LESLIE PHILLIPS

*Shrewsbury, Massachusetts*
*January, 1968*

# ACKNOWLEDGMENTS

In writing this book, I have borrowed from many sources. As a consequence, I am obligated to many people, not all of whom are aware of their contribution. I want to take this opportunity to acknowledge my debts to them.

A glance at the references at the end of each chapter will indicate the many contributions that my co-workers have made to the fashioning of this book. I am particularly indebted to Edward Zigler and Juris Draguns with whom I have worked most consistently over the past several years. The reader will also have no difficulty in recognizing the influence of the late Heinz Werner on the theoretical framework in which this work is couched.

This is an opportunity to warmly acknowledge the support for my research that Dr. Bardwell H. Flower provided as Superintendent of Worcester State Hospital. Throughout his administration Dr. Flower has encouraged the atmosphere of study and investigation that has been traditional at his hospital. The research program reported on here would also not have been possible without long-term funding by the United States National Institute of Mental Health. During the last five years, a grant-in-aid from this agency, MH-06369, has provided part of the financing that made this research possible.

I most appreciate the patient typing and retyping of innumerable chapter drafts first by Mrs. Madeleine Blair and later by Mrs. Carolyn Pezanelli. Mrs. Marian Gurnick was most helpful in preparing the references for each chapter.

I also welcome this opportunity to acknowledge publicly the depth of my appreciation for the efforts that William Vogel made toward the completion of this manuscript. Dr. Vogel read innumerable drafts of chapters, bringing to bear a razorsharp mind to cut through their obscurities. It was surprising to find that such a warm person could act as so stern a taskmaster, but whatever clarity is to be found in the text is owed in good part to his analytic powers.

Finally, a special debt is owed to both my wife and children who accepted this book with such grace as an uninvited house guest during the years in which it was written. I am most impressed and deeply appreciative that my wife could continue to live not only with the book but with me in this time of trial.

I wish to express my appreciation for permission to quote from the following articles and books:
Barbu, Z. *Problems of historical psychology*. New York: Grove Press, 1960.

Fishwick, M. The twist: brave new whirl. *Saturday Review*, March, 1962, 8–10.

Freud, S. Some psychological consequences of the anatomical distinction between the sexes. *International Journal of Psychoanalysis*, 1927, **8.**, 133–142.

Hyman H. H. The value systems of different classes: A social psychological contribution to the analysis of stratification. In Bendix, R. & Lipset, S. M. (Eds.) *Class, Status and Power.* Glencoe, Ill.: Free Press, 1953. Pp. 426–442.

Knupfer, G. Portrait of the underdog. *Public Opinion Quarterly*, 1947, **11**, 103–114.

Leighton, D., Harding, J. S., Macklin, D. B., MacMillan, A. M., & Leighton, A. H., *The character of danger. The Stirling County study of psychiatric disorder and socio-cultural environment.* Vol. III. New York: Basic Books, 1963.

MacIver, R. M. *Society.* New York: Farrer and Rinehart, 1937.

May, H. *The end of American innocence.* New York: Alfred A. Knopf, 1959.

Merton, R. K. *Social theory and social structure.* Glencoe, Ill.: Free Press, 1957.

Mills, C. W., *The sociological imagination.* New York: Oxford University Press, 1959.

Money, J., Hampson, Joan G., & Hampson, J. L. Imprinting and the establishment of gender role. *American Medical Association Archives of Neurology and Psychiatry*, 1957, **77**, 333–336.

Peters, R. S. *The concept of motivation.* London: Routledge and Kegan Paul and New York: Humanities Press, 1958.

Piaget, J. *The origins of intelligence.* New York: International Universities Press, 1952.

Roe, A. *The psychology of occupations.* New York: Wiley, 1956.

Srole, L., Langner, T. S., Michael, S. T., Opler, M. K., & Rennie, T. A. C. *Mental health in the metropolis: Midtown Manhattan Study*, Vol. 1. New York: McGraw Hill, 1962.

Warner, W. L. & Lunt, P. S., *The social life of the modern community.* New Haven: Yale University Press, 1941.

Warner, W. L., Meeker, M. G., and Eells, K. *Social class in America.* New York: Harper, 1960.

Wheelis, A. *The quest for identity.* New York: W. W. Norton and London: Victor Gallancz, Lawrence Pollinger, 1958.

White, R. W. Competence and the psychosexual stages of development. In M. R. Jones (Ed.) *Nebraska symposium on motivation*, Lincoln, Neb.: University of Nebraska Press, 1960. Pp. 97–141.

# CONTENTS

# HUMAN ADAPTATION
# AND ITS FAILURES

# 1/SOME KEY CONCEPTS

In this book we shall explore a set of related propositions that concern the field traditionally conceived as comprising psychiatric normality and psychopathology, a field considered here under the title "human adaptation and its failures." The term "human adaptation" refers to a person's response to the complexities of living in society. The intent is to consider pathological reactions, that is, unsuccessful and potentially destructive responses to the human condition, in the context of more positive, adaptive forms of human living. A general theory of success and failure in human adaptation would provide a unitary framework within which both effective and ineffective participation in society can be understood. This book offers such a theory and presents the evidence that supports it.

What constitutes effective adaptation? There is no one answer to this question. The most general requirement is that the person meet at least the minimal expectations set by society. Expectations differ with age and become increasingly complex as the individual grows up. The infant will be provided total care. But at each successive stage less and less will be done for the person while more and more will be expected of him. He is expected to pass from a stage of complete dependence to one not only of independence, but of acceptance of responsibility for the welfare of others.

With growth, the life-styles of the two sexes increasingly diverge. Both boys and girls are expected to become responsible citizens, but men are prodded to give major emphasis to work and career, women to be concerned with home and family. These commitments, of course, differ only in their relative emphases. Most women will be gainfully employed at some time in their lives, and most men will marry, support a family, and be concerned about its welfare. Finally, no person can successfully adapt in society by living out some single role. Life is too involved for that. With

1

each new stage of life new roles are expected to be added to the person's repertoire. The child entering school adds the pupil role to that of "mother's helper," younger or older sibling, that of friend to boys or girls outside the family, and perhaps others. With growth, some roles are expected to be dropped, but others become increasingly intricate and through the mature years more are always added than are relinquished.

In our view adaptation implies two divergent yet complementary forms of response to the human environment. The first is to accept and respond effectively to those societal expectations that confront each person according to his age and sex. Included here, for example, are entering school and mastering its subject matter, the forming of friendships, and later, dating, courtship, and marriage. In this first sense, adaptation implies a conformity to society's expectations for behavior. In another sense, however, adaptation means more than a simple acceptance of societal norms. It implies a flexibility and effectiveness in meeting novel and potentially disruptive conditions, and of imposing one's own direction on the course of events. In this sense, adaptation implies that the person makes use of opportunities to fulfill internally established goals, values, and aspirations. These may include any of a universe of activities, as for example, the choice of a mate, the construction of a house, or the assumption of leadership in an organization. The essential quality common to all such activities is the element of decision making, of taking the initiative in the determination of what one's future shall include.

What are the requirements for a theory that will provide both understanding and prediction in the sphere of human adaptation and failures in adaptation? Does this theory now exist? The writer believes that an adequate and sufficiently comprehensive theory of adaptation is not yet available. The intent of this book is to contribute toward such a theoretical system, one that is directed at the prediction of future patterns of living, the likelihood for deviant or pathological reactions, the forms these will take if they occur, and the likely outcome of such aberrations. From this point of view the significance of an individual's past and present styles of life lies in their latent potential for predicting the person's likely future life pattern.

There is no easy way to predict the individual's future pattern of behavior, for no simple parallels ordinarily exist in the ways a person acts in successive periods of his life. A twenty-year-old, for example, tends to act in a quite different fashion from a ten-year-old individual. Further, some people will show response patterns that are aberrant even for their own age group, and their behavior at that time will certainly differ drastically from that of an earlier period in which they acted in a socially adaptive manner.

The key to the prediction of future effectiveness in society lies in asking: "How well has this person met, and how well does he now meet, the expectations implicitly set by society for individuals of his age and sex group?" What we need to learn is the person's *relative potential* for coping with the tasks set by society, compared to others of his age and sex status. Expected patterns of behavior change with the person's age. Presumably, relative potential for meeting those expectations remains far more stable. Thus, to the extent that an individual's relative standing in adaptive potential remains constant, we should, in principle, be able to predict his future effectiveness in adaptation to society. The pragmatic question in need of resolution is the extent to which relative adaptive potential does, in fact, remain constant. Only to this extent are we in a position to predict the person's future. In this book, we shall explore some of the empirical data bearing on this question.

What method of analysis will permit us to transform past and present adaptive patterns into a measure of future coping potential? The writer proposes that this index lies in the psychological resources that *currently* inhere in the individual personality for coping with adaptive complexity. It is these psychological resources that continue to maintain their existence when the present has been swept into the past and, therefore, no longer has a concrete existence, and when the future has become the present.

Nevertheless, not just any psychological theory and not just any measures of psychological function will contribute to the prediction of future effectiveness in adaptive behavior. Some logical correspondence is required between the psychological processes and their measurement and the future degree of competence in adaptation that are to be predicted. How are we to construe this vital intermediary psychological link between present and future social behaviors? Two requirements must be met. The first is the exploration of those aspects of psychological function upon which effective social adaptation is based, and the provision of techniques for their measurement. The second is the formulation of a common conceptual framework for the study of psychological organization and social adaptation.

A person's effectiveness in social adaptation is expressed in the degree of competence attained in two areas of function. These are (1) the impersonal world of technological and socioeconomic activities, in which the person acquires an education, develops work skills, and insures the well-being of himself and his dependents, and (2) the world of personal relationships, of intimate contacts with others, which require an abundance of sensitivity and awareness of human motives and an intuitive grasp of the subtleties of human relationships. This is expressed in the degree of social participation and the acceptance of responsibility for both one's own fate and that of others—either of one's immediate dependents, or more broadly, of one's community.

What psychological constructs can account for degree of efficacy in coping with societal expectations? Certainly it is reasonably for us to hypothesize that intellectual processes constitute one such determinant of adaptation. The term "intellectual processes" is intended to convey far more than the significance ordinarily assigned in American psychology to intelligence as measured by the Stanford-Binet test or the Wechsler-Bellevue, and more than is implied by the "g-factor" of Spearman. Intellectual processes correspond to Piaget's formulation of intelligence, that is, as a psychological force for the cognitive articulation and mastery of the world and the whole pattern of one's relations with it. As Piaget (24) has observed: "Intelligence is an adaptation . . . its function is to structure the universe just as the organism structures its immediate environment . . . organization is inseparable from adaptation: They are two complementary processes of a single mechanism, the first being the internal aspect of the cycle of which adaptation constitutes the external [second] aspect".

Intellectual mastery of the objective world is a necessary but not sufficient pre-condition for successful coping with the world of social relationships. People of the same level of intellectual prowess differ in their sensitivities and effectiveness in relating to others. This psychological sophistication in the sphere of interpersonal relations is what we shall call *social development*.

A reasonable degree of intellectual and social development are necessary but again are not a sufficient guarantee that participation in society will be effective. Successful relating to others requires that the person be able to transcend his own idiosyncratic view of the world and to recognize and interpret situations as they are seen by others. Society itself is based on the capacity for mutual understanding, for societies are moral orders, networks of mutually contributing relationships. Individual morality is an expression of a willingness to accept responsibility both for the consequences of one's own actions and for the welfare of others. The degree to which the person is psychologically capable of accepting reciprocal responsibilities with others we shall call his achieved level of *moral development*.

The writer uses the term *psychological development* as a general representative of development in the intellectual, social, and moral spheres. It is proposed that psychological development is a major determinant of effective adaptation in society. The higher the achieved level of psychological development, the more effective will adaptation tend to be. *Achieved level of psychological development is identical with the person's adaptive potential.*

In this book we are concerned with the prediction of behavior in society. Prediction requires the quantification of those processes relevant to that behavior. How are we to measure achieved level of psychological development, that is, the person's adaptive potential? Two techniques will be described that provide an estimate of psychological development. From these we may hope to predict the effectiveness of future social behavior. The first technique is based on an analysis of the effectiveness of the person's past optimal performance in society. This optimal effectiveness is measured in terms of a construct of social competence.

Individuals can be rated as measurably different in the level of social competence that they have achieved up to the present. Some adults will have failed to complete grade school; others attempt and complete graduate studies; some become skilled machinists; others remain day laborers. Differences also appear in the sphere of interpersonal interaction. For example, people differ markedly in the degree to which they show leadership and responsibility in their social relationships; they differ, too, in the age at which they achieve independence from parents; finally. they differ in the age at which they undertake marriage and in the maturity and responsibility that they bring to it.

Society sets very modest standards for acceptable social performance. The artist, scientist, and successful businessman go far beyond the requirements for social survival. Similarly, the person who is active in the community more than meets its requirements for social acceptance. Those who are less economically and socially skilled have the greater risk of failing to meet society's expectations.

The second measure of psychological development is based upon an analysis of perceptual performance as sampled in a standardized laboratory task. This method of behavior assessment is more concerned with the formal characteristics of perceptual performance than with that specific knowledge of the world that is available to the individual.

A developmental emphasis is central to psychodynamic theory, which now dominates clinical psychiatric thought in the United States. Similarly, this emphasis is central to the psychology of Piaget (25) and Werner (32), which is focused largely on an analysis of intellectual development and process, but is concerned also with social and moral development. In its general sense, the developmental orientation is not so much a theory as a framework of thought. It is a way of viewing and organizing the data of a science. Unlike a formal theoretical structure, which provides a set of organizational principles to a given set of empirical data, it does not in itself lend either explanatory or predictive power to any of the disciplines within which it is employed. Its value, rather, lies in its emphasis on the historical development of systems, whether these be biological, psychological, or social. The developmental orientation suggests that animate systems, in particular, can be adequately understood only in terms of their historical evolution. This formulation is not, of course, subject to direct test; it is of heuristic value only.

The writer is committed to a developmental analysis of psychological and social behavior, and of adaptive and maladaptive functioning. Nevertheless, the writer's approach differs from that of other developmentalists in its focus upon hypotheses that are subject to empirical test and that concern the real-life behavior and problems of adult human beings. This approach leads to the following emphases in the writer's theoretical orientation.

1. A commitment to historical analysis does not imply a concern for the specific events that the individual has encountered in his past. Such events no longer have any real existence. Their present significance lies in the changes they have wrought in the person's psychological structure and the environment in which he has lived. Analysis, therefore, is focused on present personality and environmental characteristics.

2. The developmental framework provides a major formal principle that is descriptive of the growth of the organism from simple to more complex and articulated forms. This principle holds whether one is dealing with the organism as a biological entity, or with its psychological aspects, or as a unit in a social structure. It states that wherever development occurs, it proceeds from a state of relative diffuseness in organization to a state of increasing differentiation and hierarchic integration.

Typically, this developmental principle has been applied in the study of children, or in comparing the behavior of children and adults. In contrast, the writer's prime interest is in adults and the analysis of adult patterns of behavior. Adults are not viewed as a homogeneous category, all of whom may be placed at some single high point in psychological development and who rate, therefore, as developmentally more advanced than children. Rather, the writer proposes that adults, both normal and deviant, may be placed along a sequence of psychological development. With increasing chronological age people are faced with life tasks of increasing complexity. Individuals can be rated in terms of the degree to which they cope effectively with these expectations. Effectiveness of performance in life is presumed to reflect the level of psychological development that the individual has reached.

3. Development progresses along more than a single path. Multiplicity in developmental forms can be seen in the different content areas of psychological function. Thus, different rates of development may appear in the intellectual, social, and moral spheres. A person may be intellectually quite superior, but this tells us little of his social skills or his sense

of moral obligation for the welfare of others. The writer's interest centers on the specifics of and complexities in the principle of psychological development, and on how it relates to actual adult behaviors in both adaptive and maladaptive states.

4. Knowledge of the social context within which the individual operates is vital to our understanding of him and his behavior. Developmental psychologists tend to concentrate on analysis of intrapsychic processes, but such knowledge is insufficient to tell us whether the person will adapt effectively. Adaptation is the consequence of organism–environment interaction. The writer, therefore, has found it essential to consider the nature of the human environment and the common crises that interaction with that environment brings about in order to explore adaptive and maladaptive behavior in adults.

Developmental level alone does not explain either normality or deviance. Psychiatric normality is a socially adaptive state; psychopathology is a socially maladaptive state. Adaptation and its failures are hypothesized as the interaction of the person's achieved level of psychological development and the degree of environmental support available to the individual. Persons of higher developmental levels with substantial support from a stable social environment are those most likely to adapt effectively in society. Those of lower developmental levels in a nonsupportive, unstable social environment are those most likely to be maladaptive. Psychological development tells us not only the likelihood for successful adaptation, but also the likely degree of effectiveness (competence) in that adaptation to society. Even in the pathological states, the individual's *potential* for effective social behavior in the future may be predicted from the level of psychological development that he achieved in the past.

5. The intent is to see theory serve the interests of a predictive science of behavior. The emphasis, therefore, is on quantification, measurement, and explicit relationships among the phenomena relevant to a general theory of social behavior. This is in contrast to the work of most theorists in psychoanalysis and developmental psychology, whose concern has been largely with the exploration of intrapsychic process rather than with its specific consequences in overt behavior. Our concern here is with the real world in which people live and with the psychological resources that are necessary in order to come to terms with that world.

## ENVIRONMENTAL FACTORS IN ADAPTATION

Effective adaptation depends not only on the level of psychological development achieved, but on the set of external conditions within which the person operates. Each individual strives to establish that type of environment and those relationships with it that provide an optimum balance between security and the fulfillment of his goals, values, and aspirations. What this balance will be is dependent on his past history and personal maturity. The immature adult, deficient in adaptive flexibility and the skills of living, is likely to opt for an unadventurous security, for he requires a stable, supportive, and cohesive environment. The mature person, confident of his powers of survival, may well adopt a more vigorous and pioneering style of life and can flourish under less stable, less rigidly defined, and more open conditions.

The feature unique to the environment of humans is active participation with other people. Psychological development is associated with a sequence of interpersonal contexts within which the individual lives and interacts. These stretch from the earliest mother-infant relationship through sibling rivalries and peer friendships, interaction patterns on the job, the dating relationship, and marriage and family patterns. Other people provide the critically significant context within which each person operates. The pattern of their interactions provides clues as to the individual's preferred ways of relating to others, and to his level of psychological development. The immature seek to establish fixed and secure relationships within which they can act as the dependent member. The mature welcome their independence while they willingly accept the dependent attachment of those for whom they feel responsible.

### NONADAPTIVE BEHAVIOR PATTERNS

So far, we have concentrated on those psychological and environmental characteristics associated with constructive and appropriate patterns of adaptation in society. In contrast, what factors are associated with failures in social adaptation, that is, ineffectual, inappropriate, or aberrant behavior states? It is proposed that adaptive failure is most likely to occur in the context of (1) a relatively low level of psychological development (i.e., of adaptive potential), and (2) disorganization of the social matrix within which the individual habitually operates.

Basic to our thinking is that the lower the level of psychological development, the more likely it is that the individual will be confronted by problems that he is unable to master successfully. Any break in the social context to which the person is adapted exposes him to situations with which he may not be able to cope. On a probability basis those individuals of lower adaptive potential are most likely to fail when their environmental context is changed.

Thus, even relatively minor changes in interpersonal relationships may be profoundly disturbing to less mature individuals. Leaving school and the loss of schoolmates, even if contacts with them have been minimal, or the birth of a child to a distant relative, or any of a myriad of possible changes in the world in which they live may have severely deleterious effects on their patterns of adjustment.

In general, the events that lead to disorganization in the person's participation in society are ordinarily no more that the usual occurrences that come to any life, and are among the inevitable changes that accompany all of human living. They may even be of a type considered happy events, such as a job promotion, an engagement, or the birth of a child. What they always hold in common is change in the individual's established pattern of interpersonal relationships.

In brief, the writer sees inappropriate and nonconstructive reaction patterns as the consequence of failure in social adaptation. This failure occurs when the complexities of a changing social context impose demands for effective response that are beyond the individual's adaptive resources. That is, the person is neither sufficiently mature nor socially skilled to devise the new patterns of behavior required by environmental novelty. The result is ineffective, inappropriate, and on the surface, often aimless and bizarre responses, in lieu of the constructive behavior that the situation demands.

These inappropriate responses share two superficially contradictory characteristics. On the one hand, they reflect the person's habitual modes of relating to others and the problems that confront him. On the other, these deviations express in their erratic and frequently bizarre character the frustrations of an individual who possesses no effective means for coping with his difficulties. The consequences of such failure are varied and may take a number of alternative forms: the person may respond with overt actions directed against society, as in delinquency and crime; he may respond primarily emotionally and intrapsychically, as in the traditional psychopathologies; or he may respond most covertly of all in some form of somatic disease.

Why does one person respond to failure by antisocial behavior, another in psychiatric disorder, and a third with some form of physical disease? It is suggested that the types of reactions that appear during a period of pathology are not happenstance, nor are they totally unique to that period. Rather, they express in a distorted and exaggerated form the pervasive life styles of individuals who lapse into pathological reaction patterns.

This is an appropriate point at which to summarize the writer's theoretical position. Certain propositions are of particular significance and the reader's attention is now drawn to them.

1. The primary concern is to relate the individual's present to his future

and not to his past. The intent is to contribute to the clinical disciplines as predictive sciences, not solely as explanatory ones.

2. The individual's past and present, whether traumatic or constructive, are seen as relevant only insofar as they influence the individual's potential for both future effective adaptation or failure in adaptation.

3. The individual's *potential* for adaptation or disorganized behavior is viewed as dependent solely on the level of psychological development that he has achieved.

4. Whether he will *in fact* manifest adaptive patterns of behavior or become disorganized in response patterns is viewed as a consequence of interaction between achieved level of personality development and the nature of the social environment with which he interacts.

5. It is essential that both achieved level of psychological development and the environmental context be conceptually organized and quantified if a predictive clinical discipline is to be achieved.

6. If pathology does occur, its form will depend on the individual's characteristic behavior style.

How does this orientation differ from present theoretical positions within the clinical and sociological disciplines? In the following section of this chapter a critique is offered of five major systems of thought through which normal and pathological patterns of behavior have been conceptually organized. This analysis permits a comparison of these systems with the present theoretical framework. Three of them, the literature on psychiatric diagnosis, psychoanalytic theory, and the "healthy pesonality," are concerned primarily with intrapsychic phenomena. Two (role theory and social systems theory) concentrate largely on interpersonal and social forces in determining behavior. Of the five systems, descriptive (diagnostic) psychiatry and psychoanalysis focus on psychiatrically deviant behaviors, and three, the literature on the healthy personality and role and social systems theory, have largely (although by no means exclusively) been concerned with normal behavior patterns.

We can also ask if the present framework contributes to an understanding and power in the prediction of meaningful behaviors in life that is any greater than we already possess through presently available theory. In considering this question the reader is asked to consider in particular in what manner and how effectively three issues are resolved within each of the available theories. These issues are: (1) the hypothesized relationship between psychological normality and psychiatric deviance; (2) the theoretical principles by which interaction between intrapsychic processes and environmental context are organized and manifest behavior is predicted; and (3) the precision with which adaptive and pathological reactions may be both measured and predicted.

A CRITIQUE OF CURRENT APPROACHES TO NORMAL
AND PSYCHIATRICALLY IMPAIRED BEHAVIORS

A general recognition exists that a substantial segment of the population fails to achieve any adequate coming to terms with society and fails to cope effectively with the problems of living. The problem of human failure is not, however, ordinarily treated as a unitary field of either investigation or social action. Indeed, we possess no satisfactory single term to encompass this panorama of ineffective and aberrant responses to the demands that living in society places on each person.

Three differing basic assumptions have dominated psychiatric thought on the nature and interrelation of mental disorder (psychopathology) and psychiatric normality (psychological "health"). The earliest, and in psychiatric practice still dominant, assumption sees psychiatric normality as the simple absence of mental disorder. In this formulation, mental disorder and psychiatric health are viewed as mutually exclusive alternatives. The position intermediary in time sees psychiatric health as the presence of positive and constructive resources within the individual's psychological makeup ("ego resources") as a major determinant of effective social participation. Within this framework, the likelihood that psychiatric normality will be dominant over any potential for mental disorder is seen as dependent on the constructive psychological resources available to the individual. These include his intellectual potential, work skills, and social sophistication. The most recent formulation proposes that what determines whether psychiatric health or disorder will predominate is the interaction of the person's psychological structure and factors in the human environment. This position adds the human environment as a potent locus of factors that, together with the relative potency of constructive psychological factors, determine psychiatric normality or, alternatively, mental disorder. We shall discuss in turn the conceptual positions associated with each of these differing formulations.

*Psychiatric Normality Equated with the Absence of Mental Disorder*

The diagnostic system (1) officially adopted by the American Psychiatric Association is the psychiatric classification scheme in universal administrative use in the United States. This system of classification elaborates Kraepelin's (16) pioneer work in the description and classification of the psychoses. The present system concentrates on the classification of the many forms of disorders presently recognized within psychiatry. It does not, of course, list any criteria for psychiatric normality.

The basis of classification is stated as a straightforward description of overt symptom manifestation. For the most part, the diagnostic criteria are those of relatively objective description: memory impairment, the presence of hallucination, sexual deviations, or drug addictions. Never theless, the diagnostic system strays from the criterion of overt description frequently and haphazardly. Sometimes classification smacks of the theoretical framework of psychoanalysis, as in the references to the use of mechanisms of defense. We find lapses, too, into judgmental attitudes, as in the definition of the sociopath as "ill" primarily because he behaves in a manner that is discordant with the prevailing cultural milieu.

Overall, the system is determinedly atheoretical and thus lacks a consistent framework to give coherence to the whole spectrum of psychiatric disorders. Thus, psychosis does not bear any systematic or theoretical relation to neurosis. At best, on quite ambiguous grounds, one can say that neurosis represents a "less severe" form of disorder than psychosis, but one is hard pressed to defend this judgment except on the pragmatic ground that individuals diagnosed as neurotic are less likely to be hospitalized than psychotics.

Professional decisions on the treatment process itself are likely to be arrived at on quite other grounds than simple descriptive classification of symptoms. Currently, psychoanalytic theory pervasively influences psychotherapeutic practice within all the psychiatric disciplines. Treatment of a psychological variety is likely to be formulated and carried out within a theoretical frame of reference, and not restricted to a simple enumeration of symptoms. As in diagnosis, however, members of these disciplines are likely to concentrate on what is wrong with the person, rather than on what is right or normal. In their attempts at understanding the current behavior of an adult, members of the psychiatric professions tend to concentrate on the person's early history and, in particular, on those early child-parent relationships that went awry, for example, living with a rejecting or seductive mother or a sadistic father. These are the kinds of early interpersonal difficulties that are presumed to explain a client's adult aberrations in motivation or cognition, such as (put into the language of psychoanalysis) oral or anal fixations, Oedipal conflict, or uncertainty in sexual identity. Once these correspondences are established, the presumed link is taken to be the "timelessness" of intrapsychic dynamics, laid down by traumatic early experience and now continuing to determine behavior in the present. The current effects of presumed childhood trauma are usually treated as if these actually parallel the original event or situation. That is, the clinician hypothesizes that the replication of some early rejection, frustration, or trauma has initiated the current psychological difficulties of his client.

Just how early trauma initiates pathology at some specific moment of time in the life of the adult is never clearly articulated. Presumably, such childhood difficulties remain psychologically active through the psychological internalization of the original child-parent relationship. In this fashion, early difficulties, whether real or imagined, are transformed into some psychological representation of them that may well remain unconscious, that is, both out of awareness and beyond the ordinary potential of the individual for being brought into awareness. In this guise, it retains its specific and idiosyncratic qualities that are unique to the individual.

In this formulation, a number of issues remain unresolved (1) What determines whether a given trauma will continue to be disruptive in the individual's subsequent life? The observation that highly effective individuals appeared to have suffered equally with the maladjusted in terms of early difficulties makes this a pertinent issue (4, 26). (2) Is it trauma per se that determines future pathology, or only some fantasy of childhood threat or provocation? Freud's (8) own experiences in the psychotherapy of adult neurotics, that is, the discovery that the recall of sexual seduction in infancy was of events that had occurred only in fantasy, makes this a particularly relevant question.

Certain additional assumptions are implicit in the traditional psychoanalytic framework: (a) man's innate character is fixed early in life (i.e., within his first five or six years) and is subsequently relatively immutable; (b) he is a passive victim of forces that are imposed by social and familial pressures, and that operate independently of his will or control, that is, he is a responding organism, rather than one that controls its own destiny; and (c) his major aim in life is conceived to be the achievement of some form of static equilibrium with these extraneous forces, at which point his activities will cease.

Clinical practice today is based on an uncomfortable marriage between the diagnostic system of descriptive psychiatry and psychoanalytic theory. Psychoanalysis is comprised of a body of abstract constructs such as the unconscious, libidinal development, the mechanisms of defense, and ego processes. However, no method for their objective description and measurement is provided. Descriptive psychiatry, on the other hand, is simply a diagnostic system based on the presence of overt and explicit bits of deviant behavior. The two systems of thought are quite incompatible, for psychoanalytic constructs represent fluid and complexly interacting covert processes without behavioral referents; descriptive psychiatry is largely constructed of a set of fixed, discrete, and conceptually independent bits of overt behavior, explicitly unrelated to any theoretical system. Descriptive psychiatry and psychoanalysis, however, share one major feature. Neither provides a method by which the person's future behavior may be predicted.

Descriptive psychiatry is intended solely as a classificatory scheme for the diagnostic ordering of a person's present overtly deviant behaviors rather than as a system of prediction. Psychoanalytically oriented psychiatry cannot serve as a predictive system on other grounds. None of its conceptual variables have been stated in an objective and quantified form. Thus, the instincts, defenses, ego, superego, fixation, regression, and so forth remain a set of amorphous constructs. Nor does psychoanalytic theory designate any set of manifest future behaviors that can be logically predicted from the theoretical analysis of a given case history. As a consequence, translation can only be carried out in the direction of behavior to psychoanalytic mechanisms, and not in the opposite direction. Thus, we can only "understand" or "explain" behavior after the fact; we cannot predict its future occurrence.

*Psychiatric Normality As a Predominance of Constructive Psychological Resources*

During the last few decades a new literature has appeared concerned with the positive aspects of human adaptation. Writers in this field reject the concept of "healthy" adaptation as merely the absence of mental disorder. For them the person is not simply a passive victim of internal and external forces that determine his behavior; rather man is seen as transcending both his biological endowment and his historical past, and as possessing the potential for actively controlling his own future destiny.

As presently used, the term "healthy" or "normal" personality tending to describe some idealized abstraction of glowing psychic health. Maslow (19), for example, found that he could classify only two historical personages as "fairly sure" "self-actualizing" (healthy) personalities: Lincoln, in his last years, and Thomas Jefferson. Maslow considered only another five as "highly probable" self-actualizers: Albert Einstein, Eleanor Roosevelt, Jane Addams, William James, and Baruch Spinoza. He believed that such eminent personalities as Walt Whitman, Henry Thoreau, Ludwig von Beethoven, Franklin D. Roosevelt, and Sigmund Freud fell somewhat short of his standards for the self-actualizing person. The healthy personality, then, connotes some Platonic ideal of what man ought to be, but which, unfortunately, he never fully achieves. It may be thought of as some idealized end state of personal evolution rather than personality-in-development. Because of this, it simply does not correspond to the psychological potential that characterizes the vast majority of the general population. Even in the absence of such utopian qualities, most adults do achieve some modicum of survival in society, some measure of satisfaction, and do contribute toward the welfare of others.

Psychoanalytic theory provides a more general conceptual framework for understanding both personality development and psychological normality. Within this system, personality development is expressed in terms of psychosexual (libidinal) development, ego maturation (i.e., development of rational psychological function), and superego maturity. The healthy personality is one that has achieved full libidinal development; that is, one that may be designated as a true genital character, characterized by an ego freed from hampering instinctual controls and able, if it wishes, to act according to rational considerations.

Both psychoanalysis and the theory provided by Maslow suffer from a lack of explicit criteria by which personality development or self-actualization may be judged. Both describes only idealized abstractions of what constitutes the healthy personality. As a consequence, neither set of constructs permits us to designate in any objective sense those individuals who should be considered psychologically healthy or, alternatively, the degree to which every individual may be considered normal. Further, neither system is sufficiently articulated to allow any but very general descriptions of what kinds of behavior may be expected of healthy personalities.

Other writings in the field of the healthy personality are essentially nontheoretical (15, 27). They consist largely of a simple enumeration of traits or attributes that various authors consider to be qualities essential to a "well-functioning" person. Nevertheless, despite the rather random and apparently arbitrary listing of desirable traits offered by different authors, a certain logical and consistent order can be imposed on the cluster of attributes that have been assigned to the healthy personality. First, this construct implies a potential for environmental mastery based on certain intellectual and affective characteristics, that is, a realistic self-appraisal and an accurate sense of reality; and, in dealing with the environment, some substantial degree of flexibility, zest, and tolerance for stress, that is an ability to face and accept a certain degree of deprivation, anxiety, worry, and conflict.

Second, attributes presumed characteristic of the healthy personality imply some optimal balance between separateness and togetherness, that is, between the traits of autonomy (independence and self-determination) and a sense of belonging.

Finally, psychological health has been taken to imply a reciprocity in the relationships of the self with others, a mutual dependence, cooperation, and acceptance. This reciprocity is expressed by an acceptance of self along with an acceptance of others, and by some judicious mixture of the gratification of subjectively felt needs and a sense of moral responsibility for the needs and welfare of others.

Three major themes, then, emerge in the attributes that have been assigned to the healthy personality: (1) a degree of intellectual and emotional development sufficient to imply a potential for environmental mastery; (2) a level of social development that permits a balance between independence and social participation; and (3) the achievement of a level of moral development that allows for reciprocity in one's dealing with others. These attributes correspond to the three dimensions of psychological development along which, as we have proposed, the adaptive potential of all individuals may be judged.

To summarize, the present diagnostic system in psychiatry represents a potpourri of symptom classification, theoretical constructs, and value judgments. Diagnosis bears little relation to case disposition other than for or against a decision to hospitalize a patient. In particular, diagnosis bears almost no relation to choice of treatment, with psychotherapeutic objectives usually determined by psychodynamic and structural analyses of personality. Both the current diagnostic system and the psychodynamic psychoanalytic orientation that dominates American psychiatric thinking are lacking in the quantification of constructs and in predictive power.

A major deficiency in both these systems of psychiatric thought is their concentration on the abnormal and deviant, with normality and constructive adaptation in society being of quite peripheral and secondary interest. In contrast, the writer proposes that a central concern with both psychiatric normality and the potential of people for effective social adaptation will tell us far more than we now know about the great mass of individuals who constitute the general population; it will tell us, too, how they find the means for psychological survival and self-fulfillment in spite of the vicissitudes and complexities of living in society. But more than this, it will tell us a great deal that is now unknown about the abnormal and deviant. In essence, the writer suggests that we invert the customary assumption in clinical thought that we learn about normality by studying the abnormal. It is proposed, rather, that the abnormal is to be better understood within the context of normality.

So far, we have spoken of psychiatric normality as the consequence of intrapsychic factors. But normality is more than a psychological phenomenon; it is the consequence of some constructive rapprochement between the person and his social environment. We now go on to a theoretical analysis of this individual–world interaction and its consequences for adaptive or maladaptive patterns of social interaction.

*Psychiatric Normality in the Context of Individual–Environment Interaction*

As a group, psychiatrists and clinical psychologists have remained relatively indifferent to the influence of social and community structures on the manifestation of psychiatric normality or disorder. The locus of concern both theoretically and philosophically has remained with individual intrapsychic dynamics. The term "the average expectable environment," coined by the psychoanalyst Hartmann (11), captures the pervasive indifference to the role that everyday situational factors may play in initiating or alleviating personality disorganization or aberrant behavior.

It is not to be gainsaid that the recent past has witnessed a whole series of investigations on the relations between social and community structure and the prevalence of individual psychiatric impairment (12, 14, 17, 18, 28). This research interest represents, however, a continued focus on individuals based on some general supposition that various patterns of intrapsychic dynamics may be differently distributed across the social strata of a community. Similarly, we must not assume that all of the recent interest in social and community psychiatry and in community mental health programs represents an aroused interest in the psychiatric consequences of individual–social structure interaction. Rather, much of this psychiatric interest in groups stems from three related sources: (1) an aroused conviction that individual psychiatric difficulties are far more widely distributed in the community than has previously been recognized; (2) the continuous expansion of psychiatric interest in ever "milder" forms of psychiatric difficulties over the last century, restricted first to the "furiously insane" and now stretched to a concern with individual reactions to the problems of everyday life; and (3) a recognition that traditional psychiatric resources cannot be expanded to match this widened vision of needed psychiatric services. The consequence is that a search has been on over the recent past for "multiplier" techniques that will provide help to increased numbers of clients. Technical innovations to this end include group therapy, educational programs in mental health offered to the community, and the interposition of a whole spectrum of therapeutic agents between the clinician (acting as a consultant) and his eventual client. These agents include teachers, clergymen, parole officers, and others who maintain some control or influence over the person in difficulty. While all these ventures imply a quite new interest in community, the focus of therapeutic intervention remains the individual client.

Nevertheless, a valid concern for the influence of social processes on individual psychological function has also emerged in recent years. Perhaps the first evidence of this is to be found in the studies on the psychiatric hospital as a social unit (6, 29). It is expressed implicitly in recent studies that indicate that psychiatric disorder repeatedly appears in conjunction with many other forms of physical and social pathology, such as chronic physical disease, broken homes, delinquency, mental retardation, and alcoholism; and that psychiatric disorder, together with other forms of pathology, appears in excessive proportion in the economically and socially deprived populations at the center of urban areas.

These observations lead to two levels of sociological theory on mental health and disorder. One level is that of role (i.e., small social systems) theory; the other is social structure (i.e., large social system) theory. Both levels of sociological theory propose that there is usually a certain logic to the behavior of people that is determined by the social context in which they are operating. The basic assumption in both these theories is that humans are "rule-following animals" (23) whose activities tend to conform to the expectations of those with whom the person interacts.

Writing within a context of role theory, Peters noted that it is frequently unnecessary to know much about a person in order to foresee his actions. It is usually enough to know the social role he is playing. For example, "we know what the parson will do when he begins to walk toward the pulpit in the middle of the penultimate hymn or what the traveller will do when he enters the doors of the hotel because we know the conventions regulating church services and staying at hotels. And we can make such predictions without knowing anything about the causes of people's behavior" (23).

"Playing a role" implies a commitment to a regularized set of behaviors that conform to particular expectations of complementary others, for example, a doctor with his patient, a husband with his wife, or a college student with his professor. An individual lives his life in a sequence of such role relationships, for example, that of child and mother, student and teacher, worker and boss, husband and wife, or father and child.

Behavior of a complementary other that deviates from the partner's expectations will force a distortion in his own role-playing behavior. Thus, the wife who is confronted by an alcoholic husband may be forced to play the role of breadwinner for the family, or may be led to dissolve the relationship entirely through separation or divorce. Any deficiency in rule-following behavior and the consequent failure in conforming to the role expectations of the complementary partner tend to impair or destroy the possibility for stable interpersonal relationships. A number of investigators have proposed that psychopathology represents such a breakdown in interpersonal or role relationships.

It appears that role theory can provide meaningful insights into the significance of interpersonal relationships for constructive or ineffectual forms of adaptation in society. When, however, we shift our focus from small groups to the larger groupings within society, we find certain deficiencies in the explanatory power of role theory. Thus, failure in interpersonal or complementary role relationships is insufficient to account for the different rates of failure to adapt that occur in various social structures. Other factors being equal, failure in adaptation should occur with equal frequency across all social groups. Yet, both incidence rates and the forms of maladjustment differ substantially between different social categories, such as ethnic groups, social classes, the two sexes, age groups, and so forth. Such differences in the occurrence and form of deviance between social strata imply that phenomena inherent in the organization of these social structures themselves favor the manifestation of particular inappropriate reaction patterns.

Judgment as to what is abnormal or symptomatic is always implicitly guided by the standards of expected behaviors for the social category of the individual who is responding. For example, middle-class people would often be considered as behaving inappropriately by those living in a slum district. In their own social milieu, however, persons in each class level tend to follow the expectations for behavior that prevail within their own group. Pathology has often been viewed as deviant, inappropriate, and ineffective reactions to societal expectations, that is, as deviations in behavior from the social norms and values appropriate for one's place in the social context (2, 3, 7, 10, 13, 15, 22, 30, 31). Pathological behavior comprises those actions that represent some lapse from societal expectations and thus "have no point or a very odd point." These are the kinds of behaviors that impel people to ask "what made, drove, or possessed him to do it?" (23).

Social structure or social systems theory is required to handle the issues raised when we posit sets of societal expectations that guide the behavior of individuals. Expectations as to behavior that are imposed upon a person by society depend on his age level, sex, social class affiliation, marital status, ethnic group, profession, and so forth.

In the past, little sensitivity has been shown by clinical psychologists or psychiatrists for the significance of the broader social context for the ways of human living. There are exceptions, of course: Fromm (9) has traced the interrelationships of economic structures to the appearance of specific human types: receiving, exploiting, hoarding, and marketing forms of character. In contrast, sociologists have long been aware of the significance of social context for molding the dominant forms of human interaction. Mills (21), for example, has noted that the biography and character of an individual cannot be explained as dependent solely on his early family experiences or his current interpersonal setting. These must also be considered as influenced by the larger social context of his period, for man is a social and historical being whose life derives much of its meaning from specific social and historical structures. His way of life is a reflection of his culture, for much of human living consists of acting roles within established social contexts. Thus, abstract concepts, such as the economist's views on Economic Man and the psychoanalytic concept of the Oedipal phase of child development, viewed as divorced from specific historical periods, cannot alone be completely explanatory of human behavior. Changes in both economic and political roles over the last century, as well as in family structure itself since the days of Victorian fatherhood, are decisive for the role functions of modern man (21).

An individual's adaptation in society depends to a substantial extent on the clarity and general acceptance or approval of a person's status in society. Certain positions in our social structure are poorly defined, such as that of aged parents or of the professionally trained woman, or the divorcee, so that considerable intrapsychic as well as interpersonal tension may arise for people occupying such positions in society. Other positions are simply disapproved, such as that of the poor, the occupationally unskilled, the school dropout, and until recently, that of such ethnic or caste groups as the Jew, Puerto Rican, or the Negro. No amount of clarity as to one's place in the social framework would help alleviate the difficulties faced by persons who occupy such niches in society. Strains are imposed on the personality organization of these people that may make it impossible for them to perform effectively in any of their interpersonal relationships.

Such difficulties may be subjectively experienced as personal troubles and be traceable to specific experiences within the life of a particular individual. That emotional troubles originate from within the person himself or follow from his own idiosyncratic experience is a central assumption in the theory and practice of psychiatry and psychoanalysis. Thus, Jones, psychoanalyst and student of Freud, wrote that people increasingly suffer from the sense of being moved by forces within themselves that remain obscure and that they are unable to define. But the sociologist Mills denied Jones' contention that "man's chief enemy and danger is his own unruly nature and the dark forces pent up within him." Rather, "man's chief danger today lies in the unruly forces of contemporary society itself, with its alienating methods of production, its enveloping techniques of political domination, its international anarchy—in a word, its pervasive transformations of the 'nature' of man and the conditions and aims of his life" (21).

The disproportionate appearance of a particular kind of personal difficulty at one point in the social structure, for example, among the extremely poor, implies that this maladjustment transcends in significance the problems of one particular individual. In the sense of their identification with particular categories in society they become, as Mills has observed, social issues. Mills has provided some illustrative contrasts between personal troubles and social issues. In marriage, for example, a husband and wife may clash with each other and subjectively experience personal difficulties. Yet, when the divorce rate climbs to 250 out of every 1000 attempts within the first four years of marriage, we have an indication of a structural problem having to do with the institution of marriage and the family and the social institutions that bear upon them. Similarly, one man out of work will suffer personal distress, but when the unemployment rate among unskilled workers climbs above a certain percentage, say 5 or 6 percent, this fact in itself reflects a social issue not soluble within the resources of any one person.

It appears that both role and social systems theory can contribute substantially to our understanding of constructive and pathological adaptations in society. Nevertheless, their exclusive concentration on the place of social processes and structures in social adaptation is as one-sided in its way as the intraindividual orientation of descriptive psychiatry and psychoanalysis is in theirs. Social structure analysis can lead to an understanding of how these structures can exert pressure upon people to engage in conforming or nonconforming activity. Such analysis can explain why certain behaviors occur at different rates in groups that differ structurally from each other (20). Sociologists abstract an interpersonal or social pattern from behaviors shared by various people in the community in order to articulate regularities in those behaviors. But, according to Sapir, such observations " . . . do not aim to be accurate about the behavior of an actual individual or individuals or about the expected behavior of a physically and psychologically defined type of individual . . . " (quoted in Merton, 20).

As a psychologist, the writer is interested precisely in the behavior of individuals, as are all those who work in the clinical disciplines. It is necessary to recognize that man is a social being and that his social context has major significance for the form his behavior may take. But the social context is not the sole determinant of his behavior. Behavior may be conceived of as an interaction between response dispositions internal to the individual and the environmental contexts that make these potentials for response more or less appropriate.

Thus, recognition of man as a social being does not limit us solely to an analysis of his life as a sequential pattern of social roles, nor to an analysis of social systems. Corresponding to these roles and systems are particular psychological characteristics, including the person's intellectual and social resources, and his sense of morality. As Piaget has noted, "The interaction with his social environment in which the individual indulges varies widely in nature according to his level of development, and consequently in its turn it modifies the individual's mental structure in an equally varied manner" (25). Analogously, von Bertalanffy (3) has observed that the development of the self as a social object coincides with the development of symbolic categories of thought. Indeed, civilization itself has been seen as based on a complex system of symbols (3, 5, 22, 33), and all human relationships as operating within the context of a symbolic system.

In principle, a theoretical position that accepts both intrapsychic processes and environmental conditions as equally valid determinants of behavior seems most fruitful heuristically. The writer believes that such a psychosocial framework will contribute most to our understanding of social adaptation and its failures. The writer's conceptual framework stresses, in particular, the centrality of achieved level of psychological development and degree of stability in the individual's social context in determining success or failure in his adaptation in society. Failure in adaptation occurs when the individual lacks the essential psychologcal resources for coping with environmental complexities or environmental change. The following chapters of this book spell out what constitute the necessary psychological resources for social survival and effective performance in life and the qualities of environment that enhance or hinder that adaptation.

## The Plan of This Book

This first chapter has set out the main themes to be explored in this book. The following chapters will articulate these in more specific detail, and more important, provide the evidence that supports them. The focus is on adult life, with adulthood viewed as an emergent from the years of childhood and adolescence. For this reason Chapter 2 examines the process of psychological development from birth to the mature years, with attention given to the way in which the sociocultural context either enhances or retards psychological growth. Chapters 3 and 4 discuss how a technique for measuring a person's coping resources may be constructed, based on the principles of psychological development enunciated in Chapter 2.

The validity of these techniques for the measurement of adaptive potential is reviewed in Chapter 5. Here the propositions are tested that an individual's placement in adulthood on an index of social competence is related to his achieved level of psychological development, and that social competence level provides some approximation of his ability to cope with stressful conditions. Chapter 6 tests a set of propositions derived from the theoretical position outlined in the present chapter. It explores the correlates of psychological development in terms of susceptibility to the onset of pathology, its severity if it does occur, and the correspondence between coping potential and remission in disorder.

Before the interrelations between psychological development and psychopathology can be adequately explored, it is necessary to define just what is meant by pathology. This issue is examined in Chapters 7 and 8. In Chapter 7, the nature and distribution of pathology within the general population is examined, and the ambiguities and limitations of our present classification procedures are detailed. An alternative approach to the traditional diagnostic categories is proposed, based on the classification of directly observable symptoms. Chapter 8 elaborates on this proposal, suggesting that individual patterns of symptomatic behaviors can be thought of as characteristic behavior styles rather than as reflecting covert and unmeasurable disease processes. Evidence is provided that traditional diagnostic categories correspond to such pathological behavior styles. Available evidence also suggests that these behavioral response patterns are associated with pervasive attitudinal sets that transcend the immediate manifestations of disorder.

The relationships between the level of psychological development achieved in the premorbid years and the forms of pathological behavior style that individuals manifest is explored in Chapter 9. So, too, is the relation between pathological behavior and outcome to disorder. The evidence supports the proposition that some long-term, and perhaps lifelong, continuity in patterns of individual adaptation transcends even the ostensibly qualitatively different behavior states of normality and pathology.

The continuity between normal and deviant behavior styles is explored further in Chapter 10. Evidence in support of such continuity is advanced, based on parallels in adaptive and deviant behavior patterns within different types of occupational grouping and within the divergent life patterns of the two sexes. The concept of pervasive "life-styles" is proposed and elaborated on in Chapter 11. Here the correspondence between the characteristics of the general cultural context and its dominant pathological forms is examined, and evidence is put forward that as shifts take place in the dominant attitudes, values, and mythology of a culture, there are corresponding changes in its common forms of pathology. Pathological forms, then, appear to reflect the overriding culture themes of a society, and indeed may be an important means for the study of culture and culture differences.

With this emphasis on the role of the cultural context in giving form to pathological reactions, the issue is raised as to the way in which environmental factors play a role in influencing the manifestation of adaptive or nonadaptive patterns of behavior. This issue is surveyed in Chapters 12 and 13. In Chapter 12 theoretical issues on the nature of environment are first reviewed, suggesting that the social context can play a critical role in determining whether the individual will behave in a normal or deviant fashion. The more cohesive and supportive the social context, the more likely it is that the individual will survive as a rational and adaptive human being. Chapter 13 examines the question whether it is the broader context of society generally, including the disruptive conditions of slum life, that directly determines susceptibility to pathology. Available evidence suggests that it does not, but rather that it is the life context of the individual and his immediate personal relationships that contribute to the likelihood that disorder will appear. The ultimate determination of whether an individual will participate effectively in the life of the community or resort to inappropriate and deviant behavior patterns appears to depend, however, on the interaction of the psychological resources he can bring into play to cope with the demands that life places upon him, with the stressfulness, complexity, or disruptive nature of his interpersonal relationships. In arriving at this formulation, we come full circle to the theoretical position outlined in this chapter.

It must be emphasized that the intent in this book is not to provide a completed theory of social adaptation and failure. Rather, it is to be seen as a report of work in progress. This is literally so. The writer and his colleagues are engaged in a number of long-term research projects that elaborate on the work reported here. Nevertheless, the writer believes that what is presented is a coherent and defensible position on the nature of effective and deviant adaptations to society, based on the knowledge now available to us. If it arouses controversy as well as clarification of issues, it will have served its purpose.

## REFERENCES

1. American Psychiatric Association Committee on Nomenclature and Statistics. *Mental Disorders: Diagnostic and statistical manual.* Washington, D.C.: American Psychiatric Association Hospital Service, 1952.
2. Benedict, R. Anthropology and the abnormal. *Journal of General Psychology*, 1934, **10**, 59–82.
3. Bertalanffy, L. von. Some biological considerations of the problem of mental illness. In L. Appleby, J. M. Scher, and J . Cumming (Eds.), *Chronic schizophrenia.* Glencoe, Ill.: Free Press, 1960. Pp. 36–53.
4. Bonney, M. E. A descriptive study of the normal personality. *Journal of Clinical Psychology*, 1962, **18**, 256–266.
5. Cassirer, E. *An essay on man*, New Haven, Conn.: Yale University Press, 1944.
6. Caudill, W. *The psychiatric hospital as a small society.* Cambridge, Mass.: Harvard University Press, 1958.
7. Devereaux, G. A. A sociological theory of schizophrenia. *Psychoanalytical Review*, 1939, **26**, 315–342.
8. Freud, S. *New introductory lectures on psycho-analysis.* New York: Norton, 1933.

9. Fromm, E. *Man for himself.* New York: Rinehart, 1947.
10. Gruenberg, E. M. Community conditions and psychoses of the elderly. *American Journal of Psychiatry*, 1954, **110**, 888–896.
11. Hartmann, H. *Ego psychology and the problem of adaptation.* New York: International University Press, 1958.
12. Hollingshead, A. B., & Redlich, F. C. *Social class and mental illness.* New York: Wiley, 1958.
13. Horney, K. *Neurotic personality of our times.* New York: Norton, 1937.
14. Hughes, C. C., Tremblay, M., Rapaport, R. N., & Leighton, A. H. *People of cove and woodlot.* Vol. II. *The Stirling County study of psychiatric disorder and sociocultural environment.* New York: Basic Books, 1960.
15. Jahoda, M. *Current concepts of positive mental health.* New York: Basic Books, 1958.
16. Kraepelin, E. *Psychiatrie.* Leipzig: Barth, 1909–1913.
17. Leighton, A. H. *My name is legion.* Vol. 1. *The Stirling County study of psychiatric disorder and sociocultural environment.* New York: Basic Books, 1959.
18. Leighton, D. C., Harding, J. S., Macklin, D. B., MacMillan, A. M., & Leighton, A. H. *The character of danger.* Vol. III. *The Stirling County study of psychiatric disorder and sociocultural environment.* New York: Basic Books, 1963.
19. Maslow, A. H. *Motivation and personality.* New York: Harper, 1954.
20. Merton, R. K. *Social theory and social structure.* Glencoe, Ill.: Free Press, 1957.
21. Mills, C. W. *The sociological imagination.* New York: Grove Press, 1959.
22. Opler, M. K. *Culture, psychiatry, and human values.* Springfield, Ill.: Charles C. Thomas, 1956.
23. Peters, R. S. *The concept of motivation.* London: Routledge & Kegan Paul, 1958.
24. Piaget, J. *The origins of intelligence in children.* New York: International Universities Press, 1952.
25. Piaget, J. *The psychology of intelligence.* New York: Harcourt, Brace, 1955.
26. Roe, A. *The making of a scientist.* New York: Dodd, Mead, 1953.
27. Shoben, E. J., Jr. Toward a concept of the normal personality. *American Psychologist*, 1957, **12**, 183–189.
28. Srole, L., Langner, T. S., Michael, S. T., Opler, M. K., & Rennie, T. A. C. *Mental health in the metropolis: The midtown study.* Vol. 1. New York: McGraw-Hill, 1962.
29. Stanton, A. H., & Schwartz, M. S. *The mental hospital.* New York: Basic Books, 1954.
30. Szasz, T. S. *The myth of mental illness.* New York: Harper (Hoeber), 1961.
31. Weinberg, S. K. Social psychological aspects of schizophrenia. In L. Appleby, J. M. Scher, and J. Cumming (Eds.), *Chronic schizophrenia.* Glencoe, Ill.: Free Press, 1960. Pp. 68–88.
32. Werner, H. *Comparative psychology of mental development.* New York: Follett, 1948.
33. Will, O., Jr. The schizophrenic reaction and the interpersonal field. In L. Appleby, J. M. Scher, and J. Cumming (Eds.), *Chronic schizophrenia.* Glencoe, Ill.: Free Press, 1960. Pp. 194–224.

# 2 / FROM BIOLOGICAL ORGANISM
# TO ADULT SOCIAL BEING

Theorists of all persuasions agree that socioenvironmental factors play a decisive role in determining the behavior of human beings. Even genetically oriented investigators concede that living in society determines how a person's inherited potential will be fulfilled. This broad generality is a far cry, however, from a knowledge of precisely how the biological organism that is the human neonate is transmuted into an adult social being. Nevertheless, among those writers who do attempt an explanation of this transformation a certain consensus has been achieved. They appear to agree on the following characteristics of the socialization process. (1) Social facility does not appear fullblown at some moment in the development of the human organism; rather, progress is uneven with adeptness in social interaction emerging gradually over the years of childhood and adolescence. (2) An essential element in the transition from a predominantly biological organism to one engaged in social relationships is the "internalization" of the major social forms as a guide to action. (3) This internalization requires a psychological organization that can somehow hold and organize the individual's impressions of and experience with the external environment. (4) This psychological structure is not innate but develops gradually over the years of childhood, adolescence, and even beyond. (5) The character of individual psychological development is greatly influenced by the social context in which the person grows up. We shall first describe the process of psychological development. Then we shall examine the influence of early environmental factors, in particular, how factors associated with social class affiliation affect the individual's early experiences within the parental family, and as a consequence, affect his rate of psychological development.

## PSYCHOLOGICAL DEVELOPMENT

That psychological development is essential to mature participation in society is recognized by such diverse writers as Freud (10), Piaget (25), and Parsons and Bales (24). Each conceives of psychological development as an essential link between the original biological nature of the individual and later adult socialization. As noted in the preceding chapter, the writer also considers this development as essential to the emergence of the fully adult human being. Intellectual, social, and moral development in particular are seen as relevant to the understanding of social adaptation. Let us consider each of these in turn.

### Intellectual Development

Intellectual development has been most extensively studied by developmental psychologists, especially by Piaget (26). According to him, intelligence grows through a series of stages that increasingly differentiate psychological functioning from the biological processes of the organism. The earliest stage of intelligence is that of the reflex, an immediate and instantaneous response to physically present stimuli. This is followed by a period of "sensory-motor" intelligence, during which the organism takes a more active role in initiating interaction with objects with which it has direct physical contact. The third stage is one of "representational" intelligence in which the appearance of perceptual imagery permits continuity of physical interaction with the external world even when the object disappears from immediate vision. Somewhat later the stage of "concrete operations" is established. This is the earliest phase of true thought in that it allows for the mental manipulation of relationships between physical objects. In performing these mental manipulations the person enters the phase of intelligent problem solving by means of a sequence of imagined trial solutions. The final stage of intellectual development is that of "abstract conceptual thought," which expresses an ability to manipulate abstract relationships among abstract symbols.

Intellectual development brings with it an increasing flexibility in the nature of thought. That is, there is an ever greater ease in both the establishment of rational relationships between objects and the ability to undo those that were previously perceived. Piaget has called this mobility and flexibility of thought "reversibility," and proposes that this is the essential characteristic of higher forms of intelligence, including all the most complex patterns of organism–environmental relations. Reversibility is expressed in that fluidity of thought that permits the solution of complex problems; in being able to adopt intellectual positions that fly in the face of manifest reality; in being able to say, for example, that the world is round when it is so obviously flat, or being able to establish a non-Euclidean geometry by asking "What are the consequences if parallel lines *do* meet?" The essence of reversibility is the subordination of what is immediately present to the potentially possible.

The growth of intelligence is the basis for an ever-expanding mastery of the objective world. This mastery permits the initiation of more and more realistic forms of action that are freed from the restrictions imposed by the concretely given, immediately present environment. Congruently, intellectual growth brings with it a growing psychological differentiation between the individual and his environment. As he grows, the child becomes psychologically more articulated and differentiated from his surroundings. He creates a concept of self, that is, a subjective sense of personal identity that distinguishes him from his physical surroundings.

Just how does the child achieve a stabilized and articulated concept of the objective environment as well as of the self and other social objects? At times this issue has been ignored and the fact simply accepted that representation of the world outside the person has somehow found subjective representation within his mind. Durkheim (8), for example, has said that "society exists only within the minds of individuals." Similarly, Parsons and Bales (24) have said that personality is a type of "mirror image" of the sequence of social systems or interpersonal relationships to which the individual has been exposed and that have been "internalized."

The problem is: How does representation of the external world become internalized? This process has been analyzed at two levels: one level simply describes the actions of the child that appear to be associated with increasing knowledge of the surrounding world; the other attempts to provide a theoretical rationale for the role these behaviors play in internalizing the subject's experiences of the outside world.

Baldwin's (1) writing of nearly three quarters of a century ago is illustrative of the more descriptive approach to the problem of internalization. He spoke of incorporation and imitation to describe the development in the child of the psychological bases of social interaction. Through incorporation and imitation the child becomes able to perform acts that previously were the behavior of someone else, so that the characteristics he comes to consider his own are also characteristics of others. Thus, the self is other people in unique combinations.

According to Baldwin, the personality of the child can be defined only in social terms. The child's social behavior is an expression of that personality and is a consequence of those early experiences that are unique to himself and that are consolidated in his psychological development. Within the limits of organic potential, specific experiences influence the emergence of psychological processes and structures, and these, in turn, permit the inner organization of the physical and social environment.

In many ways, the work of Baldwin anticipated the recent more theoretical constructions of Piaget (25), who has provided us with the most systematic analysis of the inner construction of the individual's world. Piaget observed that the development of intelligence proceeds from the need to impose order and coherence on the world and one's relation to it. Awareness of self–world relations begins with a lack of such awareness and develops through two complementary activities, the assimilation (or incorporation) of objects to oneself and, conversely, the accommodation to the nature of objects.

Play and imitation are the overt means whereby the processes of assimilation of and accommodation to the objective world come about. Through active play, internalized schemata of the physical qualities of objects are created, first in terms of direct physical contact and object manipulation, later through inner perceptual representation. From a need to conserve and stabilize self–world relations, play will tend to assimilate all that is new to the older established schemata. It is the function of imitation to overcome the distorting effects of assimilation and to accommodate or modify established inner schemata in accordance with external reality.

Intelligence is the creation of ever more far-reaching and increasingly abstract forms of assimilation and accommodation. Intelligent adaptation is the consequence of an equilibrium between these two complementary processes. It is important to note that through assimilation and accommodation, the organism does more than respond to the external world; it becomes an organized totality of its experiences of the physical and social words, first through direct body contact and then through perceptual and symbolic representations of the world outside the self.

*Social Development*

Social development presupposes certain achievements in the sphere of the intellect. Before meaningful social relationships can be established, perceptual function must have arrived at a stage of object constancy. That is, the individual must be able to recognize objects under a wide range of environmental contexts and this must hold for human beings as well as inanimate objects.

Essential, too, is the clear and stable articulation of the self as a fixed physical entity. The newborn infant has no such sense of his body boundaries. Presumably the infant learns what is "me" and "not-me" through his bodily activities, his increasing control over them, and through such sensations as pain and changes in body temperature.

A further prerequisite for social development is the ability to categorize objects and to have some grasp of the system of relationships within which they exist. For the infant, objects first come to be recognized in terms of what they do to him—the bottle feeds, the crib warms, a person holds; but they also become known in terms of what he does to them—a toy is thrown, a face is touched, a pacifier is sucked. A basic knowledge of the infant's immediate world, then, is achieved through his body experience. Gradually the infant becomes aware of a constancy about objects, based on the way they are related to him in function. For example, the baby's hunger initiates this usual sequence: he cries, is picked up, and then is fed. Or, he kicks a toy and it moves until it is stopped by another object. The infant eventually recognizes that there is regularity in the sequence of most events, his expectations are reinforced, and consequently he finds that much of his world falls into predictable relationships.

But social development transcends the elaboration and stabilization of the relations between objects in space and time, even while it is dependent on such intellectual accomplishment. Effective participation in society implies that the world of social objects has likewise become stabilized; that is, persons must come to be recognized as individuals independent of the environmental and social context in which they appear. The first relationship to become established with another person is that with the mother. Very soon thereafter follow regular and subsequently expected interactions with the father and siblings. Thus is born the notion of one's family as a unifying theme that discriminates between those within and those outside the family circle. Eventually, awareness of society expands until it encompasses the world. The degree of sophistication achieved by adults about society in general, of course, varies enormously between one person and another. The president of the United States is expected to have a far firmer grasp on the scope of relations between nations than most people can hope to achieve.

Beyond any knowledge of overt relationships, effective social participation requires a sensitivity in response to the intangible, covert, yet vitally significant motivations that color all interpersonal relationships. To be at one with people is to be sensitive not only to what they say and do, but also to what they wish and desire. This by no means signifies the necessary granting of these wishes, even if one is in the position to do so; it means that one sees the other person as worthy and significant. People differ a great deal in their ability and willingness to support and enhance a sense of self-worth in others.

How does our awareness of this social world come into existence and how do we become part of that world? The infant and child achieves certain expectations about the behavior of others, behaviors that are specific to given individuals and to the contexts in which they occur, for example, the mother feeding her infant or the playfulness of a brother or sister. The "other" becomes known and understood primarily through the actions of the self. One's own behavior articulates a knowledge of the world in two ways: first, in the gradual molding of organized patterns of behavior in response to the actions of others. In a real sense, the person is his regularized ways of response. Second, and more important, knowledge of the world comes about through the repetitive imitation of those actions by others that are pleasure giving or tension reducing for the self. In these imitations, the infant appears to substitute himself magically for the "beneficent other" when that "other" is not present. Such actions are repeated endlessly in play until they become truly a part of oneself (25). One has only to witness little girls playing "mother" to grasp the significance of such rehearsals for the later successful fulfillment of that role. Gradually the child builds up a repertoire of roles internalized from interaction with other human beings. More than this, the child learns the social context that can appropriately elicit a given role behavior.

Roles are ordinarily played in complementary sets—the interaction of the self with another. In order to interact effectively, the individual must learn to sense in an empathic way the motives and feelings of others in given types of situations, such as eating, fighting, and playing. Only when correct anticipations are established of how others will act in known situations is it possible to form stable and successful personal relationships. Constructive and successful early social experiences foster the development of a personality structure of sufficient complexity and flexibility to adapt to the problems of living in society. It is essential that the persons with whom the growing individual relates and with whom he interacts in complementary interpersonal sets themselves be integrated members of the larger community. If the complementary other is himself alien to the larger society, the growing individual will establish for himself ways of relating that are not effective for establishing rewarding interactions with those who live in the larger society. Such "errors" in social learning are common in any socially alienated or disorganized community. As we shall discuss in a later chapter, social alienation and disorganization are common precursors of various forms of individual pathology, including psychiatric disorder and delinquency.

Maturity in social development requires an extensive internalized repertoire of possible role relations and behaviors. Increasingly, the person must learn to select and act in those roles for the self that are appropriate in relation to specific others (e.g., persons of the other sex, of certain age groups, within or outside the family) under a given set of circumstances. (See Chapter 3, Societal Expectations and Sex Differences in Social Competence).

Over the years of social development the person internalizes an idiosyncratic framework of complementary role relationships. This inner organization of complementary roles corresponds to the individual's network of overt relationships within society. Both the inner and outer sets of role relationships are built upon earlier experiences of social interaction, first within the parental family and later within the wider community. With appropriate earlier experiences the individual should be able to live out effectively the key adult roles expected of him according to his age and sex, for example, as friend, worker, spouse, and parent.

*Moral Development*

Implicitly, two standards for behavior guide the actions of each individual. One standard is external to the person and includes (although it is not restricted to) the expectations shared in society for each person's actions and style of life according to his age, sex, and status. The other is identified with the person and is embedded in his code of morals. To the extent that external and internal influences are not at war with each other, the person can live in harmony with his society. This section is devoted to a brief review of what constitutes a person's code of morality. In the second half of this chapter we shall deal with the influence of early experience on its development.

In common usage morality means both "the quality of that which conforms to right ideals or principles of human conduct" as well as "that which instills moral lessons" (34). The general use of the term morality leaves unclear whether the locus of control over conduct is within the person or is to be found in the mores of the society within which the person lives. The writer defines morality as a set of rules internalized by the individual for the regulation of his own behavior. Thus, the writer distinguishes between personal morality and the external constraints upon his behavior that are imposed by social convention.

Failure to distinguish between morality as a personal attribute and social convention obscures the problem of choosing a standard of behavior by which one must live. Unfortunately, there exists an all too frequent contradiction between actions that a society will reward and those that most individuals, given freedom of decision, would choose as truly moral. Certain extreme situations may indicate more clearly the problem of choice between social conformity and private ethics. For example, is betrayal of one's close relatives to authorities, or committing murder in response to command by authority, an appropriate obedience to social ethics, or are they a violation of what we would consider an appropriate personal morality? These are actions that were approved in Nazi Germay only a few decades ago.

Thus, socially accepted rules for behavior do not necessarily coincide with the inner moral standards of many members of that society. Most of the day-to-day standards by which men live, as well as their values, change over time and differ from one society to another. Great differences exist within our own society between the values espoused by the various social classes and ethnic groups. Ambiguities appear even within sub-cultures as to what constitute honored values. For example, the American middle class tends to give lip service to the inculcation in the young of attitudes of modesty and humility, and yet the contrary attitudes of ambition and achievement are actually reinforced. But all this is an aside. Our concern here is not with the variation in social taboos and customs over time and in different societies, but what constitutes the nature of personal morality and its development.

What about the nature of that inner morality that ideally guides adult conduct? Clearly, this is not the place to review the various theories that have been developed to explain man's conscience and the various explanations that have been put forward over the centuries as to where lies the responsibility for his actions. We shall not be able to settle here whether conscience is innate or more the by-product of experience, and whether the individual or society should serve as the ultimate judge of moral principles.

We are not interested in adopting some abstract system of ethics against which the morality of individual behaviors may be judged. Our interest lies in a study of morality as an inner or psychological attribute. Our concern is focused on precisely how a sense of morality does emerge in the maturing individual, and the form that moral sense tends to take in present-day Western society.

Piaget (27) has provided the most systematic account of the psychological aspects of moral development and of the transformation of morality in the period from childhood to adulthood. His analysis is based on a detailed and systematic examination of the game-playing behavior of children. Piaget interviewed the children used in his studies in regard to their assumptions as to the rules that govern games. It was from these empirical observations that Piaget abstracted a conceptual framework for the understanding of moral development.

Moral development, in the sense maintained by Piaget, is not to be understood as the internalization of a set of specific rules for behavior. That is, morality is not the internal analogy to the customs of the society within which the person lives. Morality is better understood as a structural concept relatively independent of particular contents. That is, a true morality does not consist solely of such specifics as remembering to contribute to Red Cross, or opening a door for older people, or helping a blind person across the street. Rather, morality may be conceived of as a set of principles that serve to guide all interpersonal behavior, principles that permit the individual to choose between alternative paths for action, even in novel situations.

Following Piaget, the writer believes that a mature sense of morality is characterized by three attributes: (1) a sense of accountability to oneself for one's actions and their consequences, independent of whether others know about these or not (i.e., the morally mature person may escape judgment by others, but he can never escape judgment by himself); (2) an obligation for the welfare of others; in particular instances, decisions may be confounded by conflicting obligations, but the intent of an obligation to others is clear. (3) Behavior should be guided by a principle of mutuality or reciprocity, that is, the rights of others should be considered as equal to one's own, with of course, the reciprocal of this also being true. Thus, one's own rights also need to be considered in decision making. Ideally, then, a mature moral sense is expressed in a set of cooperative interpersonal relations in which a balance is struck between the fulfillment of one's own needs and aspirations and acceptance of responsibility for the welfare of others. The transformation of the individual from a self-centered and demanding child to a responsible, socialized adult is the external witness to a profound inner development in conscience and morality (9).

The problem of what constitutes a socially acceptable sense of adult morality can only be understood in relation to the expected sequence of moral development within a given society. In turn, the development of a mature sense of morality is a part-aspect of general psychological development. Moral development depends on a concurrent maturing of, first, intelligence, and second, social adaptability.

*Moral and Intellectual Development.* A mature moral sense depends on intellectual development since it requires an ability to recognize one's own intentions, to appreciate the possible consequences of one's intended actions, to delay action, and to choose between alternative courses of behavior. Moral judgment of this order requires a growth in the individual's ability to inhibit and control his actions. It requires, too, an ability to take oneself as an object, to judge oneself, and to be objectively self-critical, enabling the person to judge his own behavior in the same way he judges the behavior of others. It also requires an adequate perception and evaluation of the intrinsic qualities of one's fellow-men and a realistic recognition of their wishes and aspirations. Piaget (27) has proposed that such a parallel exists between moral and intellectual development so that we find a kinship between ethical and logical norms; that is, a mature moral sense does presuppose some substantial level of intelligence.

A moral society, as we know this among human adults, is inconceivable among either animals or young children, for it implies a highly articulated system of personal values and norms, and these in turn require a shared symbol system, the activation of processes of inner deliberation and judgment, and a personality structure that can activate or inhibit various types of behavioral tendencies. The person must be able to foresee distant ends to his behavior and be capable of purposive control over his own intentions.

At this point, it may appear that the development of morality is inherently tied to the development of thought and reason. Nevertheless, intellectual development does not of necessity presuppose the establishment of an effective moral sense. A mature morality is dependent on, but is not identical with, an ability to think logically on complex problems, for the latter are often saturated with an intense emotional tone of gratification or punishment.

Morality can be deficient in the person for whom intelligence and its use for efficient living are quite intact. Thus, a confidence man may understand with exquisite sensitivity the motives that drive people on, but his comprehension does not lead him to act any more responsibly toward them. In contrast, there is also an inappropriate and excessively harsh and self-punitive form of morality that swings to an arbitrary and overweighted emphasis on the rights and privileges of others, while disregarding one's own wishes and aspirations. This imbalance characterizes the morality of the overly scrupulous adult who has a potential for depressive and guilt-ridden psychopathological reactions. These are a caricature of mature moral development.

*Moral and Social Development.* Those investigators who have written on the emergence in the child of the concepts of social rules, morality, and justice all agree that these developments are centrally dependent on the internalization of "law-giving" parental figures. Different writers, however, have taken divergent positions on what parental attributes are likely to be internalized.

Freud, who held quite pessimistic views of man's morals and values, developed a concept of "superego," a psychological function that serves to inhibit and control the individual's behavior in accordance with socially approved constraints (12). Freud thought that some basic antithesis divided the individual and his society. He believed that society exists primarily to insure that men will not injure or kill each other, and that religious forms are a means of internalizing a rigid and controlling parental figure (with God equal to father) in order to prevent people from transgressing the bounds of a restrictive morality. Man's nature was viewed as intrinsically demanding and destructive so that he can participate in society only by relinquishing, suppressing, or repressing these fundamental features of his being. Consequently, Freud proposed that societal taboos are internalized by the individual in order to prevent the breakthrough into action of primitive, selfish, and destructive fantasies (11).

Baldwin (1) took a more optimistic view of the nature of man and stressed the more positive attributes of the internalized regulators of behavior, which he subsumed under the concept of the "ethical self." The ethical self may be characterized as an ego ideal, with a sense of the kind of person one ought to be and a sense of obligation for the rights and welfare of others.

Piaget's (27) thinking implicitly reconciles these ostensibly contradictory positions on the nature of internalized regulators of behavior. He conceived of morality as evolving in a developmental sequence from a morality of constraint to a morality of cooperation. In the period of constraint the child responds and adapts to the prohibitions and sanctions imposed by authority figures by accepting these as moral absolutes. In this phase, decisions of right or wrong are governed by whether or not the behavior conforms rigidly to a set of fixed rules rather than by the spirit of the law or the intent of the doer. Subsequently, the child enters a period of cooperation in which his actions and interpersonal relationships are based on mutual trust and acceptance. The child comes to appreciate that rules are conventions rather than absolutes, and that they exist in the interests of the general welfare and not as immutable givens. Ideally, behavior becomes guided by a desire for reciprocity and equity, and others are judged by their intentions and not by the results of their actions.

The various theoretical positions just outlined on the origins of morality and its social expression differ as to whether it is rigid and punitive or more flexible and idealistic in nature. Although these interpretations differ, each has been put forward as the universal internalized guides to human action. They do not explain why individuals, even of the same level of intellectual development, differ in their moral attributes. The evidence on this point is deficient, with only an occasional study of any relevance. It can only be suggested that people who differ in their sense of morality and justice differ also in the types of parental or authority figures whom they have internalized in a role of superego or ego ideal. If the models upon which the self is patterned are rational and share the values of society, then the future bodes well. If the person draws his identifications from individuals whose values are alien to the culture and antisocial in intent, then his future social relations are less promising (2).

An ideal state of moral development is not, of course, achieved by all adults, nor is it undeviatingly adhered to in all circumstances when it is achieved. Nevertheless, it is toward this acceptance of mutuality that moral development generally appears to tend. It is a standard, therefore, against which individual moral development may be judged.

## EARLY EXPERIENCE AND PSYCHOLOGICAL DEVELOPMENT

To this point we have examined an idealized model of how psychological development proceeds in the absence of disruptive conditions. Conditions of life, particularly in the individual's early years, can, however, profoundly alter the rate at which individual psychology will progress. The personality attributes of parents and their behavior in the home, the individual's place in the sibling hierarchy, fortuitous events, social class, and ethnic background, and the wider sociocultural context within which the family is set can all influence the child's psychological development.

In later chapters we shall discuss in more detail the implications of the wider cultural context for individual adaptation and for adaptive failure. Here the writer wants to review the influence of parental social class level on the child's psychological development. The influence of class on individual development is chosen for examination because "it defines and systematizes different learning environments for children of different classes" (7). This formulation implies that the experiences of the child within the parental family serve to inculcate those ways of thought, habit patterns, and personal and social values that correspond with his own social class level.

There is no extensive literature that relates earlier family experiences within the various social classes to personality development. However, the writer has made an effort to bring together what information is available and will describe psychological development as it appears to proceed at different class levels. Obviously these descriptions will not characterize each individual within a given social class, nor can they be considered even as modal or typical pictures of the membership of these classes. Our information is too sparse to make that presumption. The most that can be claimed is that particular family experiences and personality attributes are more commonly associated with one social class level than with another. We shall first consider how middle- and lower-class identification is reflected in family behavior patterns and attitudes. Before doing so, however, let us adopt some consistent measures of class level. Sometimes, as in the "Midtown Manhattan" study (33), three levels of social class are categorized: manual workers or a low, "blue-collar," or "working" class; a middle or "white-collar" class (including professionals); and an upper class distinguished by its wealth and power. Hollingshead (14), on the other hand, has divided the class system into five categories. The Midtown low social class is equivalent to Classes IV and V as used by Hollingshead, and to the term "lower class" as used more generally in sociology. Hollingshead's Class V consists primarily of both unskilled and semiskilled manual workers and those in service occupations (waiters, etc.), with an educational achievement averaging the completion of grade school or less. The middle class of the Midtown study corresponds to Hollingshead's Classes II and III, and the high social class to Hollingshead's Class I. The Midtown study makes use of the terms "socioeconomic status" or "SES" as well as "social class," and we shall use these three terms interchangeably.

Class V has been reported as providing the highest proportion of psychiatrically impaired individuals. Nevertheless, most persons in this category are not institutionalized with psychiatric difficulties. It is important, therefore, to see if we can distinguish within this segment of the population groups of individuals who differ in their ability to adapt effectively in the community.

Class V includes a very wide spectrum of occupational stability, which ranges from those who are regularly employed and live in moderately comfortable working-class circumstances to the chronically unemployed slum dweller or transient resident. In reviewing the literature, the writer has been able to distinguish between three groups of lower-class individuals, in terms of their economic mobility. Miller (23) has proposed a somewhat similar, although four-category, distinction. The present writer's classification follows.

1. The first category comprises economically stable low-income groups who inhabit the poorer sections of our larger cities. They are often ethnically homogeneous settlements, composed of Irish, Italians, Poles, or similar groups, who feel comfortable in the culture of their past and tend to reject the imperatives of an achievement-oriented larger society. These ethnic enclaves are subject to attrition by the pull of the values of the general community on the younger generation and are gradually being assimilated into that community.

2. The second category is an upwardly mobile one within each of the foregoing ethnic groups consisting of those who have come to live by the

achievement ethic of American society. The offspring of such a family tend to leave the slum or lower-class areas in which they were born, often to reside in well-to-do suburbs.

3. The third is an economically impoverished or slum category that includes the "outcasts" of the community, including the Negro emigrants from the South who have been moving into Northern cities in large numbers ever since World War II. (Even if Negroes succeed economically, it is difficult for them to find housing outside the Negro ghettos.) Then there are the downwardly mobile "failures," who are either disinterested in work or have difficulty in finding work. Many of these are social isolates, transients who move often from one rooming house to another.

No sharp cutoff line can be drawn at some specific level of SES that will distinguish the personality and behavior patterns of those who fall above it from the patterns of those who fall below it. The distinction between low, middle, and high status is itself an arbitrary one, drawn primarily for convenience in analysis. Distinctions in behavior patterns become clear-cut only when there are substantial differences in socioeconomic status.

The most relevant social and personality data for our understanding of normal adaptation and psychopathology center on the middle and lower classes. We shall therefore compare the attributes of the middle and lower classes (as defined in the Midtown project) in that order. Because of the particular significance of slum living for personality development, the consequences of this way of life will be described separately.

*Early Family Experiences*

We shall report in sequence on the behavior patterns of middle-class, lower-class, and slum families, and attempt to relate the relevant observations as best we can to the three dimensions of psychological development discussed in the first section of this chapter. These data are summarized later in Table 2–1.

*The Middle Class*

*Intellectual Development.* In the middle class there is great emphasis on verbal communication, and many authors (21) have reported a positive relation between socioeconomic status and language development in the child. Language facility develops earlier in middle-class than in lower-class children, and even children under 1 year of age, surpass their lower-class counterparts in the amount of vocalization and range of sounds employed (16). All through childhood and adolescence middle-class parents encourage high educational achievement and look forward to seeing their children well educated (28).

*Social Development.* In middle-class families the channels of communication between child, parents, and other family members tend to be quite open. The tone of family living is generally one of hope and optimism, and a rich and complex pattern of family "rituals" binds its members into a cooperative "togetherness." Children of the middle class tend to feel themselves as loved and secure, to see their parents as acting together and trustworthy, and to regard their discipline as reasonable. Some investigators have considered middle-class training as more severe than that in the working class, but Bronfenbrenner (5) has suggested that middle-class practices have become progressively milder since the end of World War II, so that these may now be generally more permissive than those of lower-class parents. For example, middle-class mothers are more likely to feed their infants on demand and to wean late. Middle-class mothers see their children as complex human beings whom it is important to attempt to understand (28). Emphasis is placed on understanding the other person, and on mutual trust and cooperation.

*Discipline and Moral Development.* In the middle class, punishment is on the basis of the child's intent rather than on the consequences of his actions (19). That is, the child will not be severely punished even if he has caused considerable damage by accident, but only when he has intended to be destructive. Discipline is directed by the desire to create in the child an internalized conscience and the potential for self-blame and guilt (21).

Middle-class mothers desire well-adjusted and successful children, and not simply children who are "good." These mothers tend to believe in a wide range of experiences for their children as the most practical basis for their development into successful adults. They consider feeling comfortable in different situations as the best basis for success, and experience is seen as providing the best instruction for distinguishing right from wrong (28).

Nevertheless, the permitted experiences of the middle-class child and adolescent are limited. Sexual desires as expressed in masturbation and petting are condoned but premarital coitus is taboo. Kinsey (18) observed that the individual's sexual history is invariably associated with his status aspirations. Boys slated for higher educational achievements are more likely to masturbate, neck, or pet, but have less frequent intercourse, a behavior that begins later and ends earlier in their lives.

The expression of aggression is also guided and controlled in the middle class. Verbal aggression against parents or other family members is tolerated but is disapproved when directed against persons outside the family. This interdiction holds in particular for physical aggression, but a critical verbal facility is likely to be especially approved.

## The Lower Class

*Intellectual Development.* Generally, parents classified as of low SES do not have nearly as high educational aspirations for their children as do parents in the middle classes. While the middle class expects its children to enter college, most parents of low SES will be well satisfied if their children complete high school. That schooling is a lower priority goal in the lowest social class is indicated by the fact that a disproportionately high number of school dropouts originate in this segment of the population.

*Social Development.* Lower-class mothers have been found to be emotionally colder to their children, according to Sears *et al.* (30), and Hollingshead and Redlich (14) similarly report that a "loveless infancy" is more common in Class V families than in those of Class II. On the other hand, Spinley (32) has found in the lower class that the first year was one of indulgence, although this often ended abruptly with the birth of the next child. In the light of findings by Bowlby (4) and others (35, 36), this sudden disruption of maternal care in the very early years can be a severely traumatic circumstance.

Working-class fathers tend to assert their authority in an arbitrary and unqualified way. The consequence is to produce in the child hostile responses and a parallel attempt at asserting his own powers of resistance (13). Implied is a greater sense of isolation from both parental figures than is general in the middle class (31).

*Discipline and Moral Development.* In the lower-class child discipline is marked by its emphasis on control, restriction, and inhibition, and is often effectuated by physical punishment. The stern father of immigrant families, in discouraging the expression of hostility against himself or other family members, reinforces the child in setting up alternative targets outside the house.

Lower class mothers appear intent on bringing up "good," upright, religious, and happy children (28). Their efforts are directed at the "control" of their children and their discipline tends to be strict. More so than in the middle class, punishment is likely to be called forth by the consequences of the child's actions rather than by his intent. The lower-class child, therefore, may continue to remain quite sensitive to the biddings of external authority, rather than relying on the internal control of a personal conscience.

## Slum Family Living

The American democratic myth promises equality of opportunity to all persons regardless of their social origins. The experience of the children of the slum poor, is often quite otherwise. Whatever their potential abilities, children of middle-class or even working-class origin are likely to succeed far better than those growing up in slum districts. Precisely because our ideology presents our society as an open one, that is, one governed by a principle of equal opportunity for all, the "failure" of the under-privileged is seen most often as a personal failure, both by the individual himself and by society at large.

*Intellectual Development.* The child of the slum poor is handicapped not alone by limited schooling and limited job opportunities; frequently he grows up in a deprived and often disorganized household headed by poorly educated, discouraged, and embittered parents. Slum families tend to live chronically at the edge of misfortune, and family life is likely to converge on the problem of self-preservation. Consequently, concerns are bound up primarily with the difficulties of the immediate present and few satisfactions are available to either children or parents (3).

*Social Development.* Family life in the slums is likely to be characterized by either instability and insecurity or their threat, and the atmosphere is often one of apprehension, pessimism, or despair. Slum children may well view their parents as alienated from each other, the mother as domi-nating and the father as a vague and tenuous or absent figure, who fails to serve as an adequate model of male authority. Human relationships, including the behavior of children, are likely to be viewed as arbitary and unpredictable, so that family relationships are frequently marked by emotional isolation and even alienation of its members from each other, and the emotional rejection of children is common.

*Discipline and Moral Development.* The slum child is subject to the further hazard of exposure to a conflict between the middle-class values and discip-linary methods employed by school teachers and clergymen, as well as social workers, psychiatrists, or judges, in contrast to those of his parents. The child of the middle class escapes this conflict in value systems, for his parents ordinarily are at one with the larger society in the assumptions that guide their relations with the child.

When we consider the circumstances of his life, it is not surprising that the child of the slums often comes to count himself, like his parents, alien-ated from the larger society. Nor is it surprising that he remains unmotivated for achievement at school or in work. He is the victim of a self-fulfilling prophecy of a failure that is foreordained almost before the child has begun his life.

*Psychological Development*

Surprisingly little study has been undertaken to relate parental socio-economic status to the child's psychological development. Available findings indicate that social class levels and psychological development

Table 2–1
CLASS DIFFERENCE IN CHILD-REARING PRACTICES AND IN EXPECTATIONS FOR CHILD

| Sphere of psychological development | Middle class | Lower class | Slums |
|---|---|---|---|
| Intellectual | 1. Verbal communication<br>2. Long-range goals<br>3. College graduation<br>4. Exposure to diversity of experiences<br>5. Desire for child who is succesful | 1. Completion of high school | 1. No incentives to achieve in school<br>2. Child expects failure<br>3. Concern with immediate present and its difficulties |
| Social | 1. High verbal interchange<br>2. Family "togetherness"<br>3. Parents act together and are trustworthy<br>4. Children feel loved and secure<br>5. Family atmosphere of optimism | 1. Relatively cold emotionally to child, or<br>2. Much indulgence first year, ending abruptly with birth of next child<br>3. Father harsh and arbitary<br>4. Sense of isolation from both parents | 1. Household disorganized<br>2. Chronic threat of unstable and insecure household<br>3. Parents and other family members sensed as alienated from each other<br>4. Father vague or absent person<br>5. Emotional rejection of children common<br>6. Human behavior appears arbitrary and unpredictable |
| Moral | 1. Discipline based on understanding, mutual cooperation, trust<br>2. Punishment based on child's intent, not consequences of his behavior<br>3. Disapproval of sexual experience, of aggression in action<br>4. Approval of verbal aggression<br>5. Desire for child who is well-adjusted, not "good"<br>6. Effort to create internalized conscience | 1. Emphasis on control, restriction, inhibition<br>2. Punishment directed at consequences of act, not intention<br>3. Physical punishment<br>4. Rejection of expression of hostility against parents<br>5. Emphasis on "good," upright, religious, happy child<br>6. Child remains sensitive to control by external authority, not conscience | 1. Conflict between arbitrary and unpredictable behavior patterns in slums and expectations of representatives of middle-class society (school teachers, social workers, clergy, police) |

are associated, although of course, much overlapping in psychological attributes occurs between classes. What information we have been able to glean from the literature covers only the offspring of middle-class and severely deprived (slum) families. The personality types differentially associated with these two SES levels are, however, quite pertinent for us. Nevertheless, the caveat is again entered that no claim is made for the universality or even the typicalness of the personal qualities to be described; we assert only that they occur with differential frequencies in the two SES.

### The Middle Class

In the middle class, the father's occupation is generally respected, and a positive identification with the family's social status is established, reinforcing a favorable self-image in the child. The higher a family on the status hierarchy, the more its children are imbued with a sense of assurance, mastery, and awareness of the ways in which power is distributed and exercised in society.

Typically, ambition and high aspirations are bred into the middle-class adolescent, as is the necessity of living up to family standards in educational and occupational achievement. There is a stress on rational rather than emotional solutions to problems in many middle-class families. The middle class tends to live in a verbal and ideational world with planning, punctuality, and self-control emphasized as the means devoted to achievement in one's work. Even leisure time is often devoted to "self-improvement."

To the extent that early training focuses on responsibility and gives emphasis to rationality and understanding, and there is parental disapproval of impulse expression and a family policy of mutual respect between parents and children, a strict conscience will tend to be created. To the extent that such a critical self-judgment is internalized, so too is the potentiality for feelings of guilt and self-blame.

### The Slum Inhabitant

The personality attributes of the person living in the slums tend to be very different from those of the middle-class individual, and presumably originate in the quite different early family experiences to which each is exposed. The sense of being identified with low-status parents who are recognized by the child as rejected or disapproved by the community, and the constant reminders in the mass media of the stigma attached to low status contribute to an emerging sense of being a "nobody" in the low-SES child. As a consequence, strong feelings of inferiority and inadequacy and low self-esteem are frequent in this class (14, 17, 21, 32).

Feelings of anomie and futility, of emotional and social isolation commonly beset the lower-class person.

Erratic patterns of child training, fluctuating from indifference and lack of parental supervision to sporadic periods of violent temper outbursts and physical punishment, result in inadequate superego formation. The slum child often fears external authority, with the result that it then becomes something to be circumvented whenever possible. In many slum children, conscience is not strongly internalized and behavior tends to be controlled not so much by the potentiality for feelings of guilt as by the fear of being caught and punished. Implied is an underlying disrespect for and suspicion of all authority, masked by a shell of superficial conformity.

For such children the consequence is an unwillingness and inability to commit themselves to the mastery of difficult situations or to work at tasks that demand a long-term commitment. Satisfactions must be relatively immediate for people without the goad of conscience, and without the sense of living in a well-ordered world where one's efforts will be consistently rewarded.

Persons living in the slums frequently anticipate failure for themselves. Thus, they are unwilling to face disturbing and unpleasant situations, since successful solutions to their problems seem too remote or unavailable to them. The frustration tolerance of slum inhabitants is often low, and they may well act impulsively in response to difficulties, with sporadic violent expressions of anger directed at others. Alternatively, they may appear as rather passive-dependent characters, for they may well lack the initiative and internal direction of the self necessary for successful mastery of the environment. The inability to meet crises and the realistic fear of failure that is based on past rebuffs can lead to a permanent lowering of the aspiration level of the person raised in the slums.

As Knupfer (20) has stated, "... closely linked with economic underprivilege is psychological underprivilege: habits of submission, little access to sources of information, lack of verbal facility. These things appear to produce a lack of self-confidence which increases the unwillingness of the low status person to participate in many phases of our predominantly middle class culture, even beyond what would be a realistic withdrawal adapted to his reduced chances of being effective" (quoted in Srole *et al.*, 33). Indeed, all the popular culture media, the movies, comic books, newspapers, and so forth, disparage low-status identification. The consequence is that low-status children are caught in a conflict in which they must accept either the values of mass media and the schoolroom, which are dominated by the aspirations of the middle class, or the values of their low-status parents. The lower the family SES, the less likely it is that such children will be able to work themselves out of their situation of underprivilege. Consequently, a high proportion of slum residents are resigned to a life of frustration and defeat. They long for money, possessions, education, and status, but they do not know how to achieve them. They are pervaded by a sense of pessimism and fatalism consistent with the hopelessness of their condition. They are likely to lack a sense of rational control over their own destiny and to be convinced that success or failure is just a matter of "luck." Thus, they tend to believe that they have no responsibility for their own fate since it is under the control of external forces (22).

## SOCIAL STATUS AS A WAY OF LIFE

We have seen that social status is associated with far more than family income. It is related to child training practices, the child's psychological development, and his internalized value system. Social status may well be perpetuated in families where given personality characteristics and habit systems pay off in desired social rewards. We now want to review briefly the ways of life that tend to be transmitted within middle-class, lower-class, and slum families.

### The Middle Class

Typically, the middle-class child is brought up to be a "somebody." The goals that are transmitted to the middle-SES child usually include advanced education and the development of work skills, ambition, and economic achievement. Values that also significantly characterize the middle class include the importance of rationality and the postponement of immediate satisfactions in the service of long-range goals, acceptance of responsibilities, and constructive use of one's time. Similarly esteemed as virtues are the control of physical aggression coupled with an emphasis on getting along with people through displaying the proper manners, courtesy, and being personable (6, 7, 21). An understanding of the inner motives and intentions of other people is commonly fostered. The worries of higher-SES persons tend to center on their work and marriage, although difficulties in these areas are, in fact, more prevalent among lower-SES individuals (21).

### The Lower Class

Lower-class men often find their social satisfactions within the kinship group, but many also identify strongly with a friendship group with whom they "hang out" on the street corner, in a bar, etc. (29). Men in stable lower-class groups value their group relationships as of far more value than economic success. Their occupational goals tend to be modest, relatively immediate, and devalued compared to participation in human relationships.

The wives of workingmen also typically limit their social experience to their homes, husbands, and children, and to close relatives such as their mother or sisters. Frequently, they feel isolated from the world of non-relatives and find it hard to get acquainted, sensing that they lack the requisite social skills. They are, however, usually more lonely than hostile, although they are highly sensitive to anticipated rejection. They are less likely than middle-class women to belong to social organizations. Although lower-class women are typically deeply religious, surprisingly they are often not churchgoers, apparently because they would feel out of place (28).

### The Slum Inhabitant

As the slum person matures he is too often brought to the conclusion that love, respect, education, and economic rewards are not his lot, for they come neither to his family nor to others whom he knows or observes. To study and to work hard are, from his point of view, basically unrewarded activities. Therefore, those who live in disorganized slum areas often take what immediate pleasures they can. The likely consequences include promiscuity, love of destructiveness for its own sake, and a penchant for sensationalism in newspaper or pulp magazine stories dealing with crime and sex. These momentary satisfactions must serve in lieu of more lasting rewards, which, realistically, the slum resident fears will never come. "To put it simply the lower class individual doesn't want as much success, knows he couldn't get it if he wanted to, and doesn't want what might help him get success" (15).

Slum individuals are often concerned with their physical health, the difficulties of making their way economically, their roles as parents, and their poor social relationships. They tend to dislike their jobs, to feel friendless and lonely, and to see life as empty and futile (21).

In the slums, relations with other people tend to be quite restricted. Contacts are usually limited to the immediate family, close relatives, or in-groups, such as gangs. "Outsiders" are viewed with suspicion and distrust, while others of the same status who attempt to climb socially are resented and considered odd (32).

What are we to conclude from this review? To the writer the following points are of greatest significance.

1. Three different dimensions of psychological development can be distinguished, namely, intellectual, social, and moral development.

2. Beyond whatever endogenous processes influence psychological development, factors in the individual's early environment can profoundly affect the rate of development in the intellectual, social, and moral spheres.

3. The social class level of parents appears to influence developmental rate, with those born into middle-class (and presumably also upper-class) levels appearing relatively more advanced and those of lower-class levels relatively less advanced in psychological development.

4. Other factors in the early environment will also be likely to influence the individual's psychological development, such as parental personality and behavior, and position in the sibling hierarchy, but the explicit consequences of these on the psychology of the child are not adequately documented with regard to the specifics of intellectual, social, and moral development.

5. Our review suggests that the adult population of the general community covers a wide range of development in the intellectual, social, and moral spheres. Individual placement on these dimensions is presumably dependent on some complex of endogenous and experiential factors.

6. It is not any specific earlier experiences, but the psychological resources that the individual can bring into operation at a given stage of life, that determine his potential for effective adaptation at that point in his life-span.

We must now see in what way achieved level of psychological development may be measured. The next three chapters are devoted to this problem.

## REFERENCES

1. Baldwin, J. M. Society as an organization of selves. In C. F. Borgatta and H. J. Meyer (Eds.), *Sociological theory*. New York: Knopf, 1956. Pp. 62–70.

2. Bonney, M. E. A descriptive study of the normal personality. *Journal of Clinical Psychology*, 1962, **18**, 256–266.

3. Bossard, J. H. S., & Boll, E. S. Ritual in family living. *American Sociological Review*, 1949, **14**, 463–469.

4. Bowlby, J. *Maternal care and mental health*. (2nd ed.) Geneva: World Health Organization, 1952.

5. Bronfenbrenner, U. Socialization and social class through time and space. In E. E. Maccoby, T. M. Newcomb, & E. L. Hartley (Eds.), *Readings in social psychology*. New York: Holt, 1958, Pp. 400–425.

6. Cohen, A. K. *Delinquent boys*. New York: Free Press of Glencoe, 1955.

7. Davis, A., & Havighurst, R. J. Social class and color differences in child rearing. *American Sociological Review*, 1946, **11**, 698–710.

8. Durkheim, E. *The elementary forms of the religious life*. (Translated by J. W. Swaine: Glencoe, Ill.: Free Press, 1947.)

9. Erikson, E. H. Growth and crises of the "Healthy Personality," In C. Kluckhohn and H. A. Murray (Eds.), *Personality in nature, society, and culture*. New York: Knopf, 1959. Pp. 185–225.

10. Freud, S. *The ego and the id*. London: Hogarth Press, 1927.
11. Freud, S. *Civilization and its discontent*. New York: Norton, 1930.
12. Freud, S. *New introductory lectures on psycho-analysis*. New York: Norton, 1933.
13. Hoffman, M. L. Power assertion by the parent and its impact on the child. *Child Development*, 1960, **31**, 129–143.
14. Hollingshead, A. B., & Redlich, F. C. *Social class and mental illness*. New York: Wiley, 1958.
15. Hyman, H. H. The value systems of different classes: A social psychological contribution to the analysis of stratification. In R. Bendix & S. M. Lipset (Eds.), *Class, status and power*. Glencoe, Ill.: Free Press, 1953. Pp. 426–427.
16. Irwin, O. C. Infant speech: The effect of family occupational status and age on use of sound types. *Journal of Speech Hearing Disorders*, 1948, **13**, 224–226.
17. Kaplan, B., Reed, R. B., & Richardson, W. Comparison of the incidence of hospitalized cases of psychosis in two communities. *American Sociological Review*, 1956, **21**, 479.
18. Kinsey, A. C., Pomeroy, W. B., & Martin, C. E. *Sexual behavior in the human male*. Philadelphia: Saunders, 1948.
19. Kohn, M. L. Social class and the exercise of parental authority. *American Sociological Review*, 1959, **24**, 352–366.
20. Knupfer, G. Portrait of the underdog. *Public Opinion Quarterly*, 1947, **11**, 103–114; also In R. Bendix & S. M. Lipset (Eds.), *Class, status and power*, Glencoe, Ill.: Free Press, 1953. P. 256.
21. Langner, T. S., & Michael, S. T. *Life stress and mental health: Midtown Manhattan study*. Vol. 2. New York: Free Press of Glencoe, 1963.
22. Lewis, O. The culture of poverty. *Scientific American*, 1966, **4**, 19–25.
23. Miller, S. M. The American lower classes: A typological approach. In A. B. Shostak & W. Gomberg (Eds.), *New perspectives on poverty*. Englewood Cliffs, N. J.: Prentice-Hall, 1965. Pp. 22–39.
24. Parsons, T., & Bales, R. F. *Family, socialization and interaction process*. Glencoe, Ill.: Free Press, 1955.
25. Piaget, J. *Play, dreams and imitation in childhood*. New York: Norton, 1951.
26. Piaget, J. *The psychology of intelligence*. New York: Harcourt, Brace, 1955.
27. Piaget, J. *The moral judgement of the child*. (3rd ed.). Glencoe, Ill.: Free Press, 1960.
28. Rainwater, L., Coleman, R., & Handel, G. *Workingman's wife*. New York: Oceana Publications, 1959.
29. Ryan, E. J. Personal identity in an urban slum. In L. J. Duhl (Ed.), *The urban condition*. New York: Basic Books, 1963. Pp. 135–150.
30. Sears, R. R., Maccoby, E. E., & Levin, H. *Patterns of child-rearing*. New York: Harper & Row, 1957.
31. Singer, J. L. Projected familial attitudes as a function of socioeconomic status and psychopathology. *Journal of Consulting Psychology*, 1954, **18**, 99–104.
32. Spinley, B. M. *The deprived and the privileged*. London: Routledge & Kegan Paul, 1953.
33. Srole, L., Langner, T. S., Michael, S. T., Opler, M. K., & Rennie, T. A. C. *Mental health in the metropolis: Midtown Manhattan study*. Vol. 1. New York: McGraw-Hill, 1962.
34. *Webster's new collegiate dictionary*. Springfield, Mass.: G. & C. Merriam, 1958.
35. Wootton, B. *Social science and social pathology*. New York: Macmillan, 1959.
36. Yarrow, L. J. Maternal deprivation: Toward and empirical and conceptual revaluation. *Psychological Bulletin*, 1961, **6**, 459–490.

# 3 / SOCIAL COMPETENCE AND
# SOCIETAL EXPECTATIONS

This chapter and the next explore the types of measures that most adequately represent achieved level of social competence. Each such measure must conform to two principal requirements: first, it must indicate the level and quality of the individual's performance in the sphere of real-life behavior. Second, it must correspond to the operation of those domains of psychological function of which social competence is the outward expression. In the light of our past discussion, a comprehensive measure of social competence is required that will permit us to assess (a) intellectual performance and its constructive applications in environmental mastery, (b) degree of social participation as expressed in interpersonal relationships within the family and the community at large, and (c) the person's sense of morality, that is, whether he willingly participates in the social ethos or is its enemy, and whether his behavior is guided by an implicit desire to serve others as well as himself.

Social competence is a comprehensive term that includes performance in both the physical (or technological) and the interpersonal worlds. Intellectual level is probably most directly relevant to the technological sphere. Achievements in the fields of education and work are substantially dependent on intellectual potential and in themselves may, therefore, serve as some approximation of this potential. Social and moral development are more directly reflected in the sphere of human relationships, and are more easily accessible to evaluation in terms of social participation, marriage, and family relationships. First, we shall consider intellectual development its effectuation in educational and occupational achievement, and its correlates in the general development of personality. Then we shall examine how social and moral development are expressed in the person's ability to participate effectively in interpersonal relationships.

Although we shall discuss behavioral indices of intellectual, social, and moral development, the writer and his colleagues have not attempted to compare individuals in these terms as independent entities of psychological development. Our objective has been more modest than this. It is simply to develop some global measure of social competence based on the evaluation of the person's effectiveness in coping with the tasks of living in an adult society. We have chosen areas of behavior in which competence could be assessed on three bases: (1) the tasks are fairly universal in our society so that nearly every adult can be rated; (2) the expected behaviors are overt and can be judged in an objective and quantifiable fashion; and (3) they can reasonably be taken to reflect the development of personality in either the intellectual, social, or moral spheres. This last requirement is an attempt to establish an index of social competence on some rational and conceptually defensible basis. Hence, we have suggested certain items for inclusion in our scale of social competence on the basis that they may reflect achieved level of either intellectual, social, or moral development. Nevertheless, no claim is made that any item proposed for inclusion in the scale of competence is in fact a specific index of any one of these forms of development. All that is hoped is that these items are reasonably acceptable as indicative of general social effectiveness. The developmental significance of our scales, even as a totality, remains only a hypothesis. Later, however, in Chapter 5, we shall subject this hypothesis to specific test.

INTELLECTUAL DEVELOPMENT

Let us look at the correlates of intellectual performance as these appear in adaptive patterns of behavior. By intellectual performance more is meant than simply intellectual potential as reflected in traditional measures of intelligence. It is the *fulfillment* of intellectual potential in which we are primarily interested. Traditional measures of intelligence have been shown to bear a substantial (although by no means perfect) relationship with educational and occupational accomplishments. Educational and occupational achievement appear, therefore, as reasonably direct measures of the adaptive uses of intelligence. Statistically, they are also highly related to each other (6). Taken together, they are the most widely used measure of social class position. A combined index of educational and occupational levels has been found to correlate + .91 with social class level, as estimated independently by sociologists (6).

We now reach a central issue in the use of educational and occupational achievement in any comprehensive index of social competence. The question at issue is whether these measures of social competence are not simply indices of the individual's social class. By implication, therefore, are not the relationships that the writer and his colleagues have observed between "social competence" and adaptive failure simply the reflection of relationships reported by others between social class and pathology?

To answer this question we need to explore further the nature of social class. Maclver (10) has defined a social class as ". . . any portion of a community which is marked off from the rest, not by limitations arising out of language, locality, function, or specialization, but primarily by social status" [italics in original deleted]. Warner also defines a social class as "a *status group* whose status ranking is determined by the evaluation of members of the community" (18).

How independent is social status from other possible defining variables of class? A number of writers have suggested that a person's social status is closely related to his economic status, and in particular, to the degree of prestige that attaches to his occupation (5). Thus, Warner (17) found a correlation of .91 between scoring on his occupation scale and on a measure of "Evaluated Participation" that was designed to estimate status-group participation. Placement on his occupation scale turned out to be the best single index (of six) for prediction of status-group placement. Hollingshead and Redlich (6) similarly have reported that occupational level alone correlates at a level of .88 with social class placement, when this is established independently on sociological grounds.

Parsons (13) has suggested that an occupational hierarchy is the *dominant* element in American social stratification. Other elements, such as community power, cultural style of life, social participation, and personal behavior, enter into determining social status but these are all related to the occupational-economic complex, although none are quite coincidental with it. The Lynds, too, regard the economic-occupational factor as the decisive element in class definition. They believe that other variables, such as psychological feelings of status, group life, and community power relationships, are dependent on a social division along occupational and economic lines (9).

In reviewing the evidence available on the interrelations of factors that determine social prestige, Kahl (7) likewise concludes that the covariation between personal and occupational prestige is higher than for most variables in which sociologists are interested. Therefore, either occupational prestige largely causes personal prestige, or both are determined by shared underlying factors.

It must be observed, however, that occupational prestige virtually coincides with degree of work skill and responsibility required to perform successfully on a job. This can be seen in the near identity of Warner's scale of occupational prestige and Roe's (15) scale of occupational level, which is based on required skill, ability, and responsibility. Thus, the most discriminating and most frequently used index of social class level is a direct measure of the person's own achievements in the occupational sphere. It might be argued that a person's occupational status is in large part dependent on that held by his father. In fact, only modest relationships have been found between parental and adult offspring occupational levels, relationships that account for little more than 10 or 15 percent of their common variance (7, 12).

In keeping with these findings, occupational and educational achievements are used as indices of a person's own accomplishments. On the other hand, sociologists have a greater theoretical interest in the social correlates of these personal accomplishments, that is, the person's prestige in the community and his style of life.

The writer suggests, therefore, that the question whether occupational level (as well as educational accomplishment) is to be seen as an index of individual competence or social status is dependent on one's professional interests. As a psychologist, the writer is more interested in individual accomplishment; sociologists tend to a greater interest in the social consequences of that accomplishment. Of course, these two uses of the occupational and educational variables are not mutually exclusive.

## SOCIAL DEVELOPMENT

Our concern is with just how external patterns of role behavior may correspond to inner social development. First we must ask what are the dimensions along which social development is to be assessed; then we can ask what kinds of social behaviors and their characteristics will allow for these kinds of evaluation. At least three qualities of interpersonal behavior appear to reflect the degree of social maturation achieved. These include: (1) degree of stability of interpersonal relationships, (2) an allied quality of closeness, intimacy, or emotional involvement in relationships, and (3) the ability to differentiate among roles adopted either by oneself or by a complementary other.

Here, then, are the characteristics of social behavior that indicate the level of social development that the person has achieved: (1) stability, (2) intimacy, and (3) differentiation. Are there directly observable facets of the individual's social behavior by which we can objectively rate the degree to which these characteristics have been achieved? If so, these will permit an assessment of the level of social development that the person has reached. The writer believes there are and has, with his colleagues, assessed these segments of interpersonal behavior in one form or another of our measures of social competence.

### Stability

Stability in interpersonal relationships is reflected in various aspects of adult behavior, for stability means only that the person tends to maintain his relations with others over substantial periods of time. The duration of almost any interpersonal relationship might serve as an index of stability, but two items that we have included in our scales of social competence are objective and easily measurable indices of that stability. These are the length of time that a person holds a given job, and the maintenance of a marriage relationship.

### Intimacy

The degree of intimacy or emotional involvement that the person can initiate and sustain in his interpersonal relations can reasonably be rated in the friendships established, and inferentially at least, by his marital history, that is, has the person ever established close and intimate relationships with members of the opposite sex, as in marriage? If so, have such relationships been maintained or dissolved? Furthermore, the holding of leadership positions in formal organizations suggests that the person is sufficiently involved with others to want to give direction to shared social forms, even if this means only that he is seeking to enhance his prestige in the eyes of others. Similarly, the frequency with which the person attends meetings of organizations in which he holds membership is at least a crude index of intensity of social participation. Degree of emotional involvement, then, may reasonably be deduced from the existence of close friendships, marital history, organizational leadership, and organizational attendence.

### Differentiation

Differentiation in role relations is implied by the diversity of relations in which the person becomes engaged. Thus, beyond the holding of a job and entry into marriage, which are almost universal commitments in our society, we can ask, to how many different organizations does the person belong, and how different are their objectives one from the other? For example, an individual presumably relates quite differently to other people as a member of a country club in contrast to his serving on the executive committee of a parent-teacher association.

No one-to-one correspondence between inner social development and overt interpersonal behaviors is to be expected. It cannot be inferred that higher levels of social development are achieved directly in correspondence with number of friends, membership in organizations, frequency of attendance, and so forth. People differ in their social styles, partly on the basis of ethnicity, their age and sex group, and their social class level. Presumably, there is some optimum balance, too, as suggested by the literature on the healthy personality (reviewed in Chapter 1), between autonomy or separateness from people and togetherness; between introversion and extroversion; and between "inner" and "outer directedness." Nevertheless, it seems reasonable to suggest that some gross deficiency of participation in the world of human relationships implies a true failure in the development of skills in interpersonal interaction.

## MORAL DEVELOPMENT

Robbery, firesetting, murder, child neglect, and other forms of antisocial and destructive behavior deviate from any reasonable moral code for adult behavior. The occurrence of any one of these, therefore, may serve as an index of failure in moral development. We are not so much concerned, however, with defining the person's moral immaturity from such lapses in behavior. Rather it is the individual's *potential* for such deviations in behavior that we are trying to predict from his level of psychological development. At this point we are concerned specifically with those characteristics of everyday behavior that may provide clues to a person's level of moral development.

Is it possible to assess a person's level of moral development by reviewing his social behavior? More precisely, can we judge, from his everyday behavior, to what degree the person acts as if: (1) he is accountable to himself for his actions and their consequences; (2) he feels under obligation for the welfare of others; (3) his conduct toward others originates in a mutual respect for the needs and wishes of each, i.e., reciprocity. The writer considers it possible to judge the extent to which the person's behavior conforms to these criteria. Below, we have grouped behavior indices according to whether they appear to best represent the personal accountability, obligation, or reciprocity aspects of moral development.

### Accountability

Scoring on several biographical items included in our scales of social competence is presumed to reflect a person's sense of being accountable to himself for his acts and their consequences. These items include a measure of a person's independence of his parents in adult life. Has he, even as an adult, remained excessively tied to them emotionally or remained dependent on them financially? For example, has he continued to live with or quite close to his parents or other relatives? The adult who continues to live in the home of older relatives may be expressing his emotional dependence upon them, that is, he may see them and not himself as responsible for the life that he is now living, as well as for his destiny.

Similarly, the individual's sense of accountability can be judged from his level of responsibility on the job. For example, we can quantify the closeness with which his work is controlled by others or, conversely, his independence from direct supervision. Again, accountability can be judged by the number of employees for whose work output the person is responsible. In industrial or commercial organizations a difference in degree of accountability is surely implied between persons who supervise no one, those who supervise only one or a few other individuals, and those who are responsible for the work of ten or more people. It is not possible, of course, to rate accountability in terms of the number of employees supervised for those whose work does not call for the assumption of such responsibility. A novelist, artist, or scientist, for example, will not ordinarily be accountable for the work of others. At the same time, the very nature of their occupation makes them intensely dependent on a well developed ability to make effective use of their own time. The creative person will, because of the very nature of his work, score high on independence from direct supervision by others.

Another index of a sense of responsibility to oneself for the consequences of one's actions is indicated by the use to which the person puts his free time. Is it frittered away, given over solely to watching television or to socializing, or is it put to more constructive uses—to such activities as home maintenance, the building of useful equipment, or some form of personal enrichment, as for example, study in the arts or sciences or of foreign languages? Degree of accountability for the consequences of one's acts appears, therefore, to be represented in (1) the exent of independence from the control and bounty of one's parents, (2) the measure of independent responsibility allowed in one's work, and (3) the uses to which leisure time is put.

*Obligation*

The person's sense of obligation for the welfare of others may be inferred from his having been assigned or voted positions of leadership in those formal organizations in which he holds membership. Organizational leadership implies that other members are willing to repose confidence in his ability to carry out organizational responsibilities. Similarly, the person's sense of social responsibility is often reflected in the kinds of organizations to which he belongs. Are these only social in nature, serving primarily to give enjoyment and meet recreational needs, or are they groups that respond to serious social issues, as for example, the Chamber of Commerce, League of Women Voters, or Parent-Teacher Association? How seriously the person takes his broader social and community responsibilities is also indicated in whether, and how often, he votes in local, state, or national elections.

The person's marital history can likewise imply some sense of whether he can tolerate or accept an obligation for the welfare of others. Thus, maintenance of a family in itself suggests acceptance of such an obligation. Organizational leadership, the type of organizations to which the person belongs, his voting record, and whether he has maintained a family all imply the person's sense of moral obligation. Finally, an item included in various versions of a scale of social competence appears appropriately representative of the person's level of moral development, yet seems to reflect aspects of both a sense of personal accountability and a sense of obligation for the welfare of others. This is the degree of regularity with which the person has been employed as compared to the employment history of individuals who have had an equal opportunity for employment. This is taken to be a measure of a person's responsibility for himself as well as for those others who are dependent upon him for their welfare.

*Reciprocity*

Reciprocity in one's dealings with others may be rated, particularly within the marriage relationship. Maintenance of a marriage in itself suggests that at least some minimal concern for the needs and desires of the partner has served to guide one's actions in the relationship. The partnership may also imply the extent to which personal relationships are motivated by a desire for equity and mutual respect. The way in which marriage partners share in such decisions as how their money is to be spent and how their children are to be guided and disciplined is evidence of the extent of mutuality. For example, a self-centered disregard for others is indicated when money is spent, or a child is disciplined, without consideration of the interests or values of the spouse. At the other extreme, a lack of reciprocity in the marriage relationship is implied when a spouse accepts no responsibility for the disposition of the family income or the discipline of a child.

It is not suggested that level of moral development shares a precise quantitative relationship with the person's job responsibilities, use of leisure time, or work in organizations, or with the way in which he responds to his marriage and family responsibilities, or the like. Particular behaviors are far too likely to differ in significance according to the specific of each individual life. The writer believes, however, that this diversity in the kinds of life behaviors sampled does reflect some general level of moral development and, more specifically, contributes to the setting up of a global measure of social competence.

To this point the intent has been to show that a systematic analysis of everyday behaviors can convey a quite remarkable degree of information in regard to personality development. In order to be as explicit as possible, the writer has erred on the side of an excessive concreteness. Intellectual, social, and moral development have been treated in relative isolation, when, of course, the distinction is one imposed on personality for heuristic purposes. These qualities of personality are more nearly relative emphases in function than truly independent basic elements out of which a personality is built. Human intelligence operates largely in a social context, and all interpersonal relations are implicitly guided by the individual sense of what is in harmony with one's values and is therefore morally right.

If it is difficult to discriminate between the operation of purely intellectual, or social, or moral properties, it follows that no one fragment of a person's way of life can represent solely the manifestation of any one of these attributes of personality. Thus, achieved level of educational or occupational skill cannot represent the operation of intelligence alone, nor does the way in which family finances are handled correspond solely to the development of individual morality. It might be more appropriate to say that in such a concrete facet of living as educational achievement, intellectual development is more easily observed and objectively evaluated than in, say, the area of family finances. Similarly, the way in which the family's money is handled may more directly reveal the moral qualities of the marriage partners, yet some intellectual adeptness is surely required if a family is to remain solvent.

SOCIETAL EXPECTATIONS

The overarching framework of theory adopted in this book is that social behavior is an adaptive process. Human behavior is seen as not simply a consequence of the individual's psychological attributes. Rather, his behavior in interaction with others is as truly the consequence of forces external to him as it is the result of his own psychological characteristics. The wishes, expectations, and actions of other people will play as great a determining role in a person's behavior as will his own wishes, expectations, and social skills.

Social competence, then, reflects more than psychological development.

It also expresses the individual's potential for meeting those expectancies for adaptive behavior that are imposed by virtue of living in society. The expectations of those other persons who make up an individual's world lead him into the performance of those behaviors that tend to increase his skills in social living. These expectations are not happenstance. There is a general consensus, subject to much local, idiosyncractic, and temporal coloring, as to what constitutes an acceptable, or at least tolerable, range of behaviors. In every society, criteria exist for judging whether a person's actions and general style of life are appropriate for his position in that society. Overtly, expectations for a person's behavior are designated by his age and sex, and covertly by his social class affiliation. The social rules may be either implicit or explicit, ambiguous or clearly articulated, and laid down by law or simply by custom. In the United States, for example, all 6-year-olds are expected to attend school. This expectation is explicit, clearly articulated, and has the force of law. Again, as an illustration, within the restrictions of the middle and upper classes, high school boys are expected to eschew marriage and defer entering into this estate until they are "well established" in a career. This expectation is more implicit than explicit, often not well articulated, and enjoys no standing in law, although it is traditional in the thinking of middle- and upper-class parents.

Each social class level is characterized by a particular style of life. Independent of class level, however, some sequence of changing expectations for behavior confront each person in society. These expectations generally involve coping with the tasks of educational and occupational achievement and interpersonal and group relationships, as well as undertaking the responsibilities of marriage and parenthood. These are major and nearly universal areas of human living, and are of central significance in the life of most people, whether they attempt much or little in any of them. Some normative (even if implicit) standards of performance exist in each of these areas of function, which nearly all people internalize and against which they will judge their own achievements. In the last chapter we considered how style of life reflects a person's social class affillation. In the next chapter we shall review societal expectations for the behavior of the two sexes. Here, the writer will discuss how such expectations for behavior are interrelated with chronological age.

Srole *et al.* (16) conceive of age levels as a universal mechanism to which every society gears role assignments and behavioral expectations. Each age level makes its own demands on the person, in terms of its own set of expected performances at school, in work, in the acceptance of the responsibilities of marriage, and so forth. These expectancies, however, are also personal commitments, first imposed by societal pressures, but subsequently internalized and made one's own. Inner acceptance of these expectations depends on a maturing sense of self and of one's relationships with others. In turn, their acceptance lays the groundwork for further maturation in personality.

A number of investigators (1, 2) have suggested that the concept of self or personal identity emerges and is continuously transformed in living through a series of life "crises." These crises are defined by the required changes in role behavior that accompany entry into successive age groups. With each change in age status the person is expected to initiate and maitain new patterns of role behavior that have not previously been included in his repertoire of roles, for example, those of pupil, worker, spouse, and parent.

Societal expectations require more than a simple change in the surface of the person's life. They demand the development of new skills, often technical and always interpersonal in nature. In entering into each new phase of life, the person himself is continuously transformed. Thus, increasing age entails far more than physical maturation. It brings an ever-increasing complexity of expectations for behavior that tax first the intellectual resources and subsequently the social and moral resources of the person. In consequence, the personality structure becomes increasingly subtle, complex, and flexible with the successful weathering of each new crisis in development. Thus, we find personality growth through the effective resolution of crises in living, and the person becomes ever more adaptive in the face of further environmental change. Inferentially, then, it follows that the older the person becomes without succumbing to some form of pathology, the greater his resources for adaptation in society, that is, the greater his social competence. For this reason, the writer and his co-workers have made use of chronological age prior to hospital admission for psychiatric disorder as one item in a scale of social competence (19).

How do societal expectations arise? On what basis does a community come to expect and implicitly to demand certain minimal standards for behavior according to age group? The writer suggests that it is out of their experience with persons in different age groups that adults come to recognize what achievements can reasonably be expected at each age level. A consensus emerges that serves as a normative baseline against which each individual is judged. Our scale of social competence provides a quantitative index of how well an individual measures up against this criterion of societal expectations. Thus, a person's standing on our scale of social competence, compared to that of other adults, provides an estimate of his coping ability relative to that of other individuals. Social competence scoring, then, can be seen as an index of relative potential for coping with societal expectations.

Each age period is confronted by different societal expectations, so that we cannot simply expect to predict a person's future behaviors from those in which he engages in the present. The writer proposes, however, that we *can* predict the individual's future behaviors on the basis of two pieces of information: (1) knowledge of the behavioral expectations associated with that age period in which our interests lie; and (2) what the individual's relative potential will be for matching those expectations. To the extent that a person's adaptive potential relative to that of others remains constant from one age period to another, his behavior in the future should be predictable from his present adaptive potential. Thus a person's present social competence (compared to that of other adults in his age and sex group) may provide a measure of future coping potential. Nevertheless, relative standing in adaptive potential presumably will change over the years based on the vicissitudes of individual life experience. Thus the precise extent to which relative coping potential remains stable is a question for empirical investigation.

In a sense, much current psychological evaluation, including intelligence and achievement testing, is based on the presumption that a stable relationship is maintained between present and future coping ability. In regard to the broader aspects of social living, prediction of future behavior has been restricted for the most part to prognostic studies in delinquency (3) and psychopathology.

In contrast, we are concerned with how general expectations for behavior are influenced by age considerations. In line with our earlier format, we shall discuss in turn the relation of intellectual, social, and moral development to age expectations.

## Intellectual Development and Societal Expectations

Intellectual development is closely paralleled by changes in society's expectations for behavior from the infant's earliest days. Achievement of object constancy and of relations between objects, whether inanimate, animate, or human, lays the basis for that knowledge of surroundings and family expected of the young child. Language development, usually beginning in the second year, is also a vital step toward entry into social relationships with others, both family and peers.

Formal schooling begins for most youngsters at 6 years of age because a mental age of 6 years is generally assumed to be a prerequisite for the eventual mastery of reading, writing, and arithmetic skills. On the basis of these fundamental educational achievements, the child is expected to acquire in the elementary and high school years a wide and systematic knowledge of the physical and social world about him. Educational demands are in process of change and in technologically advanced societies there is a tendency to increase the minimum number of years of schooling required. In the United States, for example, there has been much concern recently about the high school dropout. This demand for more years of education parallels the increasing level of technical skills required to participate in the industrial and commercial life of this country. Education itself then serves largely to prepare the person for an occupation. This is true especially for men, although women, too, are taking increased advantage of educational opportunity for entry into a career of work, rather than a simple continued acceptance of their traditional role of mother and homemaker.

During the elementary and high school years the demand for intellectual accomplishment through education is almost universally imposed on the young in our society. Only retarded or other obviously incapacitated persons are exempt from this injunction. The end of the secondary school years marks the point at which the life paths of our youth diverge into more specialized directions. For girls, this is often the end of intellectual ambitions, for a majority of females are married by their twentieth year (4). After marriage, the majority of women leave the labor force to live simply as housewives and mothers. Nevertheless, more and more influential voices on the American scene are being raised to decry the loss to our society that is represented in this intellectual withdrawal of women. Certainly the climate of opinion is coming to favor a higher level of education for women as well as men and the continued employment of women after they marry and begin to raise a family. Increasingly, married women remain in or reenter the labor force, and women as a group now constitute approximately one third of the working population in this country.

Men are expected to work for a living, although their time of entry into the world of work varies. Many go into an occupation directly from high school. Others, and the proportion is rising rapidly, enter college or some other specialized form of further training. The societal expectation that influences each person's decision is that he will fulfill his intellectual potential to the maximum. Those who enter into an occupation are expected to improve their skill level and advance in the occupational hierarchy. Those who go on to college are acting in consonance with the continuously reiterated theme that advanced education enriches the individual's work and income potential.

College, of course, is meant to do more than this. This academic experience is intended to broaden intellectual horizons, to free thought from simple settled convictions, and to permit the person to become a constructive innovator, whether in work or the community.

From early adulthood to retirement the person is expected to increase his occupational skills. The individual is constantly judged by his peers and superiors as to his competence on the job, with outstanding effectiveness often rewarded by promotion. The competent nurse, inspired teacher, and productive scientist are likely to be assigned administrative and supervisory positions even when they are not suited for this advancement and not particularly happy in it. Those who are judged able are expected to proceed up the hierarchy of occupational advancement until the time of their retirement.

Some occupations have a niche for their "elder statesmen," those mature and successful career men who represent experience and accumulated wisdom. Whether he be a janitor, a skilled machinist, a teacher, or a scientist, the older established worker is expected to serve as mentor to the younger and less experienced employee. In fields that have no provision for elder statesmen, retirement has frequently been a time of difficult readjustment, a period of stress that the older person has found hard to tolerate. With a constantly larger proportion of our population living into their sixties and beyond, an increased concern is evident for what we euphemistically call our senior citizens. Communities are beginning to find that they can use the accumulated skills of these people in a variety of capacities. But the difficulties that often face the older, retired person as he passes from the intense competition of the economic world into abrupt intellectual and occupational inactivity are far from eliminated.

## Social Development and Societal Expectations

Very early in life, the individual is expected to master three prerequisites for further social development. These are: (1) to establish a sense of self-identity; (2) to articulate his sex identity; and (3) to learn that he is a member of a family group in which he holds a particular place. In a narrow sense, these expectations are met by nearly everyone. The child achieves recognition of what is physical "self" and what is "not-self" probably before the end of his first year (see Chapter 2). A sense of one's maleness or femaleness has been reported as usually fixed within the second or third year (11). Recognition of just who constitute one's immediate family, or of the boundaries that distinguish family from nonfamily, is also achieved early in the preschool years. These accomplishments set the stage for successful social experiences with one's age peers.

Two quite different aspects of social and interpersonal developmental need to be considered in relation to societal expectations. In the one, we concentrate on the person in terms of marriage and family; in the other we see him in more formal social relationships and as a participant in the larger community. We shall discuss the latter pattern of relationships first.

*The Person in Society.* During the school years societal expectations for social behavior correspond to a normative level of social development. Early in the school years middle- and upper-class children, in particular, are encouraged to form friendships. These informal personal relationships outside the bounds of the family are the precursors of entry into more structured social relationships. Various clubs and other forms of extramural activities are associated with the American high school and are designed to engage the interests of this age group. Thus, almost universal in the American high school is a school band, social and dramatic clubs, and athletic teams. The pattern of organized activity that is encouraged during the adolescent years often sets that lifelong pattern of organized social and community participation that more than a century ago DeToqueville found to distinguish the American way of life.

Participation in some formal organization is very nearly universal during adulthood. Thus, in 1962, the churches claimed a total membership of 118,000,000 persons, or about two thirds of the population of the United States. Labor unions report a total membership of approximately 14,500,000; a large proportion of businessmen belong to their local Chambers of Commerce; and most scientists and other professional people are members of their national and regional associations. Although these institutions bring together people of like minds, they exist for more than social purposes. Much pressure is exerted to belong to these institutions, that is, to attend church, for the worker to join a trade union (this may be a requirement for holding a job), and for the businessman or professional to hold membership in his associations.

During the mature years of adulthood the effective person is expected to do more than simply participate in social and community organizations. There is increasing pressure on him to continue to assume greater responsibility to advance their objectives. Eventually, the active older adult will be expected to groom younger members for carrying on the work of their organizations.

*Person and Family*. Personal relationships, however, are more than purely social in nature. They are very much determined by the biology of sex differences. With the onset of puberty, personal relationships bifurcate into two qualitatively different forms. While the adolescent, and subsequently the adult, is expected to continue and to expand his social contacts, it is also assumed that each individual will develop a special interest in persons of the opposite sex.

It is during adolescence that there ordinarily occur the preliminary trials and experimentation of heterosexual experience. At first, this is likely to remain only social in form, although sharp social class differences appear in this regard (8). In the lower class sexual intercourse is experimented with earlier and for more frequently than in the middle and upper classes. In the latter, adolescent boys are expected to delay sexual gratification, as well as marriage, in the interests of their career. For girls, particularly, premaritial sexual experience is considered taboo. Nevertheless, far greater sexual freedom is the order of the day for adolescents and the college age adult. It has been reported (14), for example, that today one out of six brides is pregnant on her wedding day.

Whether deferred or not, the married state is the universally approved way of life for adults, and 93 percent of the population eventually conform to this expectation. The girl who does not marry is the object of conern and perhaps pity; we have no equivalent concept of "confirmed spinster" to that of "confirmed bachelor." The older unmarried male is regarded with some ambivalence, disapproved of in his current unencumbered state and looked on as a "catch" for some "deserving girl."

Thus, there is a difference in the relative values that men and women are expected to assign to community activities in contrast to a concern with marriage, family, and home life. Motherhood and family life are the traditional cornerstones upon which a woman's world is built. Even when she participates in community organizations, she will be expected to manifest family-related interests. Thus involvement in the work of parent-teacher associations is a common community activity for housewives. Upper-class women may generalize their interests in the home through memberships on the boards of societies that deal with such problems as the unmarried mother or runaways from home. Participation in such purely community-minded organizations as the League of Women Voters is usually restricted to college-trained or other intellectually oriented women.

As children grow older and their lives more complex, parenthood becomes correspondingly a more complex and often stressful undertaking. Parents become involved in a multitude of decisions in regard to the educational experiences and social lives of their children. As the youngsters reach early adulthood and independence, however, this direct parental involvement with their children's lives should stop. At this time, the parental role is expected to change relatively abruptly. This calls for a transformation in parental interests, values, and style of life that often requires some substantial change in self concept. This period of transition is frequently a time of soul searching and emotional difficulty for the adult.

*Moral Development and Societal Expectations*

Moral development is based on the internalization of societal expectations. As we have indicated earlier, however, a true morality is not a simple accumulation of specific knowledge as to how one should behave in a given set of circumstances. Rather, morality represents a general set of principles that can serve to guide behavior in quite novel situations.

Morality is derived and abstracted from one's experience and societal expectations; it is not identical with them.

How, then, do societal expectations influence the development of a sense of morality? The specific mode of action depends on the developmental stage that the individual has achieved. Only concrete rewards and punishments can influence the behavior of the young child, and then only in the immediate instance. Thus, food and warmth can comfort a baby, or holding him can prevent an action that could lead to injury. In the first months of his life there is no hope or intent to develop any general principles of behavior except perhaps an attempt to regularize the baby's sleeping and eating cycles.

In the child's first years parents concentrate largely on helping him gain physical control over his body, for example, in learning to walk and talk and in toilet training. The insistent parental concern over toilet activities differs sharply from the desire manifested by parents for the child to develop in language and motor skills. Parents tend to feel more anger at lapses in toilet training, and more anxiety if the child is retarded in walking and talking. Retardation in the latter skills is likely to be seen as a deficiency in development with which the child is to be helped. In contrast, failure to become toilet trained represents a violation of a social taboo and is therefore subject to punishment.

The years of infancy are dedicated to mastery of the body; the school years to mastery of the mind. In school the child learns the technical skills for coping with his world. But he is expected to learn more than that. It is essential that he learn how to apply himself systematically.

Western society represents the concretization of the Protestant ethic. Success within this society requires acceptance of its cardinal principle: responsibility for one's salvation depends on one's own efforts. Both in school and at work the person must come to feel accountable for the use of his time. Western society takes self-application so much for granted, considers it so much a natural way of life, that it is difficult for us to recognize how relatively novel is this style of living, or how strange and distasteful it can appear to the peoples outside the Western orbit.

Our society expects each person from adolescence on to assume increasing responsibility for his own destiny. This includes making decisions as to one's career, friends, marriage, and family. Parents recognize that the autonomy of their offspring is inevitable, but in response their attitudes may range from resistance through impatience to resignation.

Adulthood brings with it obligations for the welfare of others. To the extent that a person succeeds occupationally (and striving for vocational success is indoctrinated early), he will be expected to become administratively responsible for the work of others. Societal expectations are more explicit and rigid when they concern the adult's responsibility for the welfare of his family. Society has always assumed that parents will provide for the material needs of their children and the law provides that parents negligent in this regard be punished. But more and more, parents are expected to be concerned about the emotional and psychological development of their children as well, so that they in turn can become responsible and productive members of society.

From adolescence on, some concern is also expected in the middle and upper classes for the general welfare of the community and of society generally. This may be reflected in the young adult's participation in civil rights activity, the Peace Corps, church groups, or in any of a multitude of "good causes." In the middle years, the sense of community obligation is more likely to be expressed by participation in causes closer to home, as the person becomes more rooted in and identified with his own community.

We have by now reviewed those aspects of everyday behavior that appear to reflect a person's level of psychological development. This discussion has suggested that it is possible to devise objective measures of a person's overt activities that reflect the inner development of personality. Indices have been presented that are presumed to tap psychological functioning in the intellectual, social, and moral spheres. Items directed at the assessment of intellectual and social performance appear to be the most direct measures of psychological function. Those concerned with morality in behavior seem most inferential. Together, these indices of performance in community living constitute a measure of the person's social competence.

A person's scoring on competence compared to that of other adults of his sex provides an index of his relative potential for effective adaptation in society. It is proposed that prediction of a person's adaptive pattern at some later period of his life is dependent on knowledge of two factors: (1) societal expectations for that age period; and (2) the person's relative standing on social competence, that is, his adaptive potential. It is suggested that to the extent that relative standing on adaptive potential remains constant, a person's future pattern of behavior is predictable.

## REFERENCES

1. Ausubel, D. P. Theory and problems of child development. New York: Grune & Stratton, 1958.
2. Erikson, E. H. Growth and crises of the "Healthy Personality." In C. Kluckhohn and H. A. Murray (Eds.), *Personality in nature, society, and culture.* New York: Knopf, 1959. Pp. 185–225.

3. Glueck, S., & Glueck, E. *Predicting delinquency and crime.* Cambridge, Mass.: Harvard University Press, 1959.

4. Golenpaul, D. (Ed.) *Information Please Almanac.* New York: Simon & Schuster, 1965.

5. Gordon, M. M. *Social class in American sociology.* Durham, N. C.: Duke University Press, 1958.

6. Hollingshead, A. B., & Redlich, F. C. *Social class and moral illness.* New York: Wiley, 1958.

7. Kahl, J. A. *The American class structure.* New York: Halt, 1964.

8. Kinsey, A. C., Pomeroy, W. B., & Martin, C. E. *Sexual behavior in the human male.* Philadelphia: Saunders, 1948.

9. Lynd, R. S., & Lynd, H. M. *Middletown in transition.* New York: Harcourt, Brace, 1937.

10. MacIver, R. M. *Society.* New York: Farrar & Rinehart, 1937.

11. Money, J., Hampson, J. G., & Hampson, J. L. Imprinting and the establishment of gender role. *A.M.A. Archives of Neurology and Psychiatry,* 1957, **77,** 333–336.

12. Morgan, J. N., David, M. H., Cohen, W. J., & Brazer, H. E. *Income and welfare in the United States.* New York: McGraw-Hill, 1962.

13. Parsons, T. An analytical approach to the theory of social stratification. In *Essays in Sociological Theory.* (Rev. ed.) Glencoe, Ill.: Free Press, 1954, Pp. 67–88.

14. Pilpel, Harriet. F. Sex versus the law: a study in hypocrisy. Harper's magazine, 1965, **230,** 35–40.

15. Roe, A. *The psychology of occupations.* New York: Wiley, 1956.

16. Srole, L., Langner, T. S., Michael, S. T., Opler, M. K., & Rennie, T. A. C. *Mental health in the metropolis: The midtown study.* Vol. 1. New York: McGraw-Hill, 1962.

17. Warner, W. L., and Associates. *Democracy in Jonesville.* New York: Harper, 1949.

18. Warner, W. L., & Lunt, P. S. *The social life of a modern community.* New Haven, Conn.: Yale University Press, 1941.

19. Zigler, E., and Phillips, L. Social effectiveness and symptomatic behaviors. *Journal of Abnormal and Social Psychology,* 1960, **2,** 231–238.

# 4 / THE MEASUREMENT OF
## SOCIAL COMPETENCE

Our task now is to assemble our behavioral measures of psychological development into a single scale of social competence. With all the benefits of hindsight it is possible to construct a scale equitably representative of intellectual, social, and moral development. As usual, however, practice has preceded insight. Much of the writer's past work required *some* measure of social competence and this was constructed from the then currently available data. The consequence is that over the last 15 years we have created four different scales social competence. Only two of these include any substantial proportion of the behavioral indices of psychological development that have been described in the previous chapters.

The failure to include them is the consequence of a number of factors. First, our four scales of competence were created at quite different times and to meet quite different research objectives. Second, the data available for rating social effectiveness varied considerably from one study to another, limited sometimes by the sparseness of routine psychiatric case histories, at other times only by the amount of time we were able to put into subject interviews. Finally, though, it must be admitted that the competence data we have collected in the past were restricted by a deficiency in conceptual clarity at the time these studies were undertaken.

Our scales of social competence include (1) the Phillips Premorbid Scale (13), (2) an index (25) based on six biographical items commonly available in routine case records of mental hospital, (3) the Worcester Scale of Social Attainment (14), and (4) our present scale of social competance, which is designed for use in studies of both normal and psychiatric populations (see Appendix). This last scale will be described first.

THE CURRENT SCALE OF SOCIAL COMPETENCE

The current scale incorporates improvements over earlier versions that result from a decade and a half of continuous research. In our most recent studies we have not been limited to the use of information collected in routine psychiatric case histories and as a consequence have been able to collect all the data we have considered relevant. Further, we have continuously revised our scale toward an increased degree of objectivity in the kind of information collected. Thus, items on closeness of friendships or experiences in the person's early years have been eliminated because of the subjectivity inevitable in the rating of emotional closeness (see the section on "Reliability of Measurement" that appears later in this chapter).

Presentation of information on items in the scale parallels their discussion in the previous three chapters. We shall look first at those items that we presume represent achieved level of intellectual development and its effectuation. Then we shall review the behavioral indices presumed to reflect social development and moral development. In the section dealing with social development, items will be organized within the catagories of stability, intimacy, and differentiation. In assessing moral development, the categories of accountability, obligation, and reciprocity will be used.

On occasion the same item appears in a number of categories and even under two or more of the major headings of intellectual, social, and moral development. This multiple use of items follows from the writer's belief that no single aspect of behavior may be assumed to express only one facet of personality development. At most we can expect that a given behavioral index mirrors one dimension of personality more sharply than another. Educational achievement, for example, corresponds more precisely to intellectual level than to social development. However, we do not know whether particular items do actually reflect specific nuances of personality, or are even accurately placed according to our logical analysis of how intellectual, social, and moral development are expressed in everyday patterns of behavior. Only future studies can answer these questions.

Scale items may be used at any of three levels of specificity. (1) The total constellations of behavioral items chosen can serve to approximate an individual's achieved level of general social competence. (2) Sets of items may be separated out to assess level of intellectual, social, or moral development. (3) Particular item clusters may be used to assess stability, intimacy, or differentiation within the sphere of social development, or accountability, obligation, or reciprocity within the domain of moral development. Whatever level of analysis is chosen, a given scale item will be used only once at that level. As an example of the multiple use of an item, let us look at item 13, that is, number of months employed during last 5 years. This is used at three points in the competence scale. It appears first as an index of the consistency with which a person's intellectual potential is applied in the economic sphere. It appears again as a measure of stability in interpersonal relationships (where the index is the number of different employers for whom the person has worked during the last 5 years). Finally, employment regularity is used as an indirect assessment of a person's sense of financial responsibility for himself and for those dependent on him.

It will be seen that if item 13 is used as an element in a total scale of social competence, it appears in that scale only once. If three component scales of social competence (i.e., intellectual, social, and moral development) are employed independently, item 13 appears in each of these separately. Finally, if the subscales of "stability in interpersonal relations" and "obligation for the welfare of others" (see below) are employed as independent measures, then item 13 likewise appears in both of these.

As a final comment, we must expect different patterns of social competence scores within the general population. Professionals, for example, are likely to score high on items presumed to tap intellectual development. On the other hand, they will tend to score as less adequate in the area of social development, since they are not prone to become active in a wide range of community organizations. A different scoring pattern may be found with businessmen. They are often socially active, although they are not likely to achieve as high a level of education as a professional person. These differences in life behavior should occasion no surprise. Developmental theory proposes that individual psychological development is not monolithic but progresses unevenly in various areas of function. Intellectual and social development, then, are not of a piece but may evolve somewhat independently of each other. If, as we assume here, competence is based on these parameters of psychological development, specialization in life-style is simply an expected outcome.

## Measurement of Intellectual Development

The first item to consider is intelligence level as measured by some standard test. This is not included in the competence scale proper, for any of a variety of measures will serve. As a minimum, the vocabulary scale of the Standford-Binet has been used. We place subjects into one of eight levels of intelligence: IQs of 69 or less; 70–80; 81–90; 91–100; 101–110; 111–120; 121–130; 131 and above.

Grades of education completed (item 11) is our second index of intellectual competence. We categorize subjects at one of the following five levels of educational achievement: none or some grade school (including ungraded or special classes); completed grade school (eight grade); some high school; completed high school; some college or more. Vocational or professional training (item 11d) counts, year for year, as the equivalent of conventional schooling.

Occupational level (item 12) serves as our third index of intellectual competence. It is scored on the basis of the subject's work history during the last 5 years. In order to assess job level accurately it is important to obtain an accurate description of the subject's work, the people whom he supervises (or who supervise his work) and what, in turn, constitutes the work of these others. Jobs are classified according to the system provided by Roe (18). She classifies occupations according to the level of skill, capacity, and responsibility that the work demands. Roe's index of occupational level conforms directly to our concept of intellectual effectuation and can serve therefore as one item in our scale of social competence.

Warner and his associates (22) devised an occupational scale as an index of social class placement. This scale is based on both the prestige and skill level of a person's job. These are related criteria. The prestige that attaches to an occupation depends mainly on the degree of skill, education, and specialization that it requires (7). It would seem, therefore, that a person's social class placement will covary with his occupational skill.

Information is gathered also on the father's occupation (item 16), not as a measure of the subject's own competence but as an index of social class of origin. The discrepancy (either positive or negative) between father's and subject's occupational level can also serve as an index of economic mobility. This may well relate to other indices of competence, but we have not as yet made use of this measure of mobility.

Regularity of employment (item 13), that is, the number of months out of the preceding 60 (5 years) in which the subject has worked, is used as a quantitative index of the consistency with which intellectual potential is applied in the economic sphere. We must be aware, of course, that unemployment is often caused by factors quite beyond the control of the person who has lost his job. Therefore months of employment should be considered only in terms of how other individuals of the same economic category stand on this index. For example, because of market demands, an unskilled laborer is less likely to be regularly employed than a skilled machinist. The employment record of a laborer, can thus be meaningfully understood as an item in his personal history only when it is compared with the employment history of other laborers, not when it is contrasted to the work history of a machinist. Medical disability (item 15) can serve to weight the validity of the employment regularity measure. If the person is severely incapacitated, it of course follows that the employment index will be rendered invalid.

Six scales have been devised for rating the person's participation in organizations and the use to which he puts his leisure time. The table for Social Competence Derived Scales (see Appendix) provide an extended list of activities that permit the scoring of all six such scales. A person's score on each of the derived scale of Organizational Activity and the Use of Leisure Time is simply the total number of all those activities in which he regularly participates that can be rated on a given scale.

The derived scale of Constructiveness permits assessment of how effectively a person makes use of his intellectual potential. Constructiveness in the use of one's leisure time includes technical or scientific self-development, such as home maintenance (e.g., installing electrical equipment or remodeling furniture), building radio equipment or reading scientific magazines; dressmaking and knitting; or cultural hobbies (e.g., listening to symphonies, or painting and photography).

In summary, effectuation of intellectual potential is represented in the present version of the social competence scale by the following items: (1) measured level of intelligence, (2) grades of education completed, (3) occupational level, rated according to the Roe scale, (4) employment regularity, and (5) constructiveness expressed in the use of leisure time. A number of competence items, e.g., degree of medical disability, help sharpen our view of the person's life pattern and should thus lead to more precise competence ratings. Other items, such as the Warner scales for rating the prestige of occupation and father's occupational level, are not directly relevant to the competence dimension. However, their inclusion will permit us to explore possible relationships between competence and other variables, for example, economic mobility or social class affiliation.

### Measurement of Social Development

In Chapter 3 we reviewed the measurement of social development under three headings: stability, intimacy, and differentiation. In the present scale of competence, stability of relationships appears implied in the average length of time for which the person has worked for each employer during the past 5 years (item 13). During this period he may well have received a promotion while remaining in the same employ. Even if he leaves a particular place of employment, it may be in the interest of obtaining more rewarding work. Nevertheless, a class of drifters exists who move haphazardly from job to job without regard to improvement in working conditions. Such people will score at a high level of job turnover.

Items that express the initiation and maintenance of close and ostensibly binding human relationships, such as becoming engaged or married (items 21a and 21b), are indicative of a degree of stability in interpersonal contact. Correspondingly, disruption of such a relationship by separation or divorce (item 21c) implies an inability to maintain close and intimate personal relationships. It is, of course, recognized that a person may break a difficult relationship, such as a "neurotic" marriage, for good reasons, and in so doing may express a more adequate personality structure than the person who remains bound in such a situation. Nevertheless, the original formation of the bond raises some question of personal immaturity. What is claimed is that, at least in a statistical sense, those who enter into and maintain a marriage are expressing a higher level of social development than those who enter into but then dissolve their marriage.

Intimacy in interpersonal relations is assessed in a number of items of the competence scale items. The items just described concerned with closeness and disruption of heterosexual relationships and marriage presumably reflect the person's ability to maintain intimate relations with others. Three derived scales also may tap this dimension of intimacy. The most obvious candidate among them is a scale of Social Participation. This enumerates such items as joining in actively as a member of any type of social or community organization. Another derived scale rates the person's relative emphasis on Participant Versus Avoidant orientation in leisure time activities. On the participant side are listed activities expressive of social integration; physical activities, such as sports; and technical-scientific and home interests. The avoidant orientation is scored in terms of aesthetic interests, as in the arts; the "escapist" reading of adventure and detective stories, and so forth; watching television, going to movies, or listening to radio; and engaging in nonstrenuous indoor games, such as playing cards or checkers.

Finally, a derived scale that identifies leisure time activity according to its Sex Identification, that is, as masculine or feminine, also may tell us something about the closeness of the person's relationships. The Sex Identification scale is scored according to the number of activities engaged in which may be clearly identified with the person's own sex, such as playing baseball for a man, or knitting for a woman. It seems reasonable that, to the extent that a person's activities are those commonly associated with his sex, he will be emotionally close to others in his personal relationships. Behavior that is typical for one's sex tends to support a person's social relations with others because his actions are concordant with societal expectations. When an individual acts in a fashion customarily associated with his sex, it is easy for others to behave effectively toward him in ways or roles that are known, comfortable, and easy to adopt. Both men and women will associate more easily with a person who consistently manifests activities that are typical for his sex.

A person's integration into the social fabric of his community is evidenced by his participation in organizations, measured in total number of meetings attended per month (item 18b). Finally, the number of positions of leadership one holds in organizations is an index of active participation with others (items 17d).

Differentiation in the nature of one's social relationships, which theory dictates as a developmentally high stage in social development, is tapped by two items in the competence scale. These are (1) the number of different organizations to which the person belongs, as an expression of variety in his social interests (item 18a), and (2) diversity in the types of these organizations according to the purposes they serve or the activities in which they primarily engage (item 17b). Some organizations—boys' clubs, or settlement houses, for example—exist primarily to serve people who need help in one way or another. Membership in other organizations, such as professional or scientific societies, expresses the work interests of the person. Again, many organizations exist simply to fulfill the social needs of the members; thus, they may hold dances or arrange bowling parties and outings.

In summary, achieved level of social development is measured in the present scale of competence by scoring on the following items: (1) average length of time the person has held a job over the last 5 years; (2) his present legal marital status, e.g., married, divorced, or single; (3) his present heterosexual activity, e.g., married, dates frequently, or does not go out socially; (4) his past psychosexual history, e.g., broken engagement, a disappointment in love, or having been deserted; (5) a derived scale of Social Participation, e.g., attending club meetings versus staying by oneself; (6) a derived scale of Participant Versus Avoidant orientation, e.g., reading technical magazines in contrast to escapist literature; (7) a derived scale of Sex Identification; (8) number of organizational meetings attended per month; (9) number of leadership positions that the person holds in organizations; (10) the number of organizations to which he belongs; and (11) the number of different kinds of organizations with which he is affiliated.

Several items dealing with marriage are included that are not directly relevant to the competence dimension. These concern age differences between subject and spouse, age and sex of subject's children, and a history in females of miscarriages. They are included to fulfill the need of other studies and appear at the particular point they do because of their logical continuity with other items concerned with psychosexual history.

*Measurement of Moral Development*

Together, accountability, obligation, and reciprocity are presumed to constitute moral development. Accountability implies a willingness to take responsibility for oneself and for the consequences of one's actions. In the present scale, accountability is measured in a number of items. The subject's type of residence (item 22) is one such item, with the subject rated high if he lives with his spouse, or supports his children; rated at an intermediate level if he lives by himself or with a friend; and at a low level if he lives with relatives or in an institution.

Accountability is assessed also by the number of people whom the subject supervises at work (item 12). Finally, the derived scale of Constructiveness may also serve to rate accountability. That is, this index tells us whether the person puts his leisure time to constructive uses or whether this time is simply filled with amusing diversions.

Obligation for the welfare of others is scored in terms of the number of positions of leadership that are held in formal organizations (item 17b). Whether or not the organizations in which membership is held are dedicated to the service of other people or the community generally also affects scoring the person's sense of obligation. Similarly, a person's voting record, that is, whether or not he has ever voted in a city, state, or federal election (item 20), reflects his sense of obligation to the community. Maintenance of a marriage and acceptance of responsibility for the welfare of children (item 21b) clearly imply a developed sense of obligation. Finally, employment regularity (item 13), to the extent that this implies an awareness of a financial responsibility for oneself and for those dependent on the self, also connotes a matured moral sense.

Reciprocity in one's dealings with others is not adequately represented in the present version of our scale of competence. Responsibility for family expressed in the scale of marital and family status (item 21b) in part reflects this attribute. That is, maintenance of one's spouse and children as an integrated unit implies some commitment to their welfare. We have dropped assessment of child discipline and the handling of family finances, as well as rating the closeness of friendships, both of which appeared in the Worcester Scale of Social Attainment. In principle, these items could tap concern for the welfare of others besides oneself. However, scoring them requires fairly subjective judgments on the part of the examiner.

In summary, a person's achieved level of moral development is represented in the present scale of social competence by the following items: (1) type of residence; (2) the number of people whose work he supervises; (3) scoring on the derived scale of Constructiveness; (4) leadership in formal organizations; (5) membership in community-minded organizations; (6) his voting record; (7) his present heterosexual activity, e.g., one continuous marriage with children versus "does not go out socially with women;" and (8) degree of employment regularity.

## SOCIETAL EXPECTATIONS

In Chapter 3 we reviewed at some length the expectations imposed by society for the person's behavior according to his age and sex group. The writer proposed that the longer a person lives free of some form of psychiatric disorder, the greater his resources for effective adaptation in society. Therefore, an item is included in the present version of our competence scale specifying either present age or age prior to onset of disorder. Our assumption is that social survival in the community implies at least minimal conformity with those expectations for behavior imposed by the community. In psychiatric cases, where psychological disorganization has taken place, age at onset of disorder must be used, and not present chronological age.

## EARLIER SCALES OF SOCIAL COMPETENCE

The following are some of our earlier forms of social competence scales. (The second and third were devised for work with psychiatrically impaired populations.)

1. *The Worcester Scale of Social Attainment.* This scale is the predecessor of our present scale of competence and is identical with the present scale in many important respects. It is mentioned here because we shall review a number of our early studies that made use of this scale.

2. *The Phillips Premorbid Scale.* The writer designed this scale in order to carry out his doctoral dissertation (12), which was concerned with the problem of prediction of outcome in the treatment of schizophrenia. The scale is a section of a more extensive rating device (13), which includes measures for assessing behaviorally deviant groups. The Premorbid Scale consists of five divisions that permit a quantitative evaluation of the following types of relationships: (a) recent sexual adjustment; (b) social aspects of sexual life during adolescence and immediately beyond; (c) social aspects of recent sexual life; (d) personal relations: history and (e) recent premorbid adjustment in personal relations. This scale has been used in a variety of studies that will be reported on below.

3. *Biographical Indices of Social Competence.* This competence index was designed by Zigler and Phillips (25) for use in a series of studies in psychopathology. In order to carry these out it was necessary to construct a measure of social competence that could be derived from routine case history records completed in a mental hospital. Six indices were chosen for our measure of premorbid social competence. These include: intelligence level; educational achievement; occupational level; marital status; age; and employment regularity.

RELIABILITY OF MEASUREMENT

The question of just how accurate and trustworthy our measures of social competence are is far more complex than that posed by conventional psychometric techniques, such as objective tests of school achievement or intelligence. The reliability of data on competence implies more than a simple correspondence in scoring by two or more raters. Reliability of social competence scores is influenced by at least three factors: (1) reliability of the basic data; (2) reliability of informants; and (3) reliability of raters. These will be discussed in turn.

*Reliability of Basic Data*

The measurement of social competence depends on an evaluation of individual social histories. Reliability in measurement is in part based on how objectively and quantitatively the different aspects of a person's biography can be assessed. His chronological age, the number of school grades completed, and his marital status are fairly direct observables and easily placed on some scale of measurement. On the other hand, when we deal with the depth of emotional ties, either in friendships or heterosexual relationships, we move into an area of subjective judgment and ambiguity in interpretation. Both kinds of indices, the relatively objective and relatively interpretative, have been used in our scales of competence.

Recency of events also plays a role in determining the reliability of case data. Happenings of today or of the past year are better remembered than those of the distant past. Information about childhood friendships, for instance, may well be distorted by knowledge of the person's present social relationships. Recency and objectivity are also likely to interact. Thus, information as to early schools attended or early places of residence may be quite reliable, whereas reports on number of, and particularly on closeness of, early friendships are subject to much retrospective distortion. In sum, data that are objective and have been written down are usually dependable; those that are recorded only in the human mind, and are thus subject to forgetting and to idiosyncratic interpretation and distortion, are not nearly as reliable.

*Reliability of Informants*

Data from which social competence is to be scored on psychiatric patients are usually obtained from two original sources: the subject (patient) himself, or close relatives. Psychiatric case records have frequently served as the actual basis for evaluating biographical data, but the subject himself or a relative is the usual source of information.

Unwittingly or not, both the subject and his relatives are biased informants, since their self-esteem is at stake in revealing the subject's history. Particularly in the case of a psychiatric patient, both he and his parents or spouse will be impelled to defend their role in his pathology. Thus, a defensive interpretation of the subject's biography is superimposed on the ordinary vicissitudes of memory. To repeat, greater consistency of report is obtained with more objective indices, such as marital status or educational achievement, than with those items more dependent on subjective interpretation.

To those who routinely collect case histories, the lacunae in information that are to be observed in the reports of relatives are astonishing. A wife, for example, may not know the kind of job held by her husband, where he has been employed over the last several years, or even how long he has been out of work. Frequently, too, a wife may know little in the way of hard facts about her husband's childhood, for example, what schools he attended or the last grade completed. Parents, too, are often surprisingly ignorant of the marital history of their offspring. In general, we have found that the psychiatric patient can provide a more complete and satisfactory history of himself than can his relatives.

A related question, although not one directly of reliability, is the theoretical bias of most psychiatric interviewers. Most American psychiatrists and psychiatric social workers are committed to the primacy of information on a patient's early childhood experiences, the constitution of the parental family and the attitudes expressed among its members, the nature of his present personal relationships and possible emotional conflicts, especially within the narrow orbit of his immediate family. Ordinarily, professional personnel are much less concerned with the specifics of the person's work history or the details of his activity in organizations. As a consequence, routine psychiatric case records are inadequate sources of the social history needed to rate social competence. They suffer from two major deficiencies: (1) Much information that is relevant to the evaluation of competence is never recorded. For instance, job descriptions are frequently insufficient to asses precisely the occupational level achieved and information on participation in social organizations is nearly always lacking. (2) Data are often recorded as the interviewer's interpretation rather than as objective facts; for example, the person will be described as "regularly employed," rather than in terms of the actual length of time that he has spent in or out of work; or he is reported as "friendly" or "sociable," without any reference to the concrete information on which such a judgment is based.

*Reliability of Raters*

Those who are called upon to rate a subject's social competence from his history have the same kinds of difficulty as the original informants in assessing the significance of the more subjective and chronologically more remote aspects of a subject's history. When judges are asked to rate recent or factual subject characteristics, they nearly always agree in their judgments; when they are asked to classify more remote events or subjective states, the correspondence in rating declines.

*Data on Reliability*

Of the four competence scales we have constructed, evidence on reliability is available only for the Phillips Premorbid Scale. The Premorbid measure, however, is relatively qualitative in character, and the reliability of the other scales of competence should, therefore, compare favorably. Solomon and Zlotowski (21) have reported on the reliability in scoring of the Phillips scale from case records by two psychologists. Rater reliability for the total Phillips scale was .81, based on a sample of 46 schizophrenics.

Garmezy and his colleagues (6) also have examined the reliability of scoring this scale on a number of small patient samples incidental to their research on social motivation in schizophrenia (16). The following information is derived from their report. The index of reliability varied according to the sources from which the data for scale scoring were derived. Two psychologists who independently rated premorbid competence of 22 schizophrenic women from the same case records achieved a scoring reliability of .86. Similarly, two second-year graduate students, in rating the competence of 15 male schizophrenics from hospital records, agreed in their ratings at a level of .90. A reliability of .92 was achieved between premorbid scores based alternatively on patient interview and on case record material. In comparing data from case histories with those from interviews with parents, a correlation of .80 was obtained. In another test of reliability in data collection, agreement dropped substantially, however, when based on case history data versus patient interview. Here, only a reliability of .62 was obtained. Similarly, when scale scorings were based on patient as compared to parent interviews, again only a reliability of .63 appeared. Apparently, parents and patients do not agree too well on the patient's premorbid history.

The source of information has a striking influence on its reliability. In independent studies, two psychologists rated patients' current marital status or personal relations with those of members of the same or opposite sex from available hospital records. In both studies, ratings coincided almost identically ($r = .95$). However, when one source of the same data is the patient and the other is a parent, reliability drops to .86.

Even more extreme discrepancies appear when subjective judgment is required on the closeness of the patient's friendships. While two raters agree moderately well when both base their judgments on the case record (in two studies $r = .76$ and .83), patient and parent simply do not agree at all ($r = .04$).

## SEX DIFFERENCES IN SOCIAL COMPETENCE

Does the concept of social competence have the same meaning when applied to men and women? Since the two sexes are brought up to live quite different kinds of lives, it seems likely that their styles of competence will be differently constituted.

At the risk of oversimplification we may say that emotional closeness and personal relationships are of more intense concern to women, work and career of greater concern to men. Parsons and Bales (11) have expressed this sex role distinction in terms of an "expressive-instrumental" role dichotomy. The "expressive" role is generally assigned to the woman as wife and mother. She is expected to be affectionate, solicitous, warm, and emotionally involved with her children—to serve as comforter and consoler. The man of the house is expected to play the "instrumental" role, that is, to serve as its leader. He is the provider and head of the household and the court of last resort in the discipline and control of the children.

However, social class differences appear in the marital roles of men and women. Working-class women tend to see men as dominant and controlling and often to feel apart from their husbands. In contrast, middle-class wives express greater confidence in their ability to assert themselves and tend not to feel so isolated from their husbands' lives. In general, sex role distinctions are less at higher social class levels (15).

Nevertheless, across the whole spectrum of social class men are generally more successful than women in their occupational careers. More than women, they fill managerial positions and work as skilled craftsmen or foremen (8). Even at the very highest professional levels men are more productive than women. In a study of the careers of 400 Radcliffe PhDs, it was found that these women published substantially less than men of comparable job and rank. Nor is this difference in output due to the double career that professional women often have to fulfill, that of housewife and mother as well as job holder. Those women PhDs who remained single published as little as those who married (2).

Relevant here are the experimental data on need Achievement (9).

Findings are based on the use of story themes as a measure of need to achieve, as this is expressed by subjects under various experimental conditions. Men show a striking increase in need Achievement when a question is raised concerning their leadership qualities or intelligence. In these same circumstances, no such increase is to be observed with women. On the other hand, when anxiety is provoked about the problem of being socially acceptable or popular, a significant increase in need Achievement has been observed with female subjects but not with males. These observations are consistent with the greater meaning of personal relations for women and of work and career for men.

## Training for Sex Roles

Men and women differ, then, in their personal commitments. They differ, too, in their subjective sense of competence. Males consistently express themselves as being more self-reliant and achievement oriented, more self-assertive and aggressive, and more hardy and fearless than females. Females rate themselves as more timid and given to loss of emotional control. Men exceed women in rating themselves, as resourceful, efficient, adventurous, realistic, logical, deliberate, and mature (19).

How do these differences in commitments and self concept come about? Clearly they have something to do with the experiences that differentially characterize the upbringing of the two sexes.

Parents tend to use a double standard for the two sexes in dealing with behaviors that they approve or disapprove in their children. By the time children are 5 years of age, boys and girls in our society are disciplined differently. The sharpest difference is in response to the child's expression of aggression, and here boys are handled with more permissiveness than girls. Those mothers who are convinced that different behavior standards should be observed for each of the sexes are those who are more insistent that girls act in conformity with the standards set by their parents (20). Similarly, Sears, Maccoby, and Levin (20) have reported that those mothers who emphasize the greatest sex role differentiation place the highest demands on girls for instant obedience. The different upbringing of the sexes stresses a more passive obedience to family rules for girls but a more active and automonous orientation for boys. Almost without exception, in societies all across the world, girls are taught obedience and responsibility for routine chores, whereas there is much more emphasis on physical skill and achievement in the training of boys.

Schooling, which is ostensibly identical for the two sexes, also imposes different self concepts on boys and girls. A report on children's readers, for example, revealed sharp differences in the way male and female characters are delineated (1). This study showed that female characters are more frequently described as sociable and kind, yet as timid, inactive, unambitious, and uncreative. The central character more frequently protects a female, suggesting the helplessness of the female, while males are more often depicted as the ones who supply vital information to central characters. Females are portrayed as lazy in twice as many instances as males, while males are much more frequently shown as achieving their goals by the socially approved route of work and effort.

There is a remarkable consistency, then, between those family and community expectations for behavior that are imposed on maturing boys and girls and the values and commitments by which they live as adults. Social competence may well show a quite different balance between the sexes. Men are likely to manifest a higher level of socioeconomic achievement, women may well average a higher degree of social participation. In any case, it seems wise to compare individuals on social competence only within their own sex group.

## OTHER APPROACHES TO COMPETENCE

Let us recapitulate the main themes that have been covered in these chapters on social competence.

1. The writer and his colleagues have provided a method for the quantitative assessment of effectiveness for a broad range of adult behaviors in the spheres of education and work, social participation, and psychosexual relations.

2. Our method finds expression in an objective scale of social competence.

3. Scoring on this scale of competence is theorized as corresponding to the individual's level of psychological development, particularly in the intellectual, social, and moral spheres.

Other writers have used the term "competence" as well as an analogous concept of "coping." The writer wants to distinguish the present use of the term "social competence" from the way in which competence and coping have been used by others.

White has used competence as an exclusively motivational construct. He sees it as a factor common to visual exploration, grasping, locomotion, language, and other activities required for effective interaction with the environment. This motivational dynamic shows itself most unambiguously in the playful and investigatory behavior of young animals and children. White proposed that "Activity, manipulation, and exploration, which are all pretty much of a piece in the infant, be considered together as aspects of competence, and that for the present we assume that one general motivational principle lies behind them" (23). In his writings he reviewed in detail an extensive theoretical and experimental literature in support of his hypothesis, but he has no explicit method for the measurement of individual competence even in the child.

A sophisticated experimental attack on the origins of "coping" potential has been carried out by Lois B. Murphy and her associates (10). These investigators, using a small number of children, undertook longitudinal studies that provided detailed observations of the childrens' responses to new situations and challenges. As defined by these investigators, the term "coping" does not include the simple use of inborn or general human abilities, such as talking or walking. Rather, coping connotes the strategies that the child employs in order to meet his needs, gain satisfactions, and come to terms with himself and the adult world. Murphy's methods of research included naturalistic observation, interviews with mothers, psychiatric interviews, psychometric and projective tests, and pediatric examinations. In this study children were observed from their second or third year up to the ages of 11 and 12. So far, the data reported are primarily on the preschool years (10).

Witkin and his colleagues (24) have developed a concept of coping similar to that of Lois B. Murphy and her associates. It is based on a program of research dealing with the interrelations of perception and personality. Both groups of investigators have operated within a general assumption that psychological development is reflected in increasing coping potential. For the Witkin group, coping is an ability to function relatively independently of environmental support, to initiate action, and to organize it effectively, as well as the power to master social and environmental forces. A major explanatory construct that serves to coordinate the results of their studies is that of "field-independence" versus "field-dependence." Witkin *et al.* employed a variety of experimental situations, including perception of the relative position of an illuminated rod in a darkened room, embedded figures, and so forth, all of which involved the perceptual "separation of an item from its context." Measures of coping capacity, independently assessed from an interview, Rorschach test performance, and a human-figure drawing test, were found to be related to an ability to perceptually separate an object from compelling background forces.

Foote and Cottrell (5) proposed a theory of interpersonal competence that is concerned primarily with personal resourcefulness and effectiveness in interpersonal relationships. These authors define interpersonal competence as the person's capability to meet and deal with a changing world, and to formulate his goals and the means to implement them. It implies, too, that the person is capable of integrating his goals with those of others and of collaborating with others. Unlike the concept of social competence, the construct of interpersonal competence is only loosely based on developmental principles, and the authors do not provide a technique for the objective measurement of adult behavior patterns.

Foote and Cottrell distinguished between two aspects of interpersonal competence, "autonomy" and "empathy." Autonomy refers to the clarity with which the identity of self is articulated and the degree to which the individual is self-directed and self-controlled in his actions. It expresses, too, his self-confidence, self-respect, and self-reliance; the extent to which he maintains an internal set of standards that guides his actions; and his capacity for realistically assessing threats against him and for mobilizing realistic defenses of the self. Empathy is defined as the ability to interpret correctly the attitudes and intentions of others, and as the accuracy with which situations can be perceived from another's standpoint, thus enabling the person to anticipate and predict the behavior of others. Empathy is basic to "taking the role of the other" and hence to social interaction.

Recently, Farber (4) has reported on a test schedule of 104 items presumed to represent competence in interpersonal relations, as this is defined by Foote and Cottrell. It must be noted, however, that the items on this schedule samples attitudes rather than real-life behaviors. Farber subjected the responses of 495 husbands to a factor analysis. He grouped the obtained factors into categories presumed to reflect empathy, autonomy, resourcefulness, and cooperativeness. On the basis of his findings, Farber proposed that interpersonal competence may consist of one general factor of competence as well as other specialized factors.

One of the few studies that has made use of an estimate of competence based on the real-life behaviors of (young) adults was carried out by Rodnick et al. (17). However, no actual scale of competence was provided by these authors. They simply selected individuals who were rated by their supervisors as either extremely high or low in work adjustment, attitudes toward fellow workers, initiative, personality adjustment, and so on. Individuals who rated highest on a composite index of these variables were found to perform more adequately on a variety of stresses than those who scored lowest. The effect of failure upon task performance was not investigated, but changes in projective test themas as a result of an interpolated failure experience were reported. The shifts in themas were interpreted by the authors to mean that under failure the better-adjusted subjects tended to maintain their self-estimation, whereas the poorly adjusted subjects suffered a decrease in self-evaluation. These two groups of subjects also were differentiated quite significantly in their performance on a hand-steadiness test under conditions of distraction stress.

Only Doll (3) has provided us with an explicit measure of social competence. However, his scale of Social Maturity is intended primarily for rating the behaviors of children. Further, it lacks a theoretical rationale as to the significance of competence and what scoring represents in terms of a child's psychological development. Items in Doll's scale are simply arranged by chronological years, in a sequence of empirically observed increasing difficulty. Represented are such behaviors as dressing and feeding oneself, walking, talking, communicating with others, and social relations.

Unlike the scale provided by Doll, the present scale of social competence is more than some arbitrary foot rule of social behavior. The items chosen for inclusion, the particular form they take, and the direction in which they are scored are all based on the belief that effectiveness of behavior in the adult years corresponds to the degree of psychological development that the person has achieved through his years of maturation and the experiences that he has undergone. Explicitly, then, scoring on this scale is conceived as an index of achieved level of psychological development.

It should be emphasized that the scale permits ratings of psychological development among adults. Adults differ among themselves in terms of their intrapsychic development; some adults are "less mature" and some are "more mature" than others. And, of course, psychoanalytic theory provides the construct of libidinal development that implies greater or lesser psychosexual maturity. In practice, however, the idea of psychological development is identified with the rapid changes of childhood, rather than with the constancy of adulthood. It is for this reason, perhaps, that other investigators, L. B. Murphy, Witkin, White, and others, who have taken a developmental view of competence or coping, have confined their studies to children. To study adults from a developmental point of view necessitates the development of techniques for their quantitative placement along a hypothesized dimension of psychological development. This, in turn, requires some comprehensive index of developmental level for adults that is independent of chronological age. Until recently, such an instrument did not exist. This situation has now changed. Our scale of social competence, as well as the Rorschach development scoring system that will be described in the next chapter, can both serve as just such indices.

### REFERENCES

1.  Child, I. L., Potter, E. H., and Levine, E. M. Children's textbooks and personality development: An exploration in the social psychology of education. *Psychological Monographs*, 1946, **60**, 1–54.
2.  Cronkhite, B. *Graduate education for women*. Cambridge, Mass.: Harvard University Press, 1956.

3. Doll, E. A. Preliminary standardization of the Vineland Social Maturity Scale. *American Journal of Orthopsychiatry*, 1936, **6**, 283–293.
4. Farber, B. Elements of competence in interpersonal relations: A factor analysis. *Sociometry*, 1962, **25**, 30–47.
5. Foote, N. N., & Cottrell, L. S., Jr. *Identity and interpersonal competence*. Chicago: University of Chicago Press, 1955.
6. Garmezy, N., Farina, A., & Rodnick, E. H. Reliability studies of the Phillips scale. Unpublished manuscript, Department of Psychology, Duke University, 1960.
7. Kahl, J. A. *The American class structure*. New York: Holt, 1964.
8. Long, L. H. (Ed.) *World Almanac*. New York: Newspaper Enterprise Assoc., World Almanac Division, 1965.
9. McClelland, D. C. *The achieving society*. Princeton, N. J.: Van Nostrand, 1961.
10. Murphy, L. B., & Collaborators. *The widening world of childhood*. New York: Basic Books, 1962.
11. Parsons, T., & Bales, R. F. *Family, socialization and interaction process*. Glencoe, Ill.: Free Press, 1955.
12. Phillips, L. Personality factors and prognosis in schizophrenia. Unpublished doctoral dissertation, University of Chicago, 1949.
13. Phillips, L. Case history data and prognosis in schizophrenia. *Journal of Nervous and Mental Disease*, 1953, **6**, 515–525.
14. Phillips, L., & Cowitz, B. Social attainment and reactions to stress. *Journal of Personality*, 1953, **22**, 270–283.
15. Rainwater, L., Coleman, R., & Handel, G. *Workingman's wife*. New York: Oceana Publications, 1959.
16. Rodnick, E., & Garmezy, N. An experimental approach to the study of motivation in schizophrenia. In M. R. Jones (Ed.), *Nebraska symposium on motivation*. Lincoln, Neb.: University of Nebraska Press, 1957. Pp. 109–184.
17. Rodnick, E. H., Rubin, M. A., and Freeman, H. Related studies on adjustment: reactions to experimentally induced stresses. *American Journal of Psychiatry*, 1943, **99**, 872–880.
18. Roe, A. *The psychology of occupations*. New York: Wiley, 1956.
19. Sarbin, T. R., & Rosenberg, B. G. Contributions to role-taking theory: IV. A method for obtaining a qualitative estimate of the self. *Journal of Social Psychology*, 1955, **42**, 71–81.
20. Sears, R. R., Maccoby, E. E., & Levin, H. *Patterns of child-rearing*. New York: Harper & Row, 1957.
21. Solomon, L. F., & Zlotowski, M. The relationship between the Elgin and the Phillips measures of process-reactive schizophrenia. *Journal of Nervous and Mental Disease*, 1964, **138**, 32–36.
22. Warner, W. L., Meeker, M., & Eells, K. *Social class in America*. New York: Harper, 1960.
23. White, R. W. Competence and the psychosexual stages of development. In M. R. Jones (Ed.), *Nebraska sysmposium on motivation*. Lincoln, Neb.: University of Nebraska Press, 1960. Pp. 97–141.
24. Witkin, H. A., Lewis, H. B., Hertzman, M., Machover, K., Meissner, P. B., & Wapner, S. *Personality through perception*. New York: Harper, 1954.
25. Zigler, E., and Phillips, L. Social effectiveness and symptomatic behaviors. *Journal of Abnormal and Social Psychology*, 1960, **2**, 231–238.

# 5 / SOCIAL COMPETENCE,

# ADAPTIVE POTENTIAL, AND

# PSYCHOLOGICAL DEVELOPMENT

The preceding chapters have been devoted to a detailed analysis of social competence and its measurement. How a person scores on the competence schedule is prima facie evidence of his achieved effectiveness in social adaptation. At a more theoretical level, social competence has been hypothesized as dependent on two equivalent constructs adaptation potential and achieved level of psychological development. On rational grounds, therefore, some relationship is to be expected between scoring on this overt index of adaptive potential and performance on experimental measures of coping ability. Conditions of experimental stress have been presumed to test precisely this ability to cope (14). The relation of how well a person scores on social competence to his performance under stressful conditions will be examined in the following sections.

It has also been possible to subject to direct test the hypothesis that achieved level of social competence is related to the person's level of psychological development. A set of indices of perceptual performance based on the Rorschach test, taken to measure achieved level of psychological development, have provided the means for this analysis. Availability of these indices has also permitted a test of the hypothesis that coping ability, as reflected in performance under conditions of experimental stress, is related to achieved level of psychological development. The relation of both social competence and stress performance to psychological development will be reported on below.

COMPETENCE AND PERFORMANCE UNDER STRESS

Effectiveness of performance under conditions of experimentally imposed stress has been explained as dependent on the individual's ability to deal with emotions aroused by conditions that he perceives as thwarting to some centrally important motive state (14, 15). Coping or control processes, which are presumed to direct or govern motivational or emotional expression, will, according to this hypothesis, determine how effectively the person behaves under such thwarting conditions.

There is, of course, no way of knowing when a particular situation will be perceived by a person as thwarting to some motive of central significance to him, thus initiating a condition of emotional arousal. People will perceive objectively identical situations in quite different ways according to their unique background of experiences. Accordingly, they will respond to some ostensibly stressful condition as conveying different levels of threat. Nevertheless, experimental tasks can be constructed that imply some degree of threat to some substantial proportion of a given subject population. Consequently, across a group of subjects who are exposed to these conditions, relative effectiveness of performance should generally correspond to individul coping potential. It follows that a person's level of performance under conditions of experimental stress should relate to his achieved level of social competence.

An experiment carried out by Feffer and Phillips (2) subjected this proposition to experimental test. Two stressful conditions were established that were designated as *task-induced* and *failure-induced* stresses (15). Task-induced stress refers to those situations in which the task itself makes excessive demands on the subject, for example, through rapid pacing of the subject or by the introduction of extraneous stimuli during the course of the task. Failure-induced stress refers to those situations in which the experimenter deliberately attempts to make the subject feel that he is not performing adequately, for example, through the introduction of false norms. By these criteria, these experiments involved performance under both task-induced and failure-induced stress conditions.

The subject population was composed of 63 normal men who were employed in industry. An attempt was made to restrict the influence of those variables that might confuse the interpretation of any obtained relationships. Thus, the group did not include extremely diverse occupational types, such as professional workers or artists. The task of comparing such individuals on level of occupational skill would have proved a formidable one. In addition, their differing class status might have been associated with differing attitudinal "sets" toward the experiment. Each subject was assigned a social competence score on the Worcester Scale of Social Attainment on the basis of a structured interview.

The subjects were randomly divided into two numerically nearly equal groups, one of which was first exposed to task-induced stress followed by failure-induced stress, while the other group was subjected to these two conditions in the reverse order. After controlling social competence scores for mental age, significant relationship between competence and performance in the task-induced and failure-induced situations were obtained.

Findings in two additional studies are also relevant, although neither made use of an adequate measure of social competence. Gerard and Phillips (7) investigated in normal men the relationship between social behavior and psychological responses to an experimental stress situation. Social behavior was rated on a scale tapping educational and occupational achievement and formal group associations. Those individuals who had more education, engaged in skilled occupations, and belonged to community service organizations were rated as higher attainers on this scale. The stress task was the Targetball, a pinball-like device manipulated by the experimenter so that the subject is made to fail after a period of successful performance. It was found that subjects with higher competence, particularly in formal group associations, showed more adequate responses to the Targetball frustration task as measured by a more realistic shift downward in their goals as the failure period continued.

An even more ambiguous competence criterion was used in a study on stress carried out by Rodnick and his colleagues (19). Their subject population was a group of young men enrolled in a work corps during the economic depression of the 1930's. They were rated by their camp counselors for work adjustment, attitude toward fellow workers, and initiative. Two subject samples were chosen that represented extremes in social adjustment and work performance, yet it is difficult to disentangle the influence of a subject's emotional adjustment from these criteria of effectiveness in community participation. This study employed several stress techniques among the experimental methods used to distinguish good from poor social performers. It was found that those individuals who were ranked as manifesting a higher degree of social and work effectiveness performed more adequately under the experimental conditions used in this study. The results of all the studies just reviewed, then, combine to indicate that adequacy of performance under conditions of experimentally induced stress corresponds to effectiveness of behavior in everyday life.

COMPETENCE AND PSYCHOLOGICAL DEVELOPMENT

Earlier it was proposed that psychological development in the intellectual, social, and moral spheres constitutes the base upon which social competence is achieved. Ideally we would like to investigate the proposition that individual competence is indeed related to achieved level of psychological development in all these spheres but we lack the tools for a test of such a wide-ranging hypothesis. It is possible, however, to assess development in the intellectual sphere in a sense far broader than is reflected in traditional tests of intelligence and relate intellectual development to achieved level of social competence. The Rorschach technique provides the means whereby intellectual potential can be comprehensively sampled. This procedure permits us to assess how the person apprehends his world through recording his interpretations of a standard set of unstructured yet complex blot forms.

The fact that perceptual analysis in the Rorschach task is based on the sense of sight is not fortuitous, for the sense of sight is more deeply involved in intellectual and cognitive processes than is any of the other senses. Thus, a test based on visual perception can be maximally sensitive and reflective of a respondent's intellectual and cognitive resources. As Schachtel (21) has noted, sight provides "a much greater wealth of sensory data than do the lower senses and . . . makes accessible to the perceiver a greater variety and richness of object qualities, especially very highly differentiated spatial patterns."

Increasing psychological development in the perceptual and cognitive spheres improves the individual's ability to articulate his environment and to increasingly respond to its subtleties and complexities. The Rorschach test, which requires subjects to impose meaning on a standardized set of unstructured blot forms, permits a comparison of how people differ in the sharpness, subtlety, and complexity of perceptual-cognitive function. Analysis of Rorschach test responses suggests that this functioning can be evaluated in terms of three different dimensions of performance: (1) the sharpness and accuracy of perception; (2) response to subtle surface qualities such as colors, textures, and form-color and form-texture relationships; and (3) imposition on the blot forms of relationships that are not directly present but are the consequence of the perceiver's cognitive processes, for example, the perception of objects in motion or of some structural hierarchy between objects perceived in the Rorschach blots.

A scoring system (17) has been devised for the assessment of perceptual-cognitive performance on the Rorschach. It presumes to measure the level of development that has been achieved by the individual in the sphere of perceptual-cognitive function. A variety of studies have confirmed the power of this scoring system to discriminate between subjects who perform at different levels of perceptual-cognitive performance. No attempt will be made to review this extensive literature, but such a survey will be found in Phillips and Smith (18). These authors report on the relation between psychological development, as measured in terms of increasing chronological age in children, and perceptual behavior on the Rorschach. Certain of these data are particularly relevant and will be summarized here. The relation of chronological age in children to three aspects of Rorschach performance will be cited. These are: (a) percentage of accurately perceived blot forms ($F + \%$) as an index of the sharpness and accuracy of perception; (b) dominance of form as a determinant of response content when form and color are both used in reporting a response to a Rorschach card ($\%FC$ in total number of color responses). This reflects psychological development in the individual's use of subtle surface qualities (c) The percentage of Rorschach responses that invoke movement in human percepts ($\%M$/total number of responses). The perception of human movement expresses an ability to impose relationships that are not directly present in these blots. This cognitive ability appears in a relatively late phase of psychological development in the child.

The data that illustrate the relation of psychological development to these three facets of perceptual performance on the Rorschach are summarized in Table 5–1. The findings on accuracy of form-level were reported by Ford (4) and are drawn from reports by a number of investigators. Those on form-color and human movement responses are derived from Hemmendinger (8). His subject population consisted of 169 children between the ages of 3 and 11 years.

Table 5–1
CHRONOLOGICAL AGE IN CHILDREN AND RORSCHACH PERFORMANCE

| Investigator | Chrono-logical (years) | Form level[a] (F + %) | Chrono-logical (years) | Total color responses[a] (%FC) | Total Rorschach responses[b] (%M) |
|---|---|---|---|---|---|
| Ford | 3–6 | 52 | 3 | 9 | 0 |
| Ford | 6–8 | 68 | 4 | 21 | 0 |
| Loosli-Usteri | 10–12 | 80 | 5 | 31 | 0 |
| Lopfe | 10–13 | 75 | 6 | 26 | 0 |
| Behn-Eschenburg | 13–15 | 71 | 7 | 41 | 2.0 |
| Hertz | 12–16 | 89 | 8 | 48 | 2.5 |
|  |  |  | 9 | 59 | 4.5 |
|  |  |  | 10 | 54 | 1.5 |

[a]Derived from Ford (4).
[b]Derived from Hemmendinger (8).

Holtzman et al. (9) have devised another inkblot technique intended, like the Rorschach, to permit the detailed study of perceptual-cognitive processes. It consists of two matched sets of 45 cards each. By means of this technique Thorpe and Swartz (24) have investigated relationships between chronological age and scoring on a series of developmental indices. Their subject population consisted of 586 psychiatrically normal subjects who spanned the age range from 4 to 22 years. These authors similarly found a close correspondence between perceptual-cognitive performance and chronological age.

Developmental theory proposes that individual psychological phenomena, such as the emergence of an idea into consciousness, the learning of a particular motor skill, or the completion of a perceptual act, appear not as final products but as developing processes, that is, as events divisible into successive stages. This development of a specific behavioral act has been called *microgenesis* (3, 22). Its experimental study permits the empirical observation of the role that the dimension of time plays as an intrinsic aspect of the development of psychological processes. Microgenetic studies have been carried out especially in the sphere of visual perception. For example, studies have been made of changes in perception when the exposure time of stimuli was increased from one successive exposure to another. The formation of percepts appears to traverse the same orderly sequence of stages in both microgenesis and ontogenesis, that perceptual development through the long period of childhood, as work by Sander (20) and Kragh (12) has demonstrated. Framo (6) applied the microgenetic method to the study of the development of individual percepts. He administered the Rorschach tachistoscopically at several exposure times to 80 psychiatrically normal adults, 20 at each exposure time. Using the same scoring system as Hemmendinger, Framo found that developmentally immature types of percepts tended to decrease with exposure levels, and developmentally more mature percepts tended to increase. Thus, the validity of the Rorschach developmental scoring system as a measure of psychological development in the perceptual-cognitive sphere has been demonstrated in terms of both ontogenetic and microgenetic procedures.

A number of investigators have explored the relation of social competence to level of perceptual development in both psychiatrically normal and pathological populations. The earliest of these studies was carried out by Lane (13) on a sample of 60 male industrial workers. Competence was measured on the Worcester Scale of Social Attainment. A composite index of perceptual performance was constructed based on Rorschach developmental indices. Higher scoring on the social attainment scale was found significantly associated with higher scoring on the Rorschach composite index of perceptual development (corrected contingency coefficient = .53), even when controlled for chronological age, intelligence, and Rorschach productivity. Similarly, it was found (5) that social competence, when assessed by means of the Phillips Premorbid Scale, was significantly associated with Rorschach developmental level in both a schizophrenic and a psychiatrically normal group of subjects.

Other investigators have explored the relation of perceptual-cognitive development as measured through the Rorschach technique to various measures of social competence or to behavior patterns that carry implications for the degree of competence that the individual has achieved. Thus, Smith and Phillips (23) related Rorschach developmental scores to placement on the Vineland Social Maturity Scale (1) among three groups of male subjects differing in chronological age spanning the age range of 11–18 years. Findings were somewhat complex with statistically significant relationships in the expected direction appearing for their youngest and oldest groups, although no significant findings were obtained with those in the intermediate age range. The authors suggested that the rapid changes in personality organization during the adolescent period might account for the diminished relationship between social maturity (i.e., social competence) and perceptual development.

Various studies have explored possible relationships between a person's ability to relate maturely and effectively to other people and the level of Rorschach perceptual development that he has achieved. The rational basis for these studies stems from the general observation that an early phase of self-centeredness in personal relationships tends to be replaced by a later period of mutually contributing relationships. Development theory suggests that this shift in personal relationships is not a change associated with age alone but corresponds to innate changes in personality. That is, adults of the same chronological age can also differ in their degree of self-centeredness and in their concern for each other's welfare. To the extent that this shift from egocentricity to reciprocity is reflected in perceptual-cognitive functioning we can anticipate a correspondence between an individual's emphasis on establishing and maintaining mutuality in his personal relationships and his achieved level of psychological development. Kaden (10) has offered findings that support this assumption. He examined the interaction within the marriage relationship of 32 psychiatrically normal men and their wives in terms of the awareness of and acceptance by these men of the motives and wishes of their marriage partner. Kaden found that the ability to accept and deal reciprocally with the spouse was significantly associated with level of perceptual performance as measured by Rorschach developmental indices. A later study (11) extended these findings to a group of married men who had formerly been hospitalized as schizophrenic patients and who had rejoined their wives in their communities.

Wilensky (25) has reported two studies that have related Rorschach developmental level to the social participation of chronic schizophrenics.

Wilensky undertook these studies in agreement with Piaget's theoretical position that, with psychological maturity, egocentric behavior gives way to both a responsibility for oneself and to cooperation with one's social group. The author tested and confirmed the hypothesis that among hospitalized schizophrenics level of perceptual development corresponded to adequacy of hospital adjustment and to their effectiveness in an experimental social situation.

Fourteen open ward and fourteen closed ward schizophrenic patients were included in the first study by Wilensky. Rorschach tests were administered and a quantified composite index assigned within which integrative responses received the highest scores and developmentally primitive percepts the lowest. This composite index was related to ward status (open versus closed), and a biserial correlation of .82 was obtained. This index was also examined in relation to performance in experimental situations that required social participation for the solution of a number of problems. Effectiveness of performance in these situations correlated .71 with Rorschach developmental level.

In a second study (25) 16 closed ward schizophrenics were similarly examined in terms of effectiveness of performance in experimental social situations that were repeated for a total of three sessions. Increasing diversity of response occurred with each exposure, and relationships with Rorschach developmental level in the last two trials moved from .58 to .86. Thus, Wilensky provided evidence that among schizophrenics, as among normal subjects, perceptual developmental level tends to be associated with effectiveness of social participation.

PERFORMANCE UNDER STRESS AND PSYCHOLOGICAL DEVELOPMENT

To this point we have shown that a person's coping potential, as indicated by the adequacy of his performance under conditions of experimental stress, and his level of psychological development, as measured in terms of a set of Rorschach perceptual indices, are both related to achieved level of social competence. Although not directly relevant to the theme of this book, it is of some interest to ask whether coping potential, measured in terms of performance under stress, coincides with achieved level of psychological development, as reflected in the Rorschach developmental scoring system. Lofchie (16) investigated this issue by means of a distraction stress technique. Analysis of the demands imposed upon the subject for effective performance under conditions of distraction stress suggests that the subject needs to discriminate between the relevant and the irrelevant stimuli that are both inherent elements of a distraction experiment. Performance level under distracting conditions should then be dependent on the individual's achieved level of perceptual and cognitive organization. The subject population used by Lofchie in the test of this hypothesis consisted of 35 psychiatrically normal adult men. Findings were confirmatory and indicated that perceptually integrative Rorschach performance is highly related to coping potential as measured by effective performance under conditions of distraction stress (tetrachoric $r$ = .91).

Thus, the hypothesized relationships between social competence, coping potential, and psychological development that were posited in earlier chapters find support in experimental findings.

## REFERENCES

1. Doll, E. A. Preliminary standardization of the Vineland Social Maturity Scale. *American Journal of Orthopsychiatry*, 1936, **6**, 283–293.
2. Feffer, M., & Phillips, L. Social attainment and performance under stress. *Journal of Personality*, 1953, **22**, 284–297.
3. Flavell, J. H., & Draguns, J. A. A microgenetic approach to perception and thought. *Psychological Bulletin*, 1957, **54**, 197–217.
4. Ford, M. The application of the Rorschach test to young children. *University of Minnesota Institute of Child Welfare Monograph*, 1946, No. 23.
5. Fowler, R. Psychopathology and social adequacy: A Rorschach developmental study. Unpublished doctoral dissertation, Pennsylvania State University, 1957.
6. Framo, J. L. Structural aspects of perceptual development in normal adults: A tachistoscopic study with the Rorschach technique. Unpublished doctoral dissertation, Boston University, 1951.
7. Gerard, D. L., & Phillips, L. Relation of social attainment to psychological and adrenocortical reactions to stress. *Archives of Neurology and Psychiatry*, 1953, **69**, 350–354.
8. Hemmendinger, L. Perceptual organization and development as reflected in the structure of the Rorschach test responses. *Journal of Projective Techniques*, 1953, **17**, 162–170.
9. Holtzman, W. H., Thorpe, J. S., Swartz, J. D., & Herron, W. E. *Inkblot perception and personality*. Austin, Tex.: University of Texas Press, 1961.
10. Kaden, S. E. A formal-comparative analysis of the relationship between the structuring of marital interaction and Rorschach blot stimuli. Unpublished doctoral dissertation, Clark University, 1958.
11. Kaden, S. E., & Lipton, H. Rorschach developmental scores and post-hospital adjustment of married male schizophrenics. *Journal of Projective Techniques*, 1960, **24**, 144–147.
12. Kragh, U. *The actual-genetic model of perceptual-personality*. Lund: CWK Gleerup, 1955.
13. Lane, J. E. Social effectiveness and developmental level. *Journal of Personality*, 1955, **23**, 274–284.
14. Lazarus, R. S. *Psychological stress and the coping process*. New York: McGraw-Hill, 1966.
15. Lazarus, R. S., & Baker, R. W. Motivation and personality in psychological stress. *Psychological Newsletter*, 1957, **8**, 159–193.
16. Lofchie, S. H. The performance of adults under distraction stress: A developmental approach. *Journal of Psychology*, 1955, **39**, 109–116.
17. Phillips, L., Kaden, S., & Waldman, M. Rorschach indices of developmental level. *Journal of Genetic Psychology*, 1959, **94**, 267–285.
18. Phillips, L., & Smith, J. G. *Rorschach interpretation: Advanced technique*. New York: Grune & Stratton, 1953.
19. Rodnick, E. H., Rubin, M. A., & Freeman, H. Related studies on adjustment: Reactions to experimentally induced stresses. *American Journal of Psychiatry*, 1943, **99**, 872–880.

20. Sander, F. Structures, totality of experience, and gestalt. In C. Murchison (Ed.), *Psychologies of 1930*. Worcester, Mass.: Clark University Press, 1930.

21. Schachtel, E. G. *Metamorphosis*. New York: Basic Books, 1959.

22. Smith, G. J. W. Visual perception—an event overtime. *Psychological Review*, 1957, **64**, 306–313.

23. Smith, L. C., Jr., & Phillips, L. Social effectiveness and developmental level in adolescence. *Journal of Personality*, 1959, **27**, 240–249.

24. Thorpe, J. S., & Swartz, J. D. Level of perceptual development as reflected in responses to the Holtzman Inkblot Technique. *Journal of Projective Techniques*, 1965, **29**, 380–386.

25. Wilensky, H. Rorschach developmental level and social participation of chronic schizophrenics. *Journal of Projective Techniques*, 1959, **23**, 87–92.

# 6 / ADAPTIVE POTENTIAL

# AND ADAPTIVE FAILURE

In Chapter 1 it was proposed that a deficiency in the individual's adaptive potential makes more likely the onset of pathology. Several testable hypotheses can be derived from this proposition. For one, in large groups, low average levels of adaptive potential are associated with a high prevalence of disorder. For another, if pathology does appear, adaptive potential sets limits on the severity of pathological response. That is, among individuals who manifest pathology, the lower the individual's coping potential, the more impaired will be his habitual pattern of social adaptation. Finally, the lower the adaptive potential, the less reversible is the pathological pattern of behavior. Stated clinically, the lower the adaptive potential, the less favorable is the outcome of disorder.

In this chapter we shall be concerned with a test of the three hypotheses just outlined. These may be restated as follows.

1. Within the general population, lower levels of adaptive potential are associated with a higher prevalence of disorder.

2. Among pathological individuals, lower adaptive potential is associated with more severe forms of disorder.

3. Among pathological individuals, lower adaptive potential is associated with less favorable outcome of disorder.

We shall now consider the supporting evidence for each of these hypotheses.

PREVALENCE OF DISORDER

In this section we shall review the relationship between coping potential and the prevalence of disorder in the general population. An adequate test of this relationship is not easily accomplished, for it requires the fulfillment of a number of highly demanding methodological criteria. These include an ample and representative sampling of the general population. Needed also is a comprehensive sample of individuals manifesting the relevant forms of pathology in which we have an interest. In the present context, these include psychiatric impairment, antisocial behaviors, and psychosomatic diseases. An adequate test also requires that objective and quantified measures be available for both coping potential and the presence of these several forms of pathology.

To date, no study has been carried out that even remotely satisfies all these requirements. Nevertheless, although the studies on which they are based do not meet these stringent criteria, certain relevant findings are available. The methodologically most satisfactory of these studies have examined the relation of placement on individual social competence indices to the proportion of persons who are classified as psychiatrically impaired. Findings from this type of study will be reviewed first. The relationships between impairment rates and the following competence indices will be discussed in turn: occupational and educational achievement (used as indices of socioeconomic status); marital status; interpersonal affiliations; leisure time activities; and age. A consideration will then be given to available data that relate social competence level to the geographic distribution of various types of pathology in a medium-sized American community, as further evidence of the heuristic value of the competence formulation.

## Competence and the Prevalence of Disorder

*Socioeconomic Status.* Most studies that have examined rates of psychiatric disorder in the general population have used occupational and educational indices as measures to designate social class level. Although no one method for translating occupational and educational achievements into a corresponding class level (that is, socioeconomic status) has been universally accepted, occupational level alone predicts social class (as assigned independently by sociologists) with a remarkably high degree of precision (22). It has been found that the combination of occupation and education scores provides an almost exact indicator of class placement, with correlations surpassing .90 (20). In turn, it seems safe to assume that socioeconomic status (SES) is an accurate index of an individual's occupational and educational achievements.

A great many studies have been concerned with the relation of SES to rates of psychiatric impairment in the general population. Many of these studies have been reviewed by Dohrenwend and Dohrenwend (9). Of the 18 relevant papers reviewed by these investigators, 14 reported the highest rate of psychopathology in the lowest SES. Correspondingly, 10 of these 14 reported the lowest prevalence rate in the highest SES.

It should be noted, however, that the relation tends not to be a simple linear one. The correspondence between SES and impairment rate appears in large part dependent on a disproportionately high prevalence of impaired individuals in the lowest SES stratum. Thus, Hollingshead and Redlich found an extremely high rate of disorder among their lowest social class (Class V), with a less clear correspondence between class and disorder among the four other social classes. Similarly, Srole *et al.* (39) reported 30.0% as psychiatrically "well" and 12.5% as severely impaired in their highest SES. The drop in the proportion of respondents classified as well and as severely impaired shifted relatively slowly through their 12 SES levels until levels 11 and 12 were reached. The change in rates was particularly marked for level 12, in which 4.6% were reported as well and 47.3% as severely impaired. A deficiency in competence alone does not appear to provide the explanation for the high rate of psychiatrically impaired persons in the lowest SES. Unstable and stressful living conditions also appear to influence the proportion of pathological individuals within the general population (see Chapter 13).

*Marital Status.* Marital status has been found highly related to rates of psychiatric disorder by a number of investigators. Married persons tend to manifest pathology least frequently, single persons most often (7, 20, 28, 39). Widowed persons show impairment rates similar to those of the married; the divorced are in this regard more nearly like the single. These observations are not unreasonable if we accept the proposition that the widowed are, on the whole, capable of maintaining a marriage relationship but are prevented from doing so by the death of their spouse. Divorced individuals, on the other hand, are more likely to be persons unable to cope with the complex demands of marriage and family relationships.

The difference in rates of pathology between the married and single are less strikingly discrepant among women than among men (7, 39). This finding presumably reflects the divergent role implications of the single state and married life for the two sexes. Many competent women prefer an independent career to what they consider the burdens and frustrations of marriage; many incompetent women marry in order to be taken care of. These considerations tend not to hold for men. Whether single or married, a man is expected to provide for himself and, beyond this, to succeed as best he can in the world of work. Further, for men, marriage is not ordinarily an avenue of escape from responsibility; on the contrary, with marriage the man explicitly accepts responsibility for the welfare of his wife and future offspring. In this light it is not surprising that less effective males cling to the single state, or having married, soon become divorced. Seemingly, only men who are able to cope with the demands of adult living can enter into and maintain a successful marriage.

*Interpersonal Effectiveness.* The correspondence between the degree of social interaction and severity of psychiatric impairment among persons living in the general community has been studied by Langner and Michael (23). They examined the degree of "interpersonal affiliations" defined in terms of number of close friends, the number of neighbors with whom the person claims to be friendly, and the number of organizations to which he belongs. A combined index of these variables differentiated significantly between low and high impairment categories, with high scoring in interpersonal affiliations associated with a low level of psychiatric impairment.

*Leisure Time Activities.* Langner and Michael also reported on the relation of how a person uses his leisure time to his degree of psychiatric impairment. People with more reported leisure time activities were the less impaired. Those whose activities involved large groups also scored as less psychiatrically impaired than those who engaged only in solitary activities.

*Age Groups.* Srole *et al.* (39) conceive of age levels as a universal category to which every society gears role assignments and behavioral expectations. With increasing age, the demands imposed on the person become more complex. New expectations for social performance appear at each age, but conceptually these can be placed in a simple hierarchy of personal fulfillment that includes educational and occupational achievement, social participation and concern for the welfare of others, and heterosexual adjustment, as expressed in marriage and parenthood. Evaluation of the individual's performance in these areas of social function may be taken as an index of his social competence and consequently of his potential for effective social adaptation.

Starting in early adolescence both men and women are faced with the vicissitudes of sexual, marital, and parental relationships, roles for which they are often unprepared. Through the years of adulthood these demands take their toll, as seen in the increasing incidence of personality deviations with age. Srole *et al.* have reported that among their 20- to 29-year-old group 15.3% were severely impaired psychiatrically, while among their 50- to 59-year-olds 30.8% were so impaired. A regular and consistent rise has also been reported in first admission rates to psychiatric hospitals with increasing age (2). This holds true for both men and women, independent of marital status.

This completes our review of those studies that have been concerned with the relation of social competence variables and the prevalence rates of psychiatric disorder. In summary, we can note a striking consistency in the direction of these relationships. Whatever index of competence is employed, whether achieved level of education and occupation (SES), marital status, interpersonal effectiveness, use of leisure time, or age at onset of disorder, the findings are consistent. Those groups capable of more effective coping with societal expectations show the lowest prevalence rates for psychiatric disorder.

### Competence and the Geography of Disorder

An attempt to relate social competence level to the distribution within a community of various types of pathology has also been undertaken (42). This study was conducted in Worcester, Massachusetts, a city of 185,000 population. It examined within each of the city's thirty census tracts the correspondence of various indices of average social competence to the prevalence of three forms of social maladjustment. Three measures of average competence, or better, *incompetence*, were derived from census data. These indices included average level of educational accomplishment, average occupational status, and the proportion of divorced persons in each census tract of the community. Educational level was measured in terms of the proportion of individuals 25 years of age and over in each tract who had not completed grammar school. Occupational level was established in terms of the proportion of persons classified in unskilled labor and service occupations. These indices of low educational and occupational achievement and failure in marriage, as reflected in the divorce rate of each census tract, were combined into a composite measure of social incompetence. The study examined the relation between level of incompetence and the number of public mental hospital admissions, the number of clients seeking treatment for alcoholism, and the number of public disturbances recorded by the police department. A combined index of maladjustment based on these three forms of personal and social difficulties was also constructed and related to the composite measures of incompetence. Results are tabulated in Table 6–1.

TABLE 6–1

INCOMPETENCE AND MALADJUSTMENT ACCORDING TO U.S. CENSUS TRACT DATA[a]

|  | Educational level | Occupational level | Divorces | Average incompetence |
|---|---|---|---|---|
| Mental hospital admissions | .61[b] | .69 | .76 | .77 |
| Alcoholic clinic referrals | .51 | .67 | .55 | .67 |
| Police disturbances | .78 | .73 | .88 | .89 |
| Composite index of social maladjustment | .74 | .80 | .88 | .88 |

p = .01 for correlations greater than .45.
p = .001 for correlations greater than .55.
[a]Based on findings in a city of 185,000 population (Worcester, Massachusetts).
[b]Rank order correlations.

It will be seen that across the census tracts of this medium-sized community all the measures of social incompetence are related to the incidence rates of quite diverse forms of social maladjustment. A most striking correspondence was found between the average incompetence level of each census tract and its overall degree of social maladjustment.

Despite the impressively high relationships observed, these findings must be interpreted with caution. They do not reveal that persons of lesser competence have the greater likelihood of manifesting some form of maladjustment, but only that people who do so tend to be drawn from neighborhoods of lower than average social competence. One among other possible explanations may be that neighborhoods that manifest lower levels of competence are marked by less close personal relationships, and that this deficiency in emotional support tends to provoke intrapsychic or behavioral problems. Further, the cases of maladjustment in this study are limited to those that have been brought to agency or public attention. We know nothing of the distribution of persons with psychological, behavioral, or psychosomatic difficulties when the presence of these pathologies is not a matter of public record.

This problem of unrecorded cases besets the majority of studies on the epidemiology of psychiatric, behavioral, and psychosomatic disorders. As noted earlier, a number of studies (4, 24, 39) have indicated that only a small fraction of psychiatrically impaired individuals come to professional attention. Some evidence is available, however, on the relation of competence level to severity of treated psychiatric impairment in the general population. A brief review of this literature will help to focus our discussion on the relevant issues.

## SEVERITY OF DISORDER

While the foregoing findings support a major hypothesis advanced in this book on the relation of coping potential to pathology, they cannot be accepted with complete confidence for two reasons. The first lies in the absence of a direct test on the relation of social competence, as explicitly measured in one comprehensive index, to the prevalence of pathology. This caveat is probably of minor import. It is difficult to believe that some overall measure of competence would provide results any different from the consistent findings with all these partial measures of competence.

The second reservation is more formidable. It concerns the confidence that we can place in reported prevalence rates of psychiatric disorder. In the following chapter we note that this form of pathology is defined ultimately only in terms of the private judgment of the psychiatrist. When, in turn, we find that observed prevalence rates for psychiatric disorders vary from 0.8% to 64.0% among the general population (9), a considerable degree of uncertainty is introduced into any conclusions drawn from findings based on these rates. Fortunately, an alternative test of the relationship between social competence and psychiatric disorder can be formulated. A reasonable hypothesis, which follows from the general conceptual position advanced in Chapter 1, is that among persons diagnosed as suffering from some form of psychopathology, those of lower competence levels will manifest more severe forms of disorder.

One difficulty lies in the way of a direct test of this hypothesis. How is severity of disorder to be measured? In proceeding to a test of the hypothesis, we assumed that forms of disorder that either (a) interfere most with the everyday life of the person, or (b) are least reversible, that is, prognostically least favorable, may be considered as the more severe forms of psychopathology. In these terms, it was felt that schizophrenia and the personality and character disorders may reasonably be classified as more severe forms of psychiatric disorder than either the psychoneuroses or the manic-depressive reactions. Having made this decision, it was possible to test operationally the hypothesis that among a population of individuals, all of whom are diagnosed as suffering from some form of psychiatric disorder, those of lower levels of adaptive potential should manifest the more severe forms of disorder, those of higher adaptive potential the less severe.

As noted earlier, two measures of adaptive potential are available: achieved level of social competence and level of perceptual development, as this is measured through the Rorschach technique. A number of studies that have related indices of premorbid social competence to severity of pathology will be reported on first. This will be followed by a review of studies concerned with the relation of perceptual development to severity of disorder.

### Social Competence and Severity of Disorder

The relation between the competence and severity variables was examined among first-admission patients who entered Worcester State Hospital during 1963 (42). The study was limited to patients living in Worcester at the time of admission who were under 55 years of age and who were diagnosed as suffering from either a psychoneurosis, manic depression, schizophrenia, or a personality or character disorder. In all, 97 men and 76 women met these criteria.

A brief social competence index was calculated for each of these subjects, based on their educational and occupational achievements, marital status, and age at hospital admission. As predicted, a significant relationship between social competence and diagnosis was observed among both men and women. Those of higher competence tended to be diagnosed as either psychoneurotic or manic-depressive, those of lower competence as either schizophrenic or as a personality or character disorder.

These findings are reinforced by those obtained earlier (43) through an examination of case history data on 793 patients admitted to Worcester State Hospital during a 12-year period (1945–1957). The patients were categorized into four major diagnostic groups; manic-depressive (37 men, 38 women); schizophrenic (165 men, 122 women); psychoneurotic (81 men, 71 women); and character disorder (197 men, 82 women). The 1950 census data for the state of Massachusetts were employed to compare the total hospital population, as well as the four diagnostic groups, to the population at large on the variables investigated.

Results indicate that these diagnostic groups differed from the general population and from one another in rather specific ways. The distributions of the manic-depressive and psychoneurotic groups on the biographical variables displayed many similarities, while they differed markedly from the distributions of the schizophrenic and character disorder categories. The psychoneurotics and manic-depressives were significantly higher in educational and occupational achievements, more regularly employed, more frequently married, and of higher average age than either the schizophrenics or those classified as personality or character disorders. Thus, we can take these studies as verification of the hypothesis that pathological individuals of higher premorbid social competence tend to manifest the less severe forms of disorder.

A somewhat parallel finding was obtained by Hollingshead and Redlich (20) in comparing the distribution of the neuroses and schizophrenia in relation to social class level (equivalent to a combined index of educational and occupational achievement). The neuroses showed a higher prevalence rate among the higher social classes, and a decline in Class V. For schizophrenia, the reverse relationship was observed, with relatively modest increments from Class I through Class IV, but a striking increase in prevalence in Class V.

A study by Fine et al. (12) attempted to relate social competence level to a person's potential for pathological behavior. In this study a Rorschach index was used as the criterion of psychiatric impairment. This score was devised by Fisher (13) as a quantitative index of maladjustment. By means of this score he was able to differentiate between groups of women classified as schizophrenic, neurotic, and normal. Thetford and De Vos (40) were able to confirm these findings on both male and female samples. In the study by Fine et al., social competence was measured by means of the Worcester Scale of Social Attainment. The experimental group consisted of 74 men drawn from the community who had been selected as subjects in a research project dealing with the relation between social and personality variables and performance under stress. The majority were industrial workers, but the sample also contained white-collar employees and a number of industrial foremen.

It was found that the higher the achieved level of social competence, the lower was the subject's score on the Fisher maladjustment index. This relationship remained stable even with intelligence level partialed out. Thus, it was possible to find a substantial correspondence between effectiveness of behavior in the community and placement on an index of intrapsychic adjustment.

### Perceptual Development and Severity of Disorder

One of the basic propositions advanced in this book is that social competence reflects the level of psychological development achieved by the individual. A test and confirmation of this hypothesis was reported in Chapter 5. We have just offered support for the proposition that severity of disorder is associated with the level of social competence achieved in the premorbid period. It follows that severity of disorder should also be related to an individual's level of psychological development, as measured perceptually through the Rorschach technique. A number of studies conducted by Frank (14), Friedman (16), and Siegel (38) have tested this hypothesis.

Among them, these investigators compared the Rorschach perceptual performance of 30 hebephrenic and catatonic schizophrenics, 30 paranoid schizophrenics, 30 neurotics, and 30 psychiatrically normal adults. All these subjects were male. The Rorschach performance of these groups was compared to that of groups of children ranging in age from 3 to 10 years. The general line of reasoning that guided these studies was that, in terms of formal perceptual processes, hebephrenics and catatonics would perform like the youngest children (aged 3 to 5 years), paranoids at a level comparable to somewhat older children, and the neurotics somewhere intermediate to the 10-year-old children and normal adults. Their findings consistently supported this formulation.

### OUTCOME OF DISORDER

Much has been written about the prediction of outcome in psychopathological states. Before we review the literature on this topic, however, it seems necessary to consider how outcome is to be defined and measured. Let us take the question of measurement first. Is outcome to be rated as favorable or not simply according to the subjective impression of the psychiatrist? Shall we make use of more objective indices, such as the length of time that the patient spends in contact with a clinic or hospital, or his failure to survive in the community and his subsequent return to the hospital? We might also consider the degree to which the patient's symptoms have diminished as an appropriate criterion of outcome. Finally, we might make use of the individual's performance level in the community subsequent to release from a clinic or hospital. Performance level can be taken to include how well the person fulfills expected role behaviors within the family, on the job, and within the community.

It can be seen that it is inappropriate to view outcome as a single, unitary phenomenon. Rather, it must be treated as a very general term for a set of widely divergent sequelae to the pathological process. Since most published studies on outcome have made use of either psychiatric judgment or the objective measures of length of hospitalization and return to hospital as outcome criteria, we shall review these traditional indices first. In a subsequent section we shall report on the use of psychiatric status and performance level in the community as outcome measures.

*Traditional Criteria of Outcome*

None of the traditional criteria in psychopathology fulfill the requirements for an objective, quantitative, and conceptually meaningful measure of outcome. We shall substantiate this judgment by considering the limitations of the two most common sets of outcome indices: psychiatric judgment and certain more objective criteria. We shall then go on to examine the relation of the individual's adaptive potential to placement on these outcome measures.

*Psychiatric Judgment.* Until recently the most frequently used index of outcome was the psychiatrist's impression of improvement in the patient's psychological state. Case histories have regularly concluded with some comment by the attending psychiatrist stating that the patient's condition has improved or remained the same. Since we usually know neither the basis for this judgment, the meaning it is intended to convey, nor to what extent psychiatrists working independently would agree in their assessments, the value of such a rating is highly questionable.

A glance through any sample of case records indicates that the psychiatric condition of nearly all patients will be rated as improved at the end of any period of observation or treatment, so that in practice, it is difficult to use this criterion of outcome in any meaningful fashion. It must be recognized that in rating the patient's condition after treatment, the psychiatrist is also rating the value and quality of his own work, so that it is not unreasonable to find that the condition of the patient is consistently judged as enhanced by psychiatric intervention.

*Objective Indices of Outcome.* A number of objective and quantified indices of outcome have been devised. The most frequently used of these measures is duration of hospitalization, but also in use is the number of subsequent readmissions that the patient has suffered, or alternatively, the number of releases as well as the length of time he manages to remain out of the hospital. Unhappily, none of these indices solely reflects the actual psychiatric status of the patient or his ability to perform effectively in the community.

As evidence for this observation it can be noted that psychiatric ideology has had a profound impact on the proportion of patients who have been released from mental hospitals over the last century and a half. In the period between 1833 and 1846, psychiatric practice at Worcester State Hospital was guided by confidence in the therapeutic effectiveness of "moral treatment" (6). During that time the proportion of patients who left the hospital designated as recovered equaled 58%. When the dominant psychiatric opinion at the hospital shifted, as it did in the period 1870–1890, to a belief that mental disorder was a virtually incurable condition, the rate of discharges classified as recovered dropped to 26% (18). In both periods "recovery" was defined as restoration to the family and social performance in the community equal to that enjoyed before hospitalization. Recent efforts to return as many patients as possible to life in the community has brought about nearly 100% return of admitted patients to the community. Indeed, current psychiatric policy is directed at preventing any period of hospitalization whenever this is at all possible, with treatment preferably based on community clinics.

Another factor appears to be at work that significantly affects the length of time that the patient is hospitalized. This is the acceptability of the patient's behavior on the ward, that is, whether he is well groomed, sociable, and willing to work. Patients who are judged as acting in a socially desirable fashion are released early; those with socially undesirable behavior tend to remain in the hospital (32). Conformity to the hospital's code of behavior, then, is a prerequisite to favorable disposition.

This observation may explain why duration of hospitalization and number of readmissions (15) or releases (26) are unrelated to each other. While the patient is hospitalized he must conform to standards of behavior that are set by the psychiatric staff. When he returns home, the behavior norm is set by his relatives (15) and these may not coincide at all with those set by the hospital. Thus, problems in managing the patient at home, as well as the presence of symptoms that immediately effect family life, such as nervousness, staying by oneself, pessimism, or being argumentative, are associated with readmission. In contrast, the presence of overt symptoms that reflect primarily the psychiatric state of the patient is unrelated to length of hospitalization (26).

It should be noted also that patients of varying levels of effectiveness in community participation may remain outside the hospital. More adequate persons do so because they can cope with the demands of adult life. Less adequate persons do so because those responsible for their welfare, such as parents, make generous allowance for the patient's deficiencies and are tolerant of his idiosyncracies (15). Similarly, for unattached individuals living alone in deteriorated rooming house areas, the quality of social participation and anonymity characteristic of these slum areas allows for the free and unhampered expression of deviant behavior (5,44).

## Coping Potential and Outcome

Yet, despite the contribution of both the dominant philosophy in psychiatric care and pressures for social conformity, both of which power-fully influence the hospitalization and readmission measures, the individual's own social effectiveness does play some role in determining his rating on these outcome indices. To some modest extent each of these measures is expressive of the individual's coping potential, so that social competence and level of perceptual development, both of which reflect the individual's adaptive potential, tend to be associated with placement on these outcome indices. We shall review in sequence studies in the field of psychopathology that relate social competence and level of perceptual development to placement on these outcome indices.

Social Competence. The earliest study (34) of outcome to employ the Phillips Premorbid Scale included a total of 31 male patients, diagnosed predominantly as cases of dementia praecox (schizophrenia). Outcome was classified by psychiatric judgment into three levels: greatly improved, moderately improved, and least improved. All patients had some form of shock treatment, either electroshock, insulin coma, or metrazol, or some combination of these. The period of 6 to 12 months after shock treatment was set as the point for the evaluation of the therapeutic results. Social competence was found to be significantly correlated with the outcome of disorder.

Bleke (2) has corroborated these findings. He examined the relationship between scoring on the Phillips Premorbid Scale and the release of schizophrenic male patients from the mental hospital. One year after the completion of an experimental study carried out with 20 of these patients, Bleke reviewed their subsequent hospital records. He found that all but one of the ten high social competence subjects had been discharged, whereas nine of the ten lows were still hospitalized.

Farina and Webb (11) also made use of the Phillips Premorbid Scale in the prediction of (a) success or failure on a trial visit back to the community, and (b) long-term hospital status, that is, whether the patient is in the hospital or community some years after his first admission. The authors gathered data on 40 patients who were young, male, diagnosed as schizophrenic, and hospitalized for less than 9 months before being placed on trial visit. They found that high social competence was associated with both success on a trial visit home and discharge from the hospital. Query and Query (36) have confirmed the power of the Phillips Scale to predict release from and subsequent return to the hospital over a period of 5 years in a group of 48 men diagnosed as schizophrenic.

Nuttall and Solomon (32) posed the question whether premorbid social competence variables, using the Phillips Premorbid Scale, would predict outcome in schizophrenic groups that were drawn from three different social class levels. Significant relationships in the expected direction were found at all three class levels, with the most substantial relationship obtained with the lowest or working-class sample and the least with the highest class group.

It has also been found (37) that premorbid social competence, as measured by the Phillips Premorbid Scale, predicts outcome of disorder among female schizophrenic patients, as it does for male patients. Other investigators (10, 27, 30, 31, 33) also have observed a correspondence between marital status and outcome in psychiatrically impaired women, and Freeman and Simmons (15) confirmed this finding for both men and women.

Zigler and Phillips (44) have conducted studies, using both male and female patients, in which premorbid social competence was related to outcome in a large sample of patients who represented a comprehensive sampling of most forms of "functional," that is, nonorganic, psychiatric disorders. Using their six-item case history index as a measure of premorbid social competence, these authors found that patients who had manifested a relatively high level of social competence were more likely to have spent a shorter time in the hospital and to have been released from the hospital, and were less likely to have been rehospitalized than patients of lower premorbid social competence. Dinitz *et al.* (8) similarly have noted that married status, educational attainment, and social class position all predict posthospital performance as measured by a combined index of three variables: rating of psychiatric status, performance of routine home duties, and social participation. The subject sample consisted of 287 married females who had been hospitalized for some form of psychiatric disorder.

Despite the consistency of findings, the nature of the relationship between social competence and outcome remains ambiguous. As reported earlier in this chapter, the diagnosis assigned a patient is related to his social competence level. Therefore, the difference in outcome for groups that differ in competence level may be the result of some difference in their diagnostic composition rather than the consequence of social competence variables. Furthermore, patients high on particular social competence indices employed to measure social competence (e.g., intelligence) may receive more intensive psychiatric treatment. It can be argued that the more favorable outcome among high competence patients is the result of such superior treatment.

A study was designed by Zigler and Phillips (44) to help resolve these issues. In this study patients in both the high and low competence groups had been diagnosed as schizophrenics, and the groups were matched for kind and amount of psychiatric treatment. Even with these restrictions, social competence level predicted outcome of disorder in the expected direction. From these findings it may be argued that competence appears as a more significant contributor to outcome than does either the amount or kind of treatment received, a position supported by other investigators (8, 15).

A number of other researchers have reported on the relation of various individual indices of premorbid social competence to outcome in psychiatric disorder, most commonly for patients diagnosed as schizophrenic. In a review of the available literature, Zubin et al. (45) reported that in six out of seven studies, the presence of heterosexual contacts or interests was associated with favorable outcome. Similarly, marriage, in contrast to remaining single, was prognostically favorable. Only one study in each of these cases reported to the contrary. Among 90 studies reviewed, 88 reported the favorable implications of a "good" social history, that is, effectiveness in interpersonal relations during the premorbid period.

Although the work of only two investigators reviewed by Zubin et al. was concerned with work history, their studies indicated that good performance in this area was related to a positive outcome. These findings were confirmed by Brooke (3) and by Wing et al. (41). Brown has reported also that occupational level is positively related to favorable outcome. This finding is consistent with the report, based on a study by Hollingshead and Redlich (20) of 725 schizophrenic patients, that concluded that social class, which is highly dependent on occupational and educational level, is also significantly associated with a positive outcome. Hardt and Feinhandler (19), reporting a study on 4000 male schizophrenics, made the same observation.

This brief review of the literature strongly suggests that several factors of premorbid experience influence outcome in psychiatric disorder. These factors include the degree of heterosexual maturation, marital status, aptitude in interpersonal relationships, and effectiveness at work. That is, the more adequately the individual is able to cope with the major facets of adult living during the premorbid period, the more favorable is his potential for recovery from psychiatric disorder.

Prognosis has also been studied in the fields of delinquency and crime. Here the major studies have been conducted by Sheldon and Eleanor Glueck (17), whose work we will review. Although not so designated by these authors, two types of variables appear to distinguish those delinquents or criminals who subsequently adapt in society from those who do not. One type of discriminating indices may be classified as measures of social competence, the other as assessments of childhood experience and family background. Here we shall consider only the competence indices.

A variety of criteria for outcome were used by the Gluecks. These include violation of probation; behavior in the reformatory, jail, or prison; social adaptation under conditions of parole; recidivism 5–10 years after completion of first criminal sentence; and whether or not a former delinquent or criminal acted in a delinquent fashion in subsequent Army service. The Gluecks took an entirely empirical approach to the use of their various predictive indices with these criterion measures. In their tables for prediction, the various indices of social competence appear haphazardly. Therefore, we shall not attempt to tie the competence predictors to individual outcome criteria, but will simply summarize the kinds of competence measures that appear to be associated with prognosis generally in delinquency and crime.

Data provided by the Gluecks suggest that the competence variables of age at onset, intelligence level, education, occupational skill, work habits, use of leisure time, and economic responsibility for oneself and one's dependents all serve to discriminate delinquents with a favorable prognosis from those with a less fortunate outcome. Thus, social competence variables are not associated as prognostic indices solely with psychiatric forms of disorder. These measures appear prognostically relevant in delinquency also. The consistency with which these variables are associated with outcome in quite different forms of pathology suggests that prognosis is more a consequence of the individual's adaptive potential than of any unique facet of deviance itself.

Finally, it should be noted that social competence variables appear to play a role in determining outcome even in the sphere of physical diseases. Berle et al. (1) studied a group of 793 patients who suffered from various stress disorders, which included irritable colon, tension headache, peptic ulcer, urticaria, ulcerative colitis, and vasomotor rhinitis. In this group they isolated a set of psychological and social variables that distinguished improved from unimproved patients. Among these items were a number that we have classified as social competence indices, such as marital status, educational achievement, and employment regularity. They crossvalidated their variables on a second group of 209 patients who suffered from asthma, migraine, and hypertension.

The Berle scale has also been found useful in predicting outcome in tuberculosis (21). It was found that marital status, occupational level and job stability, and outside interests predicted treatment success or failure in this disorder. This finding parallels a finding by Moran et al. (29) that social competence level predicted those tubercular patients who remain in treatment until this is successfully completed from those who do not. These authors comment that, for the patient with an ineffectual life history, hospitalization is only the most recent of a long series of life situations in which he has failed to make an adequate adjustment. This conceptual position parallels that adopted here: pathology is only one phase in the life pattern of the individual, and one that bears the imprint of his characteristic life style.

*Perceptual Development and Outcome.* A limited number of studies have explored the relationship between psychological development, as measured by Rorschach developmental indices, and outcome in disorder. In one such recent study (35), the present writer examined Rorschach protocols[1] taken prior to electroshock treatment on schizophrenic patients who were subsequently assigned to three levels of improvement in psychiatric status: not improved, moderately improved, and markedly improved. Eleven, 19, and 15 patients, respectively, were placed in these improvement categories. Scoring on developmentally high Rorschach indices significantly discriminated between these three outcome groups. Levine (25) observed a similar correspondence between Rorschach developmental level and shortness of psychiatric hospitalization within a psychiatric population that included both schizophrenic and nonschizophrenic patients.

## *Psychiatric Status, Performance Level, and Outcome*

In the previous section we discussed the observed relationships between adaptive potential, measured in terms of either social competence or perceptual development, to traditional measures of outcome in psychopathology. We have noted a surprising consistency in findings despite the limitations that inhere in these outcome criteria. Ultimately, these traditional measures are presumed to reflect either the posttreatment psychiatric status of the patient or his performance in the community. Why, then, have not any more direct measures of improvement in psychiatric status or post treatment performance level come into more common use? Each of the latter types of assessment for outcome has limitations that have restricted its general application, and these will be discussed in turn.

*Psychiatric Status.* The use of posttreatment psychiatric status has immediate appeal. If a patient's psychiatric condition could be reliably rated and quantified, it would mean that standards could be set for release from the hospital, or more generally, for treatment programs. Unhappily, we are not in a position to establish objective standards for either the degree of psychiatric impairment or intactness. Earlier in this chapter we referred to the ambiguity of psychiatric ratings, and to the uncertainty of the extent to which pathology is distributed in the general population.

---

[1] The writer wishes to express his appreciation to Dr. Rosaline Goldman, who made available the Rorschach protocols on these patients.

Estimates have ranged from 0.8 to 64% (9). Clearly we do not possess any stable or generally accepted foot rule for the presence or degree of psychopathology. Indeed, it will be remembered that ultimately the presence of pathology devolves on the unrestricted judgement of the individual psychiatrist (24, 39). Even under the most favorable of conditions, and working from identical data, psychiatrists fall far short of perfect agreement in assessing the presence and level of psychiatric impairment. If we are unable to judge with any certainty whether a person is pathologically impaired or not, or to what degree this may be true, it follows that it is not possible to judge with any certainty the degree of improvement in psychiatric status.

*Posttreatment Performance Level.* The limitations that apply to psychiatric status as an outcome criterion do not beset performance level as a posttreatment measure. Performance level in the community, both prior to the onset of pathology and subsequent to treatment, can be rated in an objective and quantifiable fashion. Further, the most powerful and consistent set of predictors for the posthospital status of the psychiatric patient are the various indices of prehospital social competence. We have already noted that competence level predicts length of hospitalization and likelihood of rehospitalization. As is to be expected, major correspondences exist between effectiveness of pre- and posthospital performance in many areas of community participation. That is, the premorbid work history, social interests, and marital status are reliable guides to the patient's style of life in the posthospital period (35).

The chief limitation in the use of posttreatment performance level as an outcome criterion appears to be quite outside its potential significance as a meaningful method for assessing outcome. It will be noted that it is the only such criterion measure that requires intensive study of the client outside the confines of the treatment setting. Considerable effort and expense is involved in seeking him out and assessing his performance in the community. It is this need to evaluate the patient as a participating member of society, combined with a concentration by psychiatric professionals on the pathological state itself, that perhaps has set limits on the use of performance level in the community as an outcome measure.

A FINAL COMMENT

It is relevant to ask to what extent the available criteria of outcome tend to coincide. If it turned out that placement on any one criterian determined scoring on all the other measures, there would be no need to choose. It happens, however, that they tend to be statistically independent of each other (26), although some very modest relationships have been observed among them. Duration of hospitalization is associated with subsequent employment regularity and with degree of participation in the social life of others. Similarly, to the extent that a patient remains symptomatic, his likelihood of readmission to the hospital is increased (15).

Because the various outcome measures tend to show little relation to each other, the question arises as to which should be chosen as the more valid index or indices of outcome. To ask this question is to pose a more general issue: what is the intent of any outcome measure; that is, to what purpose may it be put?

Outcome measures may be used in a variety of ways: Change in the behavior of one particular patient may be of interest, or we may want to compare the relative effectiveness of one treatment procedure over another for various types of patients. In order to establish an appropriate index of change or outcome the therapist must ask himself what kind of change he is seeking. Is the patient expected to be a less troubled or happier person; is he to become more psychologically "normal;" or is he to become a more effective and responsible participant in community life? These aspirations are not mutually exclusive, but they can differ in their importance to the therapist. Certainly, their achievement must be assessed in very different ways.

The clinician in private practice who treats effective but troubled clients on an outpatient basis may consider an improvement in their subjective emotional state as a primary goal. The therapist who is responsible for the welfare of seriously disordered and hospitalized private patients needs to be concerned with their psychiatric condition. For the practitioner who works in the public mental hospital the primary goals are to keep the patient's hospital stay as short as possible, to prevent rehospitalization, and to enhance insofar as possible the patient's effectiveness as he participates in the life of the community. Since 98% of hospitalized psychiatric patients in the United States are housed in public mental hospitals, the significance of these variables concerned with hospitalization and performance in the community appear central to assessing both the patient's status and the effectiveness of the treatment programs to which he is subjected.

In the present chapter we have been concerned with the relation of coping potential to prevalence, severity, and outcome in psychopathology. But what *is* psychopathology? There is no simple answer to this question. The next chapter is devoted to a review of the issues involved in its definition.

### REFERENCES

1. Berle, B. B., Pinsky, R. H., Wolf, S., and Wolff, H. G. A clinical guide to prognosis in stress diseases. *Journal of the American Medical Association*, 1952, **149**, 1624–1628.
2. Bleke, R. C. Unpublished data referred to by E. H. Rodnick and N. Garmezy. In M. R. Jones (Ed.), *Nebraska symposium on motivation*. Lincoln, Neb.: University of Nebraska Press, 1957. P. 142.

3. Brooke, E. A national study of schizophrenic patients in relation to occupation. Congress Report. Vol. 3. Second International Congress for Psychiatry, Zurich, 1957.
4. Brugger, C. Psychiatrische Bestandesaufnahme im Gebiete eines medizinisch-anthropoligischen Zensus in der Nähe von Rosenheim. *Zeitschrift für die gesamte Neurologie Psychiatrie*, 1938, 160. In A. H. Leighton, J. A. Clausen, & R. N. Wilson (Eds.), *Explorations in social psychiatry*. New York: Basic Books, 1957.
5. Cohen, L. Los Angeles rooming-house kaleidoscope. *American Sociological Review*, 1951, **16**, (3), 316–326.
6. Dain, N. *The rise and fall of moral treatment*. New Brunswick, N.J.: Rutgers University Press, 1964.
7. Dayton, M. A. *New facts on mental disorders*. Springfield, Ill.: Charles C. Thomas, 1940.
8. Dinitz, S., Lefton, M., Angrist, S., and Pasamanick, B. Psychiatric and social attributes as predictors of case outcome in mental hospitalization. *Social Problems*, 1960–1961, **8**, 322–328.
9. Dohrenwend, B. P., and Dohrenwend, B. S. The problem of validity in field studies of psychological disorder. *Journal of Abnormal Psychology*, 1965, **70**, 52–69.
10. Dunham, H. W., & Meltzer, B. N. Predicting length of hospitalization of mental patients. *American Journal of Sociology*, 1946, **52**, 123–131.
11. Farina, A., & Webb, W. W. Premorbid adjustment and subsequent discharge. *Journal of Nervous and Mental Disease*, 1956, **124**, 612–613.
12. Fine, H. J., Fulkerson, S. C., & Phillips, L. Maladjustment and social attainment. *Journal of Abnormal and Social Psychology*, 1955, **50** (1), 33–35.
13. Fisher, S. Patterns of personality rigidity and some of their determinants. *Psychology Monographs*, 1950, **64** (1, Whole No. 307).
14. Frank, I. Perceptual structurization in certain psychoneurotic disorders: A genetic evaluation by means of the Rorschach test. Unpublished doctoral dissertation. Boston University, 1951.
15. Freeman, H. E., & Simmons, O. G. *The mental patient comes home*. New York: Wiley, 1963.
16. Friedman, H. Perceptual regression in schizophrenia: An hypothesis suggested by the use of the Rorschach test. *Journal of Genetic Psychology*, 1952, **81**, 63–98.
17. Glueck, S., and Glueck, E. *Predicting delinquency and crime*. Cambridge, Mass.: Harvard University Press, 1959.
18. Grob, G. N. *The state and the mentally ill*. Chapel Hill: University of North Carolina Press, 1966.
19. Hardt, R. H., & Feinhandler, S. J. Social class and schizophrenic prognosis. *American Sociological Review*, 1959, **24**, 815–821.
20. Hollingshead, A. B., & Redlich, F. C. Social class and mental illness: A community study. New York: Wiley, 1958.
21. Holmes, T. H., Joffe, J. R., Ketcham, J. W., and Sheehy, T. S. Experimental study of prognosis. *Journal of Psychosomatic Research*, 1961, **5**, 235–252.
22. Kahl, J. A. *The American class structure*. New York: Holt, 1964.
23. Langner, T. S., and Michael, S. T. *Life stress and mental health*. New York: Free Press of Glencoe, 1963.
24. Leighton, D. C., Harding, J. S., Macklin, D. B., MacMillan, A. M., & Leighton, A. H. *The character of danger: Psychiatric symptoms in selected communities*. Vol. III. *The Stirling County Study of Psychiatric Disorder and Sociocultural Environment*. New York: Basic Books, 1963.
25. Levine, D. Rorschach genetic level and mental disorder. *Journal of Projective Techniques*, 1959, **23**, 436–439.

26. Levine, D. Relations among criteria of improvement in functional psychoses. In Proceedings of the 73rd Annual Convention of the American Psychological Association, 1965.

27. Linn, E. L. Patients' socioeconomic characteristics and release from a mental hospital. *American Journal of Sociology*, 1959, **65**, 280–286.

28. Malzberg, B. Important statistical data about mental illness. In S. Arieti (Ed.), *American handbook of psychiatry*. New York: Basic Books, 1959. Pp. 161–174.

29. Moran, L. J., Fairweather, G. W., and Morton, R. B. Some determinants of successful and unsuccessful adaptation to hospital treatment of tuberculosis. *Journal of Consulting Psychology*, 1956, **2**, 125–131.

30. Morgan, N. C., & Johnson, N. A. Failures in psychiatry: The chronic patient. *American Journal of Psychiatry*, 1957, **113**, 824–830.

31. Norris, V. A statistical study of the influence of marriage on the hospital care of the mentally sick. *Journal of Mental Science*, 1956, **102**, 467–486.

32. Nuttall, R. L., & Solomon, L. F. Factorial structure and prognostic significance of premorbid adjustment in schizophrenia. *Journal of Consulting Psychology*, 1965, **29** (4), 362–372.

33. Pascal, G. R., Swenson, C. H., Feldman, D. A., Cole, M. E., & Bayard, J. Prognostic criteria in the case histories of hospitalized mental patients. *Journal of Consulting Psychology*, 1953, **17**, 163–171.

34. Phillips, L. Case history data and prognosis in schizophrenia. *Journal of Nervous and Mental Disease*, 1953, **6**, 515–525.

35. Phillips, L., and White, W. C. Unpublished manuscript, Worcester State Hospital Psychology Department Library, 1967.

36. Query, J. M. Neale, C. R., & Query, W. T., Jr. Prognosis and progress: A five-year study of forty-eight schizophrenic men. *Journal of Consulting Psychology*, 1964, **28** (6), 501–505.

37. Rodnick, E. H., and Garmezy, N. An experimental approach to the study of motivation in schizophrenia. In M. R. Jones (Ed.), *Nebraska symposium on motivation*. Lincoln, Neb.: University of Nebraska Press, 1957.

38. Siegel, E. L. Genetic parallels of perceptual structurization in paranoid schizophrenia: An analysis by means of the Rorschach technique. *Journal of Projective Techniques*, 1953, **17**, 151–161.

39. Srole, L., Langner, T. S., Michael, S. T., Opler, M. K., & Rennie, T. A. C. *Mental health in the metropolis: The midtown study*. Vol. 1. New York: McGraw-Hill, 1962.

40. Thetford, W. N., & DeVos, G. Personal communication to Fisher, S. in Patterns of personality rigidity and some of their determinants. *Psychology Monographs*, 1950, **64** (1, Whole No. 307).

41. Wing, J. K., Denham, J., & Monro, A. B. The duration of stay in hospital of patients suffering from schizophrenia. *Journal of Prevention of Social Medicine*, 1959, **13**, 145.

42. Worcester Area Mental Health Survey, May 1966. Available through the Worcester State Hospital Psychology Department Library.

43. Zigler, E., & Phillips, L. Case history data and psychiatric diagnosis. *Journal of Consulting Psychology*, 1961, **25** (5), 458. (a)

44. Zigler, E., & Phillips, L. Social competence and outcome in psychiatric disorder. *Journal of Abnormal and Social Psychology*, 1961, **63** (2), 264–271. (b)

45. Zubin, J., Sutton, S., Salzinger, K., Salzinger, S., Burdock, E. 1., and Peretz, D. A biometric approach to prognosis in schizophrenia. In P. H. Hoch & J. Zubin (Eds.), *Comparative epidemiology of the mental disorders*. New York: Grune & Stratton, 1961. Pp. 143–206.

# 7/THE DEFINITION AND MEASUREMENT

## OF ADAPTIVE FAILURE

To this point we have been concerned with the individual's ability to cope with the complexities of life in the community, that is, to live up to or surpass the expectations that society sets for the behavior of each adult according to his age and sex. The task undertaken in this chapter is to discuss the nature of adaptive failure, its distribution in the population, the forms that it may take, and techniques for its measurement.

When a person is unable to master the problems that beset him, any of a number of inappropriate and nonconstructive ways of behaving may ensue. Sometimes these are expressed in those bodily dysfunctions that are known as psychosomatic disorders. Alternatively, these failures in life find distorted expression in some type of psychological abnormality; or again, failure to cope effectively may precipitate some form of delinquent or criminal activity. All these varied types of response to failure may be defined as pathological in the sense that they constitute ineffective, inappropriate, and, on the surface, often aimless and bizarre activities in lieu of the constructive response that society expects and the situation demands.

The problem of human failure is not, however, ordinarily treated as a unitary field of either investigation or social action. Indeed we possess no satisfactory single term to encompass this panorama of ineffective and aberrant responses to the demands that living in society places on each person. Here we shall use the term psychopathology, or for the sake of brevity, pathology, as a single, comprehensive designation for all these diverse forms of deviant, inappropriate, and ineffectual responses to the problems of human living. This chapter and the next are devoted to identifying the major types of pathology, the problems inherent in its classification, and the conceptual issues involved in its definition.

## MAJOR FORMS OF PATHOLOGY

Pathological reactions are personal tragedies not only for their victims but for their families as well. Yet, it can be asked if the number of such cases and the potential danger for their victims as well as others make their existence a serious social problem. A review of the available data leaves no doubt that this is the case. Here we want to provide a brief survey of the evidence that supports this conclusion. We shall first present statistics for those deviant reactions conventionally classified as psychiatric or mental disorders. Data on other forms of pathological reaction that increasingly are recognized as inappropriate responses to the dilemmas of life are also relevant. These include a wide spectrum of behaviors that are classified as antisocial in nature, and those disturbances in bodily function that are categorized in psychiatry and medicine generally as psychosomatic disorders. Findings on these forms of pathological reaction will also be presented.

### Psychiatric Disorders

According to statistics released by the American Hospital Association, about 51% of the 1,400,000 patients who comprise the average daily census in all hospitals are patients in psychiatric care (11). Thus, patients suffering from mental disorders occupy more hospital beds than persons with polio, cancer, heart disease, tuberculosis, and all other physical diseases combined.

More than 98% of these psychiatric patients are in public mental hospitals. Of all first admissions to state and county hospitals, the largest percentage are patients diagnosed as schizophrenic (23%) and those classified as suffering from the organic disorders of cerebral arteriosclerosis, other circulatory disturbances, or senile brain disease (23%). Because of the relative youth of schizophrenic patients on admission to hospitals, those schizophrenic patients who are not discharged tend to accumulate from year to year and make up approximately half of the resident population of these hospitals. On the other hand, patients with circulatory and senile brain diseases constitute only about one seventh of the resident population of these mental hospitals because, being old, they often die soon after admission.

Other frequent causes of first admission to mental hospitals include alcoholism (15%), psychotic disorders other than schizophrenia (8%), personality disorders (7%), psychoneurotic reactions (7%), and mental deficiency (3%). The various psychological disturbances tend to develop at different times during the life cycle. In the age range 14–44 years, schizophrenia and personality disorders predominate. During the next decade of life the involutional psychoses and alcoholic psychoses become relatively common. In the sixties, psychoses with cerebral arteriosclerosis and senile psychoses assume prominence, and these mental disorders of the senium continue to rise relative to other disorders until the end of the life-span.

In addition to hospitalized cases of mental disorder, approximately 400,000 patients per year receive psychiatric care in outpatient psychiatric clinics. Further, there are reported to be 3,800,000 problem drinkers in the United States, of whom 950,000 are chronic and severe alcoholics. In addition, 50,000 persons are presumed addicted to narcotics. That is, there are approximately as many cases of severe alcoholism in the United States as all other cases of psychiatric disorder combined, both inpatient and outpatient. In contrast, in terms of the number of people affected, the problem of narcotic addiction is of relative minor significance.

At least 250,000 children with less serious disorders also receive treatment each year at child guidance clinics throughout the country (18). At the present time it is estimated that the annual cost of mental illness is apprximately $4 billion (19). This figure includes the total maintenance and operating expenditures of public and private mental hospitals, the cost of public assistance to mentally disordered and intellectually retarded persons, and the estimated income losses of patients in mental hospitals.

The foregoing statistics are based on the prevalence of treated mental disturbances. Several attempts have been made to ascertain the overall rate (including both treated and untreated cases) of psychiatric disorder in the general population. Estimates have varied widely, ranging from a low of 0.8% as psychiatrically disordered (25) to 64.0% (16). These figures derive from studies conducted around the world. Nevertheless, even when consideration is limited to urban United States, the range is still very wide, with a  minumum estimate of 1.8% (15) and a high of 32.0% (5). The uncertainty that accompanies the proportion of persons who are to be classified as psychiatrically disordered is strikingly demonstrated by the variation in rejection rates, based on grounds of psychiatric disability, at United States Army induction stations during World War II. These rates varied from one station to another from a low of 5% to a high of 51% (24).

What determines this wide variation in reported rates of disorder? At least three factors appear to influence the magnitude of these findings. First a difference in rates appears according to whether investigators made direct contact with the subjects of their studies or relied on written records or informants. Higher rates tend to appear with direct contact. The median rate of disorder found in six studies based on records or informants was

2.15% with a range from 1.1% to 9.0%. In direct contact studies, the median rate of recorded psychiatric cases was 13.6%, with a range from 1.1% to 64.0% (6).

The second factor that appears to influence the observed rate of disorder is the recency of the study in which it appears. Even when we restrict ourselves to studies based on direct interview, those carried out prior to 1950 averaged a median of 3.55% cases of psychiatric disorder in the general population. Those conducted from 1950 onward reported a median of 18.0% of disorder (6). The reason for this striking increase in recorded rates does not seem to lie in a true upsurge in the prevalence of mental disorder. Rather, it appears to be accounted for by differences in intent between earlier in contrast to later studies. By and large, earlier investigators were guided by a desire to avoid overestimation, later investigators by a determination to achieve a complete enumeration of cases.

A third variable that influences the proportion of reported cases of psychiatric disorder in a community is the ambiguity that surrounds the definition of mental disorder. When the investigator adopts a strict standard, reported rates tend to be low. When the standard is less restrictive, rates tend to be high. Thus Essen-Möller (8) recorded a rate of 13.6% for "diagnoses constituting the main subject of most psychiatric population studies." This rate jumped to 54.7% for all those subjects in whom some degree of pathology could not be definitely ruled out. Similarly, Srole *et al.* (22) reported that 2.7% of their general population sample were psychiatrically "incapacitated," a designation that they considered as equivalent to the level of psychiatric disorder manifested by hospitalized psychiatric patients. Another 20.7% were classified as either "markedly" or "severely" impaired, equivalent to the severity of disorder to be found among psychiatric outpatients. However, these investigators reported that 81.5% of their total sample suffered from at least some mild degree of psychiatric impairment, or symptom formation, and only 18.5% could be considered as psychiatrically "well," that is, as totally nonsymptomatic.

*Antisocial Behaviors*

Over the past several decades increasing interest has centered on individuals who manifest any of various forms of sociopathic personality disorders, that is, forms of pathology that are defined in terms of behaviors that deviate from prevailing social standards. These types of disorder are increasing in frequency, an observation that may be associated with reported recent increases in criminal and delinquent behaviors.

Each year more than 2 million crimes are reported in the United States (27), of which over 90% are against property (e.g., burglaries, larcenies, auto thefts, and robberies), the residual being directed against persons (e.g., aggravated assaults, forcible rapes, and murders). Each year also more than 750,000 children come before the juvenile courts because of alleged delinquent behavior. It is now estimated that one boy in every five is brought into court during his adolescence on a delinquency charge, including traffic violations (21). It is estimated that the cost of juvenile delinquency to this nation's economy currently runs about $4 billion a year (9).

*Psychosomatic Disorders*

Large numbers in the general population suffer from physical diseases that are now considered psychosomatic in nature. Thus, of all the patients annually admitted to general hospitals, it is estimated that 6 million are suffering from serious mental and emotional disorders that are, at least in part, responsible for their physical condition (18). For example, in the age range 45–64 years, 5 of the 12 types of disabling illnesses with the highest annual rated per thousand of the population are usually regarded as psychosomatic diseases. These include diseases of the heart, functional digestive disturbances, arthritis and chronic rheumatism, hypertension and arteriosclerosis, and headache. The average number of cases per thousand persons for each of these 5 categories of disorder varied from approximately 9 to 23. Thus, about 1–2% of the middle-aged population is disabled annually by each of these deseases (17).

The data just presented imply that an impressive proportion of the general population of the United States manifests some form of psychopathological reaction of sufficient severity to have come to professional attention, whether this be a psychiatric agency, some representative of the law, or a practitioner of physical medicine. It is impossible to determine with any degree of accuracy the number of persons involved in such institutional contacts within any given year. A review of the available literature suggests that the cases handled within such a period in any one community may equal one twentieth, or 5%, of the total population. Information is unavailable regarding the extent of overlap among these cases. Certainly, there are many "repeaters," persons who even within as short a period as a year are seen more than once by the same institution and who are counted as a corresponding number of cases. Many people are registered with more than one agency, sometimes on a referral basis, and are counted in the statistics of each of the institutions involved. In one crisis episode, for example, a person may be seen by quite different types of agencies, such as the police, a clinic for alcoholics, and a psychiatric facility, and thus may appear as a separate "case" for ostensibly quite different forms of pathology in the several agencies.

We are in the dark as to the proportion of pathological individuals who become known cases by virtue of referral to some agency to the number who remain among the "invisible" cases of pathology because their disorder remains undetected. As we have seen, estimates of the true proportion of known to unknown cases vary. Available evidence suggests a ratio of one to five or six registered to unregestered cases (4, 22). If the number of detected cases of pathology were no greater than the number of pathological individuals, this ratio would imply that, at a conservative estimate, as many as one person in four, or 25% of the population, manifests some severe form of disorder, whether this be psychiatric, antisocial or psychosomatic. On the face of it this estimate appears to be unreasonably high. Where are all these cases of pathology to be found? Surely they are not randomly distributed throughout the community. Evidence that we shall present later shows that they are not. Even so, it is difficult to believe that one person in four manifests some form of severe disorder.

In the light of the great variability in reported rates of disorder and the wide diversity in its forms, a basic conceptual issue needs to be raised—how is disorder to be defined? Does it imply an inability to participate effectively in the community, an assumption that appears reasonable in cases of profound intellectual retardation or of those who carry out physically or sexually assaultive acts? Alternatively, is it possible to conceive of disorder as simply some intangible or covert "emotional" disturbance that does not necessarily infringe on the person's ability to fulfill responsibilities at work or to maintain satisfactory interpersonal relationships, although it may impair the establishment and maintenance of close emotional ties? Is the term psychopathology to convey a meaning intermediate between these two formulations? Undoubtedly many people successfully fulfill their major responsibilities on the job and within the sphere of family living and yet are involved in some pattern of aberrant activities, such as a homosexual relationship, bouts of heavy drinking, or drug addiction. Others may fulfill all their responsibilities and more, and yet lead lives of intense desperation, laboring under a sense of futility and aimlessness. Can any one definition of psychopathology be assigned to all these variants of deviance? The next section of this chapter is devoted to a discussion of this issue.

## PROBLEMS IN CLASSIFICATION

Scrutiny of the relevant literature suggests that psychiatric disorder is to be defined only in terms of a psychiatrist's judgment that such disorder is present. In the words of D.C. Leighton and her colleagues (14): "It is essentially that collection of behavioral pattern occurring among human beings with which psychiatrists are usually concerned." And Srole *et al.* (22) say "mental health is a nonmetric, constellational variable and as yet can only be classified by refraction through the lens of the psychiatrists' perceptual and judgemental processes."

What kind of independent validation lends weight to the highly subjective basis of psychiatric classification? Unfortunately, very little. The methodology adopted in two recent major community studies underscores the subjective and arbitrary nature of psychiatric classification. In both these studies interview items on which psychiatric judgments were to be based were chosen from objective tests of psychiatric status, such as the Neuropsychiatric Screening Adjunct (23). Preliminary validation studies indicated that certain of the selected items were able to discriminate groups of individuals independently diagnosed as suffering from psychiatric disorder from persons living in the community who were not victims of any known psychiatric condition. These discriminating items were retained in the final study instruments, but so too were items that failed to distinguish between the psychiatric and community samples, on the basis that the latter items were considered by psychiatrists participating in these studies as valid indices of mental pathology. Further, it is not possible to enumerate the precise symptoms manifested by a patient who has been diagnosed as a schizophrenic, alcoholic, or any other type of deviant individual. Thus, these classifications provide only a very general guide to the overt characteristics of pathology. Yet, in order to achieve a sound understanding of disorder, a precise and detailed description of its manifestations is essential. That is, the observation and cataloguing of deviant behaviors, or "symptoms," is a first and necessary step toward the understanding of psychopathology.

It should also be noted that the traditional categories of disorder bear a variable relation to symptomatology. For action disorders, the only useful criterion for the presence of disorder is the occurrence of its manifest symptoms. Thus, a drug addict is to be defined by his use of drugs not called for by his physical condition. A person may also be defined as a drug addict, even though no longer using drugs, if he must take explicit steps to prevent a relapse into their use, as in avoiding acquaintances who are continuing the use of drugs, or any situation that has been associated with their use. In contrast, to call an individual a drug addict when he has never been overtly addicted to drugs is an exercise in futility. We possess no direct measure of a latent tendency, or a potential, for addiction that would permit us to include in this syndrome those individuals who are not now nor have ever been overt addicts, yet who may become such in the future.

The situation is quite otherwise in regard to those physical diseases that have come to be labeled psychosomatic, such as ulcers or arthritis. The process may have impaired the body's functioning and yet a person may be quite unaware that he is a victim of illness. In this case, the only indication of the presence of disorder is found in subtle biochemical indices of physiological imbalance. These signs will, of course, indicate that some physical disease is present. They will not provide proof that the appearance of certain physical diseases is fostered either by particular personality characteristics of the victim or the traumatic situations to which he has been exposed. Indeed, it must be observed that no consensus has been achieved on the hypothetical psychological origins of the various forms of psychosomatic illness. That these exist as physical diseases is unquestioned; the precise role played by psychological factors in their origin is still uncertain.

The situation in regard to the more directly psychological and emotional disorders that are defined in terms of the patient's psychological state is even more ambiguous. Significant differences of opinion exist regarding the meaning and classification of these forms of pathology. A major question at issue is whether these disorders are to be thought of as "disease" processes, analogous to physical diseases, or as the behavioral reactions of individuals who have been pressured into inappropriate and inadequate behavior patterns by events that are beyond their coping potential. The concept of mental disorders as disease processes favors an organic basis to these disorders and encourages a physiological approach to their investigation. Yet it must be noted that, ideally a physical disease is defined in terms of a triad of criteria that includes a specific symptom syndrome, a specific course, and a specific etiology. None of these criteria can be satisfied for any of the aberrant reactions that constitute the field of mental disorder (2). Indeed, we can diagnose the presence of some specific form of psychiatric disorder only when overt deviations in thought, emotion, or behavior such as hallucinations, explosive emotional outbursts, or seclusiveness, are present. No tests are available that, on the basis of sampling the covert psychological or emotional state of the individual or his physiological functioning, permit us to decide on the presence or absence of psycho-pathology.

Thus, to ask whether schizophrenia, or any other form of mental disorder, is to be defined by the presence of its overt symptoms or in terms of some assumed covert process is futile. Even if we assume that the onset of overt psychiatric symptoms is the consequence of some distortion in the individual's psychological or somatic processes, the mere *hypothesized* presence of such distorted processes cannot serve to define a disorder. Only when these causal factors have been demonstrated and measured can we relinquish overt behavior as the only acceptable criterion for pyschiatric diagnosis. Thus, for the present at least, psychiatric disorders must be defined simply and directly in terms of the symptoms that appear in the person's behavior.

Recent years have witnessed a decline in the commitment to the definition of mental disorders as disease processes. The American

Psychiatric Association nomenclature, published in 1952, uses the term "mental disorders" rather than "mental disease," and defines psychopathology as a set of descriptive entities rather than as causally differentiated categories. Mental disorders are also conceived in this diagnostic system as "reactions" (i.e., as schizophrenic, neurotic, and depressive reactions, and so forth). Indeed, rejection of the disease concept in mental disorder has gone so far that Bleuler (3) was able to say, in regard to schizophrenia, that most investigators no longer consider this a disease entity, an inherited disorder, an expression of a somatic disease, or a disease susceptible to a specific somatic treatment.

In practice, *The Diagnostic and Statistical Manual for Mental Disorders* of the American Psychiatric Association (1) strays far from its ostensible commitment to psychiatric diagnosis as a simple organization of the patient's symptoms. It is true that its classificatory criteria are, for the most part, those of relatively objective description: memory impairment, the presence of hallucinations, or the sexual deviations and drug addictions. At other times, however, the criteria invoked smack of the theoretical framework of psychoanalysis, as in references to the individual's use of (psychoanalytic) "mechanisms of defence." Typically, the tone is objective, but we find lapses also into judgmental attitudes, as in the definition of the sociopath as "ill" primarily because he behaves in a manner that is discordant with the prevailing cultural milieu.

These various interpretations of the nature of psychopathology result in widely divergent criteria for pathological behavior: sometimes as the manifestation of demonstrable psychological phenomena (e.g., memory impairment), or the use of certain hypothesized mechanisms (e.g., dissociation or displacement), or disorders of personality organization, or alternatively, as some behavioral disharmony with the prevailing social mores. That is, the present relatively heterogeneous system of psychiatric diagnosis lacks a consistent theoretical framework that might give coherence to the various disorders. Cases of schizophrenia, for example, do not bear any systematic or theoretical relation to cases of manic depression. At best, on quite ambiguous grounds, one can say that the neuroses represent a "less severe" form of disorder than the psychoses, but one is hard pressed to defend this judgment except on the pragmatic ground that individuals diagnosed as neurotic are less impaired in their everyday functioning and are less likely to be hospitalized than psychotics.

Even if the basis of diagnosis were restricted to those symptoms that are manifest in the behavior of the patient, the ambiguities that inhere in the diagnostic process would not be fully resolved. In the field of psychopathology, the term "symptom" itself is remarkably open to divergent interpretations. As we have noted, symptoms are often viewed as the surface manifestations of some covert disease process. Widely used textbooks of descriptive psychiatry (20) exemplify this approach. Delusions, hallucinations, depersonalizations loom large among the defining criteria of several kinds of mental illness; one looks in vain for references to the diagnostic value of such behavioral indices as physical assault or a suicidal attempt in the traditional descriptions of psychiatric disorders.

For purposes of conventional classification, the task of the diagnostician is to elicit and to describe directly as comprehensive and explicit a sampling of the aberrant reactions of the patient as possible. Since the disease is presumed inherent in the individual, the diagnostic process will most likely be modeled after that followed in physical medicine, that is, the observation of the patient's behaviors and verbalizations through interview. During this diagnostic session, the patient's thought processes and emotional reactions will be probed, his attitudes and actions examined, even his somatic responses to the stress of his present situation explored. The clinician will look for the presence of such deviant reactions as hallucinations or delusions, anxiety or depression, overactivity or seclusiveness, headaches or sleeplessness, and other signs of disturbed organismic functioning. The guiding principle implicit in such an interview is to ascertain how deviant the human organism has become in its response patterns under the influence of some covert disease process.

It is possible, however, to view symptoms in a quite different light. They can be seen as the expression of an implicit yet guiding set of attitudes that govern the person in periods of both deviant and adaptive behaviors. On this assumption, the diagnostician will look for evidence of the way the person tends to act in the world outside the hospital. He will be particularly interested in what was aberrant in the behavior of the patient before he was brought to the attention of the authorities. The diagnostician's interest in such inappropriate and pathological responses as hallucinatory activities or mood disturbances will be in how they may reflect some existing disturbance in the patient's emotional ties and how their presence may further disrupt his emotional ties with others. The diagnostician will be concerned, then, with whether the patient has threatened or attempted assault, whether he has entertained thoughts of suicide or made a suicidal attempt, or has revealed other ideational, verbal, or behavioral evidence of disorganized interpersonal relationships. Such deviations in behavior are scarcely to be thought of as symptoms in any conventional sense, that is, as representing some inner and covert disease process.

Such a broad-gauge interpretation of the nature of pathological reactions is adopted in this book. It includes but goes much beyond the range of symptomatic reactions that will be *directly* elicited in a conventional diagnostic interview. A term other than "symptom" that would be more precisely indicative of that broad range of deviant response patterns available to the human organism in its interpersonal transactions would be preferable. Such a term does not exist, and "symptom" is firmly ensconced in the language of psychopathology. With some misgivings, then, the term symptom will be retained in the following discussion.

### PROBLEMS IN RELIABILITY

Other difficulties beset the classification of psychiatric disorders. One finds, for example, that diagnosis bears no one-to-one correspondence to symptom manifestation and that most symptoms appear in the wide variety of cases that together constitute the spectrum of diagnostic classification. The occurrence of hallucinations, delusions, blunted affect, inappropriate affect, seclusiveness, or suspicion is common in cases diagnosed as schizophrenia. However, this diagnosis may be assigned because of the occurrence of any one or more of this list of symptoms. That is, one individual classified as schizophrenic may appear seclusive and deluded but not hallucinated nor given to inappropriate or blunted affective responses. Another schizophrenic, however, may be so categorized because of hallucinations and blunted affect. Cases bearing identical diagnoses, then, can show quite different symptom pictures (7, 13, 30).

Alternatively, identical symptoms can appear in cases classified as falling into different diagnostic syndromes. The appearance of any specific set of symptoms is a highly unreliable guide to even the major diagnostic classifications (30). Zigler and Phillips examined the psychiatric case records of nearly 800 patients who had been categorized as either manic-depressives, schizophrenics, neurotics, or personality or character disorders. The frequency of occurrence of 35 common symptoms was investigated in each of these four groups. These authors found 67 relationships between individual symptoms and particular diagnostic categories. The degree of relationship between symptom and diagnosis, however, turned out to be quite small. For 33 of these relationships the absolute magnitude of this relationship was .10 or less. In only one instance did a magnitude greater than .30 appear. Thus the association between specific symptoms and a given diagnosis is so small that symptomatology is an unreliable guide to diagnosis, and vice versa. These findings are in agreement with those of earlier studies (10, 29).

It is not surprising that a high degree of unreliability has been found to characterize psychiatric classification. Such inconsistencies in classification may in part be blamed on inadequate professional technique, but much of this diagnostic variability has been traced to the obscurity and ambiguity inherent in the standard classification system itself. In a study of the basis for disagreements in classification, Ward and his co-workers (28) reported that one third of the disagreements in diagnosis were caused by variability on the part of the diagnostician, including differences in eliciting covert material, and by contradictory decisions as to what should be considered the dominant pathology in mixed symptomatology. Two thirds of the disagreements, however, were ascribed to inadequacies in the classification system, including impractically fine distinctions, the requirements of unnecessary decisions in weighting, as in a forced decision between dominance of either neurotic symptoms or personality disorder when both were in evidence, and the lack of clear criteria for distinguishing between psychiatric categories.

The unreliability of conventional diagnoses is illustrated by the study of Hunt *et al.* (12), which involved the psychiatric classification of nearly 800 enlisted men who were first seen by a psychiatric unit at a naval precommissioning installation and who were subsequently transferred to a hospital for medical evaluation and separation from the navy. Diagnoses at the two installations were compared. Overall agreement on specific diagnoses was found in only 32% of these cases, while agreement increased to 54% for the broad classifications of psychosis, psychoneurosis, and personality disorder.

In contrast, individual symptoms can be rated for their presence or absence in a far more reliable fashion than can the traditional more global psychiatric diagnoses. Ullmann and Gurel (26) have reported a study in which different psychologists rated symptoms from 120 summaries of psychiatric admission notes. Agreement on the presence or absence of individual symptoms was quite substantial, with psychiatrists who worked independently making parallel choices for almost all symptoms. It appears that the diagnostic process is at best only modestly reliable, and that only for the major nosological categories. In contrast, specific symptoms are recognized and enumerated quite consistently by psychiatrists working independently. Another advantage that accrues to the use of symptoms as the measure of pathological behavior is their manifestly closer relation to the subject matter of pathology—the actual behavior of the patient. This would appear an overwhelming advantage at a time, as today, when the profession of psychiatry has become uneasy at attaching any etiological significance to the standard diagnoses. Since some implication of the substantive existence of these disorders inevitably continues in the use of the standard diagnostic categories, why does not the profession accept at face value its own prescription—that its syndrome classifications are simply descriptive entities—and, recognizing the unreliability of such classification, go on to a straight enumeration of the symptoms of each patient? This would provide a far more reliable solution for the presumed intent of the present nosological scheme, that of descriptive classification.

Why such a system has not come into being is unknown. It can only be suggested that the simple enumeration of the details of a patient's pathology does not provide a sufficiently comprehensive grasp of the individual's disorder. The clinician appears to prefer some universal method for cataloguing the various forms of disorder as these are idiosyncratically expressed in the behavior of different patients. In this need, clinicians respond as do all other observers of natural phenomena; they are impelled to classify what they see. Man has achieved his present status by his capacity to organize conceptually the workings of the universe, and his own behavior is no exception to this human need for ideational organization. Conventional psychiatric classification reflects this behavioral principle at work and, with all its deficiencies, no alternative proposal for organizing the subject matter of psychopathology has yet been put forward that serves in nearly as adequate a fashion as do the conventional psychiatric syndromes.

Nevertheless, the conceptual ambiguity of the present conventional diagnostic system and its unreliability warrant an attempt to establish an alternative method of case classification. The logical base for such a system is the recording of symptoms, for this implies no commitment concerning their origin and is a highly reliable procedure. The simple enumeration of symptoms is not, however, an adequate method of case classification. Some procedure for ordering them is essential if a heuristically satisfying and viable diagnostic method based on symptom occurrence is to be created. An attempt to interpret the meaning of symptoms and certain proposals for their classification are elaborated in the next chapter.

### REFERENCES

1. American Psychiatric Association Committee on Nomenclature and Statistics. *Mental disorders: Diagnostic and statistical manual.* Washington, D.C.: American Psychiatric Association Hospital Service, 1952.
2. Bertalanffy, L. von. Some biological considerations of the problem of mental illness. In L. Appleby, J. M. Scher, & J. Cumming (Eds.), *Chronic schizophrenia.* Glencoe, Ill.: Free Press, 1960.
3. Bleuler, M. Research and changes in concepts in the study of schizophrenia. *Bulletin of the Isaac Ray Medical Library,* 1955, **3**, 1–132.
4. Brugger, C. Psychiatrische Bestandersaufnahme in Gebiete eines medizinisch-anthropoligischen Zensus in der Nähe von Rosenheim. *Zeitschrift für die gesamte Neurologie Psychiatrie,* 1938, 160. In A. H. Leighton, J. A. Clausen, & R. N. Wilson (Eds.), *Explorations in social psychiatry.* New York: Basic Books, 1957.
5. Cole, N. J., Branch, C. H. H., & Orla, M. Mental illness. *A.M.A. Archives of Neurology and Psychiatry,* 1957, **7**, 393–398.
6. Dohrenwend, B. P., and Dohrenwend, B. S. The problem of validity in field studies of psychological disorder. *Journal of Abnormal Psychology,* 1965, **70**, 52–69.
7. Enright, J. B., and Jaeckle, W. R. Psychiatric symptoms and diagnosis in two subcultures. *International Journal of Social Psychiatry,* 1963, **9**, No. 1., 12–17.
8. Essen-Möller, E. Individual traits and morbidity in a Swedish rural population. *Acta Psychiatrica et Neurologica Scandinavica,* 1956, **100**, Supplement, 1–160.
9. Fogarty, J. E., Chairman. Statement at U.S. House of Representatives Appropriations Sub-Committee for Departments of Labor, Health, Education, & Welfare, Opening special hearing on Juvenile Delinquency, March, 1960.

10. Freudenberg, R. K., & Robertson, J. P. S. Symptoms in relation to psychiatric diagnosis and treatment. *A.M.A. Archives of Neurology and Psychiatry*, 1956, **76**, 14–22.
11. *Hospitals.* August 1, 1963. Guide Issue. Chicago: American Hospital Association.
12. Hunt, W. A., Wittson, C. L. & Hunt, E. B. A theoretical and practical analysis of the diagnostic process. In P. Hoch and J. Zubin (Eds.), *Current problems in psychiatric diagnosis.* New York: Grune & Stratton, 1953. Pp. 53–65.
13. Katz, M. M., Cole, J. O., & Lowery, H. A. Nonspecificity of diagnosis of paranoid schizophrenia. *Archives of General Psychiatry*, 1964, **11**, 197–202.
14. Leighton, D. C., Harding, J. S., Macklin, D. B., Macmillan, A. M. & Leighton, A. H. *The character of danger.* New York: Basic Books, 1963.
15. Lemkau. P., Tietze, C., & Cooper, M. Mental-hygiene problems in an urban district: Second paper. *Mental Hygiene*, 1942, **26**, 100–119.
16. Llewellyn-Thomas, E. The prevalence of psychiatric symptoms within an island fishing village. *Canadian Medical Association Journal*, 1960, **83**, 197–204.
17. *Medical Almanac.* Compiled by P. S. Nagan. Philadelphia: Saunders, 1961–1962.
18. National Association for Mental Health. *Facts about mental illness.* Washington, D.C., 1956.
19. National Committee Against Mental Illness. Inc. *What are the facts about mental illness in the United States?* Washington, D.C., 1964.
20. Noyes, A. P. *Modern clinical psychiatry.* Philadelphia: Saunders, 1934.
21. Report to Congress on Juvenile Delinquency, February, 1960. U.S. Department of Health, Education, and Welfare Washington, D.C.
22. Srole, L., Langner, T. S., Michael, S. T., Opler, M. K., & Rennie, T. A. C. *Mental health in the metropolis: The midtown study.* Vol. 1. New York: McGraw-Hill, 1962.
23. Star, Shirley A. The screening of psychoneurotics in the army: Technical development of tests. In S. A. Stouffer, L. Guttmann, E. A. Suchman, P. F. Lazarsfeld, S. A. Star, & J. A. Clausen (Eds.), *Measurement and prediction.* Vol. IV. Princeton, N. J.: Princeton University Press, 1950. Pp. 486–547.
24. Stouffer, S. A., Guttman, L., Suchman, E. A., Lazarsfeld P. F., Star, S. A., & Clausen, J. A. *Studies in social psychology in World War II.* Vol. 1. The American soldier: *Adjustment during Army life.* Princeton, N.J.: University Press, 1949.
25. Uchimara, Y., Akimoto, H., Kan, O., Abe, Y., Takahashi, K., Inose, T., Shimazaki, T., & Ogawa, N. Über die vergleischend psychiatrische, und erbpathologische untersuchung auf einer Japanischen insel. *Psychiatria et Neurologia Japonica*, 1940, **44**, 745–782.
26. Ullman, L., & Gurel, L. Validity of symptom rating from psychiatric records. *Archives of General Psychiatry*, 1962, **7**(8), 130–134.
27. U.S. Bureau of the Census. *Statistical abstracts of the United States.* (86th Ed.) Washington, D.C., 1965.
28. Ward, C. H., Beck, A. T., Mendelson, M., Mock, J. E., & Erbaugh, J. K. The psychiatric nomenclature. *Archives of General Psychiatry*, 1962, **7**, 198–205.
29. Wittenborn, J., Holzberg, J., & Simon, B. Sympton correlates for descriptive diagnosis. *Genetic Psychology Monographs*, 1953, **47**, 237–301.
30. Zigler, E., & Phillips, L. Psychiatric diagnosis and symptomatology. *Journal of Abnormal and Social Psychology*, 1961, **63**, 69–75.

# 8 / CONCEPTUAL ISSUES

# IN ADAPTIVE FAILURE

In the past few decades several attempts have been made, through factor-analytic techniques, to provide more objective and quantitative methods for describing symptom manifestation in the behavior of the patients. These techniques measure the tendency of specific symptoms to co-occur in the behavior patterns of individual patients. This method of analysis is the machine equivalent of the knowledge built up over centuries from the observations of generations of clinicians. There is no guarantee that syndromes computed by machine will in practice overcome the unreliability and inconsistency that inhere in the use of the present diagnostic method. Certainly several decades of such attempts have not produced any new classification system of general appeal to the psychiatric profession. One reason, perhaps, is their very objectivity. Investigators who report these statistical clustering of symptoms tend not to build on them any more subtle conceptual edifice than the real existence of these symptom factors.

SYMPTOM PATTERNS AS BEHAVIOR STYLES

A review of factor-analytic studies does suggest that the broad outline for such an organizing conceptual scheme may be derived from the results of empirical investigation. In brief, the findings imply that symptomatic behaviors reflect a person's pattern or style of relating to other people. For example, in a study by Lorr (1) on 250 psychotic patients, first- and second-order factors implied three primary symptom clusterings: (a) depression with guilt, and a pathological intropunitiveness with a self-directed hostility; (b) thought and personality disorganization with associated social withdrawal; and (c) a hostile belligerence or irritable combativeness. In another study carried out by Lorr and his coworkers (3) symptom factors obtained on male psychiatric inpatients were also divided into three major clusters. These include: (a) a set of affective factors (i.e., manic-depressive or tense, agitated, depressive); (b) factors indicative of social withdrawal and seclusiveness; and (c) a series of factors suggestive of resistiveness and belligerence.

Implied by these studies is a strong thread of disorganization in interpersonal relations. In a very general way, one can summarize these findings as indicative of three quite different role orientations in symptom manifestation: (a) self-directed hostility and guilt with associated depression; (b) social withdrawal and seclusiveness, accompanied by thought and personality disorganization; and (c) hostile belligerence and combativeness.

Factor-analytic studies of symptom manifestation have also been undertaken among children. The forms of deviant behavior that brought a large number of children to a guidance clinic for help were subjected to analysis by Lorr and Jenkins (2). Their analysis yielded five common factors, which the authors labeled as encephalitis or brain damage, unsocialized aggression, socialized delinquency, overinhibition, and schizoid character. Second-order factors were termed rebellion and schizoid disorganization. Apart from brain damage, three themes of interpersonal relationships somewhat similar to those observed among adult psychiatric cases emerge among these children. These are: (a) aggression, delinquency, and rebellion; (b) schizoid character or disorganization (loss of social contact); and (c) overinhibition. This last differs from the self-directed hostility, guilt, and depression more characteristically found in adult psychiatric cases.

Two factors emerged for Peterson (4) when he had teachers rate over 800 kindergarten and elementary school children drawn from the general community on 58 clinically frequent problems. Remarkable consistency in symptom factors appeared across all age groups. The first factor implied a tendency to express impulses against society, the second suggested (a) low self-esteem, depressed mood, and (b) social withdrawal. Here, too, even among these normal children, appears a triad of ways in which distorted interpersonal relationships are expressed symptomatically: in either a turning against others, a turning against the self, or a social withdrawal.

A study carried out by Phillips and Rabinovitch (6) explicitly supports the assumption that symptom manifestation reflects three major ways in which the pathological individual relates himself to others. This investigation, based on a total sample of over 600 psychiatric patients, involved the analysis of the statistical relationships to be observed among 46 symptomatic behaviors. The investigation proceeded by randomly dividing the total sample into two numerically equal groups. The first, or pilot group, provided the initial data on which the symptom categories were based. The other group of subjects were reserved for later use in testing the stability of these observed categories.

Thirty-nine of the original 46 symptoms appeared at a sufficiently high frequency to warrant statistical analysis. Of these, 31 evidenced either positive or negative relationships with one or more other symptoms. Interpretation of these data led to the organization of 25 symptoms into three categories based on the following considerations: (a) each symptom appears in only one of these categories; (b) only positive relations occur among symptoms within each category, whereas no positive relations appear between symptoms in different categories; and (c) for a given symptom, negative relations occur only with symptoms in the other two categories.

A rational analysis of the three symptom clusters thus formed suggests the following interpretation of their significance. Category 1 appears to imply a Turning Against the Self, expressed either directly in action or thought (e.g., suicidal attempt, depreciatory ideas against self), in mood (e.g., depression), or in suffering expressed somatically (e.g., bodily complaints, insomnia). The second category comprises a group of symptoms that may be categorized either as actions or thoughts signifying a Turning Against Others (e.g., threats assault, temper outbursts, robbery), or as self-indulgent and socially disapproved behaviors (e.g., drinking, perversions). The last of the three categories was taken to represent an Avoidance of Others, either directly (suspiciousness, withdrawal) or in distorted fantasy (e.g., hallucinations, sexual preoccupations, bizarre ideas). Results with the second group were in agreement with findings observed in the pilot sample. In summary, findings from the series of studies just reviewed imply that the various common symptom patterns manifested by patients express diverse behavioral styles. These occur in three major forms: as a Turning Against the Self, a Turning Against Others, and an Avoidance of Others.

A different facet of behavior style may also be reflected in symptom manifestation: the individual's preferred mode of self-expression, that is, in thought, in the emotional sphere (affect), or in overt behavior (action). This method of symptom classification has been called Sphere Dominance by Phillips et al. (5). These authors describe a Sphere Dominance score, which expresses the tendency of a patient's symptoms to appear primarily in thought (e.g., suicidal ideas, sexual preoccupations, hallucinations), affect (e.g., depression, tension, temper outbursts), or action (e.g., suicidal attempt, assault, drinking).

BEHAVIOR STYLE AND PSYCHIATRIC DIAGNOSIS

In the previous chapter two alternative positions on the significance of psychiatric symptoms were contrasted. On the one hand, it was proposed that symptoms express some form of disease process, separate from the person yet somehow within him, of which he is an unwilling and usually unwitting victim. On the other, it was proposed that symptoms reflect the behavioral style of the person whose whole personality is mobilized in an attempt at coping, however inappropriately, with some problem in his life. Conceptually, these positions seem quite divergent. In practice, they may not be as far apart as they at first appear.

This last statement needs both explanation and demonstration. In explanation it may be observed first that the present classification system for mental disorders accepts the substantive reality of the unique forms of mental "illness" that it enumerates and describes. Although the causal basis for these disorders is explicitly left open, their existence is not.

The "behavior style" position finds no such general nor official commitment within the mental health disciplines. It is proposed that, nevertheless, the clinician implicitly makes use of behavioral style constructs in arriving at the diagnosis of a specific mental illness.

In the study now to be described, the author and his colleagues (5) attempted to demonstrate that the clinician, in diagnosing mental illness, does so by classifying the patient's behavioral style. In defense of this proposition, these authors noted that the predominant interpersonal or role relationships of a patient, as well as the predominant sphere in which his symptoms are expressed (i.e., in action, thought, or affect) are of prime concern to the clinician in arriving at a diagnosis. On the basis of this observation, they hypothesized that quantitative indices of a patient's preferred Role Orientation and of his dominant sphere of symptom expression are related to the diagnosis assigned by the clinician. A central thesis was that it is not so much the presence or absence of particular symptoms within any role or sphere that determines diagnosis, but the expression of symptoms predominantly in one role and sphere rather than in the other two alternative roles and spheres.

In a test of this hypothesis, the authors of this study examined the relation of Role Orientation and Sphere Dominance scores to diagnosis as assigned independently by psychiatrists in over 500 hospitalized patients, both male and female. On rational grounds symptoms were classified according to sphere of expression into Thought symptoms (e.g., delusions, self-depreciatory, threatens assault), Affect symptoms (e.g., apathetic, maniacal outbursts, tense), and Action symptoms (e.g., assaultive, drinking, homosexuality).

The symptoms included within each of the Role Indices of Turning Against the Self, Turning Against Others, and Avoidance of Others follows from the work of Phillips and Rabinovitch (6), reviewed earlier. These Role scores were modified to make them more explicitly representative of social role and to provide an approximately equal representation of Thought, Affect, and Action symptoms within each of the three role categories. The symptoms included within each of the three role categories are

(1) Turning Against the Self: suicidal ideas, suicidal attempt, self-depreciatory, depressed; (2) Turning Against Others: threatens assault, assualt, robbery, temper outbursts and (3) Avoidance of Others: suspicious, perplexed, hallucinated, withdrawn, apathetic. Predominant Role and Sphere Dominance scores were calculated for each patient. Patients also were classified into one of four major diagnostic categories as manic-depressives, schizophrenics, personality and character disorders, or psychoneurotics.

The crucial question in this study was whether the magnitude of the observed relationships was sufficiently large to indicate that the style variable is an important component underlying the known reliability of psychiatric diagnosis. Findings in this study confirmed this possibility. The relationship between Sphere Dominance and diagnosis was .60. The distribution of the three Role Orientation groups across the four diagnostic categories was also substantial (coefficient of contingency .71). Indeed, the combined relation of Sphere Dominance and Role Orientation to diagnosis appeared to be capable of accounting for virtually all that is reliable in psychiatric diagnosis (multiple $r = .75$). The results of this study lend considerable credence to the presumption that psychiatric diagnosis, as assigned by the clinician, corresponds in substantial degree to some regularity in the behavior pattern of the patient. That is, the clinician appears to be substantially influenced by the patient's behavior style in reaching a decision as to the "mental illness" of which the patient is a victim. Thus, while the clinician ostensibly makes use of symptoms as indices of illness, he appears to derive from them inferences about the patient's general style of behavior. Our measures of Role Orientation and Sphere Dominance make explicit this relation between symptoms and behavior style. For example, suicidal attempt and suicidal ideas both indicate a role orientation of Turning Against the Self, but suicidal attempt is categorized as sphere dominant in Action, whereas suicidal ideas are classified as sphere dominant in Thought. It is not any simple summation of individual symptoms that corresponds to diagnosis; rather it is particular behavior styles, as inferred from specific constellations of symptoms, that are related to the psychiatric diagnosis assigned by the clinician.

This observation might explain why there is virtually no correspondence between individual symptom manifestation and the diagnosis assigned. Reliability in the assignment of diagnosis appears to follow from the consistency with which diagnosticians can independently infer styles of behavior from symptom manifestation. This organization of symptoms to reflect particular behavior styles may be what Thorne (8) has called the "feel of the case," which leads clinicians to agree on the diagnosis to be assigned.

The conventional mode of diagnosis requires considerable training and always remains to some substantial extent unreliable. In contrast, the Sphere Dominance and Role Orientation Indices are objective and quantitative expressions of symptom manifestation. Since the combination of Sphere Dominance and Role Orientation accounts for diagnosis at the upper limits of diagnostic reliability, the remaining variance in conventional diagnosis may well represent random error inherent in assigning diagnoses on an intuitive and subjective basis.

At the risk of repetition, a major theme of this and the preceding chapter may be summarized as follows. The dominant assumption in the field of psychiatry is that a patient's "symptoms" are the external indicators of some form of inner pathological process. The intent of the conventional system of psychiatric diagnosis is to aid in the classification of the various possible forms of these pathological processes, which are variously termed "mental diseases," "mental illnesses," or "mental disorders." In practice, or course, the clinician can classify only the deviant observables in the patient's behavior. The notion that these reflect an "illness" is based on the conceptual scheme within which the field of psychiatry operates.

It is generally recognized that the act of diagnostic classification requires more than an enumeration of the symptoms that are listed in the diagnostic manual as defining a disorder. A number of studies have shown that no one-to-one relationship exists between individual symptoms and given disorders, for the whole spectrum of symptoms appears in relation to all disorders. The simple tabulation of symptoms would result in a nearly random assignment of patients among the various disorders.

Inferentially, then, clinicians impose some order on the observed symptoms in a manner not spelled out in the standard diagnostic manual. No consensus exists as to the precise nature of the organizing principles used by the clinician. He does appear to respond to whether symptoms appear predominantly in action or thought; how emotionally responsive the patient is; the extent to which physical symptoms are part of the presenting picture; and whether the patient tends to be directed against himself or others in his pathology. This type of analysis seems to be carried on in a subjective and intuitive fashion, and constitutes part of the "art" of clinical practice.

Clinicians believe they are classifying mental disorders. They are, of course, classifying behavioral styles, that is, consistency in the ways in which patients tend to act. That clinicians can to some degree agree in their observations is indicated by some modest consistency in at least the broad classifications to which they assign patients. Indeed, the degree of agreement is surprising when we recognize that individual symptoms are rather randomly related to diagnosis and that the specific rules for classification are nowhere spelled out.

It must be emphasized that agreement on the presence or absence of individual symptoms is substantially higher than the diagnoses that are subsequently deduced from these symptoms. What the writer and his colleagues have attempted to provide is an objective and quantitative system for the classification of behavior styles as these are expressed in symptoms. That the obtained indices of behavior style correspond to those imposed intuitively by the clinician is demonstrated by their power to predict assigned diagnoses. Thus, it has been shown that at least in this phase of clinical practice, the computer serves as a reasonably adequate substitute for the art of the clinician.

So far, we have stressed only the communality between conventional diagnosis and our indices of significant behavioral style. The central issue is whether there is any difference between the two systems of diagnosis other than the distinction in their degree of objectivity and quantification. It is proposed that major differences between the two lie in (1) the conceptual framework within which each is embedded and (2) the purposes that they are intended to fulfill.

The diagnostic process concentrates on the classification of "illness" or disorder. Ultimately, perhaps, the system may be intended to provide a rational guide to etiology and treatment, but until now it has not fulfilled these ambitious objectives. At best, the assigning of psychiatric diagnoses fulfills legal requirements in the administrative handling of patients; it does not ordinarily advance the therapeutic efforts of the clinicians. Indeed, a widespread belief in psychiatry is that diagnostic procedures are empty and futile gestures that might well be discarded.

What is wrong with the diagnostic enterprise as it is now practiced? First, diagnosis treats the pathological behavior of the patient as a unique condition, unrelated to his normal pattern of behavior. That is, the pathological state is treated as autonomous and isolated from "normal" behavior. Further, the classification of psychiatric disorder tends to be treated as an end in itself. It does not provide practical guidance about the problems of patient care, nor has it seen general use as a means to advance theoretical knowledge about psychopathology.

In contrast, the Role Orientation and Sphere Dominance Indices are embedded in an explicitly investigatory framework. These measures are intended to "say something" meaningful about psychopathology and to aid in the accumulation of additional knowledge of its nature. Creation of these indices represents a commitment to the objective and quantifiable interpretation of pathological behavior as an aspect of the patient's behavior style. Further, this style is assumed to represent only one episode in the individual's life pattern. The intent is to explore continuities between adaptive and nonadaptive patterns of behavior, to examine relationships between pre- and postmorbid styles of life and pathological behavior style, as expressed in the Role Orientation and Sphere Dominance Indices. In this sense, these indices are presumed to measure a particular facet of the individual's life style. We will describe the relationships observed between these indices and pre- and postmorbid behaviors in the next chapter. Here we want to explore some psychological correlates of the behavior styles that symptoms express.

## ATTITUDINAL SET AND BEHAVIORAL STYLE

The last few decades have witnessed the discovery of a number of unexpected and at times baffling concomitants of psychopathology in the realms of perception, cognition, learning, and sensation. Many of these findings have been subsumed under the heading of stylistic factors in behavior. We propose that just such stylistic factors account for the particular symptom pattern manifested by the patient. That is, his pattern of pathological behavior is the overt expression of a pervasive and dominant attitudinal set. It is as if over time these attitudes bring into being a specific, yet limited, repertoire of behaviors. The choice of which precise behavior is to be activated depends on the particular situation within which the person finds himself. By the same token, a given individual's dominant attitudinal set precludes, or at least makes highly unlikely, other patterns of response.

As a specific illustration of this thesis, we may consider the self-critical individual who is faced by the threat of profound failure. In such circumstances he is likely to feel self-depreciatory and self-critical, to believe that he is responsible for his failure and, consequently, to suffer from a sense of guilt. Depending on circumstances, he may consider the idea of doing away with himself, even perhaps going to the extreme of making an actual suicidal attempt. Given his guiding set of attitudes, he will not be so likely to blame others for his failure, to express resentment over being mistreated or tricked, will not threaten others with retribution, and almost certainly will not attempt actual destructive activities against others, such as firesetting or physical assault.

Given a contrary set of guiding attitudes, almost the reverse hierarchy of response pattern is to be anticipated. That is, when a person's attitudinal set is one of resentment over mistreatment, a whole spectrum of antisocial behaviors may ensue. Similarly, it is unlikely that such a person will verbalize self-critical attitudes, fantasy self-destruction, or make an actual suicidal attempt.

To the extent that the construct of dominant attitudinal sets is valid, it minimizes the unique significance of any particular symptom studied in isolation. That is, it suggests that the presence or absence of a specific symptom is of little significance, for its appearance or nonappearance depends on a combination of two circumstances: (a) its relevance to the individual's dominant guiding set, and (b) given this set, the appropriateness of the symptom to the environmental context within which the person finds himself. Thus, a self-derogatory and guilt-ridden person is not likely to attempt suicide in the presence of other people, although he may well do so alone; nor is the provocatively resentful person likely to threaten or attempt physical assault on a bigger, stronger, and aggressive individual.

We have suggested that the individual symptoms manifested by a patient reflect his particular behavior style and that, in turn, behavior style expresses a pervasive and dominant attitudinal set. Nuttall, Rosenfield, and Phillips (7) undertook a test of the proposition that symptom pattern and attitudinal set bear a consistent relationship to each other in a sample of over 200 men hospitalized for the first time in their lives for psychiatric difficulties. None of these patients were being treated with psychoactive drugs at the time of interview. Each was administered individually a personality schedule consisting of 289 one-sentence statements that were to be designated as either true or false. Most items in the schedule concern the respondent and the greater proportion touch on everyday or psychiatrically "normal" activities (e.g., "I like working with theoretical ideas" and "I dislike introducing the speaker at a meeting"). Some, however, sample personal difficulties, such as, "I have had periods of days, weeks, or months when I couldn't get going," and "My skin seems to be unusually sensitive to touch."

Following administration of this schedule, the patient sample was divided randomly into two numerically equal groups. Role scores were computed for each patient based upon the symptoms that he had manifested. Each patient was assigned three role scores, which designated his relative standing on the roles of Turning Against the Self, Turning Against Others, and Avoidance of Others. The symptoms chosen to reflect the three Role Orientations were essentially identical with those included in these role categories by Phillips, Broverman, and Zigler (5). One of the two groups of patients was chosen arbitrarily for study and correlations were run between the three sets of patient role scores and answers to each of the 289 items in the personality schedule. By this procedure three sets of items were extracted from the schedule, scoring on each of which was correlated at the .15 level or better with placement on one of the three Role Orientations. Inspection of the sets of items associated with the role symptom scores differed substantially from each other in their characteristic tone. This tone bore an obvious and reasonable correspondence with the role or behavior style with which it was associated. Thus, schedule items correlated with a symptomatology of Turning Against the Self reflect feelings of depression, hopelessness, pessimism, despair, loneliness, apathy, or disinterest; of tension, worry, or anxiety; or of an insecure self-criticalness. Items related to the Role Orientation of Turning Against Others convey the qualities of suspiciousness, hostility, and deficiency in conscience; or alternatively, of energy, enthusiasm, and expressive self-assertiveness.

Items related to the Role of Avoidance of Others imply a sense of emotional isolation; of self-effacement or a pollyannaish denial of anger and hostility; or a dependence on eating as a means of coping with emotional upset. On observing this correspondence between attitude and symptom expression, the decision was reached to establish three item pools composed of those items correlated at .15 or better with any one of the three symptom Role Orientations and whose content reflected the feelings that had been found associated with the corresponding Role Orientation.

The three pools of personality schedule items found associated according to these criteria with the three symptom Role Orientations were designated as attitude scales. A total of 25 items constituted the Turning Against the Self attitude scale, 19 items the Turning Against Others scale, and 16 items the Avoidance of Others scale. These three sets of items, and the direction of their scoring (as either true or false), which correspond to placement on its associated Role Orientation, are listed in Tables 8–1, 8–2, and 8–3.

TABLE 8–1
TURNING AGAINST THE SELF ATTITUDE SCALE

| Statement | Score |
|---|---|
| 1.  Most of the time I feel blue. | True |
| 2.  I have periods of such great restlessness that I cannot sit long in a chair. | True |
| 3.  I can concentrate as well as other people can. | False |
| 4.  I have met problems so full of possibilities that I have been unable to make up my mind about them. | True |
| 5.  I enjoy life. | False |
| 6.  I seem to have enough confidence in myself. | False |
| 7.  Life is a strain for me much of the time. | True |
| 8.  I seldom feel blue. | False |
| 9.  I am happy most of the time. | False |
| 10.  I sometimes am afraid that others might think me stupid or ignorant. | True |
| 11.  I feel I daydream too much. | True |
| 12.  I often feel as if things were not real. | True |
| 13.  I frequently find myself worrying about something. | True |
| 14.  I think the future is going to be a pretty exciting time for me. | False |
| 15.  I don't seem to care what happens to me. | True |
| 16.  I have strange and peculiar thoughts. | True |
| 17.  I feel anxiety about something or someone almost all the time. | True |
| 18.  I feel that I can usually make up my mind with great ease. | False |
| 19.  I dread the thought of the future. | True |
| 20.  My daily life is full of things that keep me interested. | False |
| 21.  I am always careful about my manner of dress. | False |
| 22.  I sometimes feel that I am about to go to pieces. | True |
| 23.  Even when I am with people I feel lonely much of the time. | True |
| 24.  The future seems hopeless to me. | True |
| 25.  It makes me feel like a failure when I hear of the success of someone I know well. | True |

TABLE 8–2
TURNING AGAINST OTHERS ATTITUDE SCALE

| Statement | Score |
|---|---|
| 1.  Whenever I've been punished there was good reason for it. | False |
| 2.  I sometimes wonder what hidden reason another person may have for doing something nice for me. | True |
| 3.  I like to be where there is something doing all the time. | True |
| 4.  Sometimes I've felt I had to do something whether I wanted to or not. | True |
| 5.  I try to correct people who express an ignorant belief. | True |
| 6.  It's rare for me to feel weak all over. | True |
| 7.  I would never think of letting someone else be punished for my wrongdoings. | False |
| 8.  I enjoy promoting a new project. | True |
| 9.  I usually work things out for myself rather than get someone to show me how. | True |
| 10.  There are many foods that I strongly dislike. | True |
| 11.  I dislike eating in new and strange restaurants. | False |
| 12.  I am seldom bothered by thoughts about sex. | True |
| 13.  Every little effort seems to wear me out. | False |
| 14.  I enjoy almost all foods. | False |
| 15.  I have had periods of days, weeks, or months when I couldn't "get going." | False |
| 16.  It is safer to trust nobody. | True |
| 17.  If I could get into a movie without paying and be sure I was not seen I would probably do it. | True |
| 18.  I enjoy making fun of people who do things that I regard as stupid. | True |
| 19.  At times I feel like picking a first fight with someone. | True |

Each patient in the first randomized sample received scores on each of the three attitude scales according to the number of these items that he had checked in the direction found by statistical analysis to be correlated with placement on the three Role Orientation dimensions. Thus, if a patient had checked each personality schedule item in the attitude scale associated with Turning Against the Self in the direction found associated with that Role Orientation, he would score at the top of that attitude scale. In the first randomized sample, placement on the three Role Orientation dimensions and each of the corresponding three attitude scales was found to be significantly associated with correlations ranging between .42 and .48.

The second randomized sample was chosen to validate the stability of these findings. Using the identical items to constitute the three attitude scales, scoring on these scales was correlated with placement on the three Role Orientation dimensions. Against significant relationships were observed between symptom dimensions and the corresponding attitude scales.

TABLE 8–3
AVOIDANCE OF OTHERS ATTITUDE SCALE

| Statement | Score |
|---|---|
| 1. I eat about as usual even when I am emotionally upset. | True |
| 2. I wish I were not so shy. | True |
| 3. The members of my family and my close relatives get along quite well. | True |
| 4. The past was a happy time for me. | True |
| 5. At times I have insisted on having things my own way. | False |
| 6. I am happiest when alone. | True |
| 7. I am always courteous, even to people who are disagreeable. | True |
| 8. I rarely get cross and grouchy. | True |
| 9. Socially, I am a poor mixer. | True |
| 10. I sometimes try to get even rather than forgive and forget. | False |
| 11. In school I found it was easy to talk before the class. | False |
| 12. I have never been in love with anyone. | True |
| 13. It is more important for a child to be bright than to be well-adjusted socially. | True |
| 14. I find that eating candy or chewing gum helps when I fell upset. | True |
| 15. I like to flirt. | False |
| 16. I am more interested in planning a project than in carrying it out. | True |

What shall we make of these findings? First, there is an immediate reasonableness to these relations between attitudes and their corresponding symptomatic behaviors. It is easy to believe that individuals governed by their particular attitudinal set would, under some particularly stressful condition in life, behave in the symptomatic fashion that they do. Second, items of a relatively mild intensity, as well as those of greater emotional significance, are both significantly associated with deviant behavior patterns. This suggests that the attitudinal sets reflected in these items transcend any specific period of pathology and provide the guiding principles for action that form the individual's life style. That is, responses to these attitude scales appear to express a set of values, attitudes, and beliefs about oneself and the world in which one lives rather than to reflect directly any specific or concrete behaviors in which one is engaged. Nevertheless, scoring on these attitude scales does correspond to particular patterns of symptomatic behaviors. These findings reinforce the hypothesis that such behaviors represent the overt realization of some guiding attitudinal set.

### REFERENCES

1. Lorr, M. The Wittenborn psychiatric syndromes: An oblique rotation. *Journal of Consulting Psychology*, 1957, **21**(6), 439–444.
2. Lorr, M., and Jenkins, R. L. Patterns of maladjustment in children. *Journal of Clinical Psychology*, 1953, **9**, 16–19.
3. Lorr, M., Jenkins, R. L., S. O'Connor, J. P. Factors descriptive of psychopathology

and behavior of hospitalized psychotics. *Journal of Abnormal and Social Psychology*, 1955, **50**, 78–86.

4. Peterson, D. R. Behavior problems of middle childhood. *Journal of Consulting Psychology*, 1961, **25**, 205–209.

5. Phillips, L., Broverman, I., K., & Zigler, E. Sphere dominance, role orientation, and diagnosis. *Journal of Abnormal Psychology*, in press.

6. Phillips, L., & Rabinovitch, M. S. Social role and patterns of symptomatic behavior. *Journal of Abnormal and Social Psychology*, 1958, **57**, 181–186.

7. Nuttall, R., Phillips, L., & Rosenfield, J. Attitudes and psychiatric symptomatology. Unpublished manuscript, Department of Psychology Library, Boston College, 1967.

8. Thorne, F. Back to fundamentals. *Journal of Clinical Psychology*, 1953, **9**, 89–91.

# 9/PATHOLOGICAL BEHAVIOR STYLE, PSYCHOLOGICAL DEVELOPMENT, AND OUTCOME TO PATHOLOGY

We have proposed that symptoms express the general themes of a person's style of life. We now want to explore the relation of life-style, as expressed in symptom manifestation, to both achieved level of psychological development and to outcome of disorder. A degree of continuity is to be expected between an individual's premorbid life pattern, the form taken by pathology, and its resolution. This continuity in life-style will be discussed from three different point of views, to each of which a section of this chapter is devoted. The first section will review the relation of two aspects of pathological behavior style, Role Orientation and Sphere Dominance, to the level of psychological development achieved by the individual in the premorbid period. The second examines the relation of behavior style in psychopathology, as expressed in Role Orientation and Sphere Dominance, to outcome of disorder. The final section is concerned with the process-reactive distinction in psychopathology. It suggests that two very different long-term patterns of behavior have traditionally been classified within the single diagnostic syndrome of schizophrenia. It further proposes that recogniton of these differences in life-style can serve to explain what otherwise remains a perplexing and unresolved issue in the field of psychopathology.

## PATHOLOGICAL BEHAVIOR STYLE AND PSYCHOLOGICAL DEVELOPMENT

We have earlier discussed behavior styles in pathology under two headings, Role Orientation and Sphere Dominance. We shall review the relation of these facets of pathology to psychological development, starting with Role Orientation.

*Role Orientation and Psychological Development*

In Chapter 4 it was proposed that a major facet of psychological development is the emergence of a moral sense, defined in terms of (1) a sense of accountability for the consequences of one's actions, (2) an acceptance of an obligation for the welfare of others, and (3) a pattern of interpersonal relationships that is controlled by a mutual respect for each other's need and wishes. Acceptance of personal responsibility for the consequences of one's actions implies a recognition that one's own decisions determine one's destiny. It means, too, a recognition that one's fate is not dependent solely on the whim of others or on accidental or impersonal forces beyond one's influence or control.

A degree of correspondence should exist between acceptance of responsibility for one's actions and a person's dominant behavior style, even among those who have failed to cope with life and who consequently are manifesting some form of pathology. Those who accept personal responsibility for their life situation will tend to blame themselves for their failures; those who reject such responsibility will blame others for their plight. That is, in pathology, those who feel they have not met their obligations and who feel they are responsible  for their failure should tend to turn against themselves in symptom manifestation; those who are relatively immature, or who feel others are to blame for the vicissitudes of their existence, should either tend to turn destructively against others, or avoid others who threaten them. The index of Role Orientation, which we have used to classify symptom manifestation, captures this assignment of responsibility for one's fate.

As we have noted, acceptance of personal responsibility corresponds theoretically to a relatively high level of psychological development. From the discussion to this point, then, we should expect that an individual's role orientation in symptomatology should correspond to his achieved level of psychological development, as this is measured in terms of either an index of social competence or Rorschach indices of perceptual development. The observed relations between role orientation and achieved level of social competence will be discussed first, followed by a review of those relationships that have been found between role orientation and perceptual development.

*Role Orientation and Social Competence.* Zigler and Phillips (44) were the first to explore the relation between role orientation and social competence. These authors hypothesized that patients who had achieved a higher level of social competence in the premorbid period should manifest predominantly symptoms indicative of Turning Against the Self; those of lower social competence should, in blaming others, either retaliate by Turning Against Others or Avoidance of Others in their symptomatology. The subject population used in their study included over 1000 hospitalized psychiatric patients of both sexes. A total of 29 symptoms of sufficient frequency of occurrence among these patients to warrant statistical analysis were employed. All these symptoms were categorized according to their placement within any of the three Role Orientations just listed. The tendency for the appearance of each of these symptoms to be associated with high or low levels of scoring on social competence indices was then examined. In both men and women, findings substantially supported the hypothesis that pathological individuals of higher levels of social competence tend to manifest symptoms reflective of a Turning Against the Self, while symptomatology associated with lower levels of competence indicates either a Turning Against Others or an Avoidance of Others.

*Role Orientation and Perceptual Development.* In the developmental view, both the symptomatic and the perceptual aspects of behavior are thought to represent expressions of the person's general developmental level. Consequently, we would expect a high degree of covariance to obtain between role orientation expressed in symptomatology and scoring on Rorschach indices of perceptual development. Specifically, we can anticipate that an emphasis in symptomatology on Turning Against the Self should be associated with high-level performance in the perceptual sphere, and both Turning Against Others and Avoidance of Others with low-level performance.

The relation between role orientation and achieved level of perceptual development has been tested only with the contrasting role orientations of Turning Against the Self and Turning Against Others (32). Groups of persons who were characterized by suicide attempt, threatening suicide, assaultiveness, and threatening assault constituted the experimental samples.[1] The assaultive group consisted of individuals who had been imprisoned for repeated physical attacks on others. The other groups were composed of individuals hospitalized for psychiatric difficulties. The two categories that deal with suicidal intentionalities clearly correspond to Turning Against the Self; the two categories that encompass injurious intent directed at others imply a Turning Against Others. The question at issue is whether Turning Against the Self, as expressed in the two suicidal groups, is related to scoring at a higher level of perceptual development on the Rorschach technique than is Turning Against Others, represented here by the two assaultive groups.

[1]The writer wishes to thank Drs. Alice Kruger and Robert C. Misch. who made available the Rorschach protocols used in this study.

This possibility was first tested separately within the overt action and within the ideational categories. That is, the overtly assaultive group was compared on the Rorschach developmental indices to the overtly suicidal attempt group; a comparable analysis was undertaken with the ideational categories, that is, those classified as threatening assault and threatening suicide. Finally, the two assault groups were combined and compared in perceptual performance to the combined suicide groups. All findings were consistent with the hypothesis that Turning against the Self is associated with higher levels of perceptual development than is Turning Against Others. Developmentally higher forms of perceptual response on the Rorschach discriminate between these role orientations at a statistically significant level. Differences in perceptual performance between the overt action and the ideational groups will be discussed in the next section.

*Sphere Dominance and Psychological Development*

Earlier we described an index of Sphere Dominance that expresses the tendency of symptoms to appear predominantly in the sphere of action, thought, or affect. Here we want to explore the relation of Sphere Dominance in symptom expression to the pathological individual's level of psychological development. We shall discuss in turn the relation of Sphere Dominance to social competence scoring and to Rorschach perceptual level.

*Sphere Dominance and Social Competence.* To date, only the correlates of the relative dominance of symptoms in action or thought have been examined. Specifically, Phillips and Zigler (34) proposed that higher levels of premorbid social competence should be associated with a tendency for symptoms to appear predominantly in thought, lower social competence with the likelihood that symptoms will occur predominantly in action.

The rationale for this formulation originates with the developmental theorists of both psychoanalytic (9, 11, 23, 36) and nonpsychoanalytic persuasion (26, 30, 41), all of whom have suggested that primitive developmentally early behavior is marked by immediate, direct, and unmodulated responses to external stimuli and internal need states. In contrast, higher levels of development are characterized by the appearance of indirect, ideational, conceptual, and symbolic or verbal behavior patterns. That is, theory suggests that a shift in emphasis from action to thought is an expression of a universally valid sequence in psychological development.

Use of such an action-thought parameter appears to allow for the derivation of certain predictions concerning the relationship between symptomatology and psychological development. More mature individuals who manifest inappropriate (i.e., symptomatic) forms of behavior should do so with relatively greater emphasis on ideational, symbolic, or verbal forms of behavior and correspondingly should show fewer symptoms expressed in direct or overt action. Alternatively, less mature persons should, in pathological states, evidence symptoms that are in the sphere of direct or gross action rather than symptoms of an ideational or verbal variety. The relevant hypothesis tested by Phillips and Zigler (34) was that individuals who manifest symptoms in the ideational and verbal sphere have attained a higher level of premorbid social competence than those who manifest symptoms characterized by overt action.

To test this hypothesis, case records of nearly 800 hospitalized psychiatric patients were examined. Social competence scoring was based on the six-item index described in Chapter 4. In addition, each of the case histories was examined for symptoms manifested by the patient. The purpose of this initial analysis was to place individuals into a pure Action, pure Thought, or Mixed group. All individuals who manifested only symptoms of an action variety were placed in the Action group. All individuals who manifested only symptoms of the thought type were placed in the Thought group. Individuals whose symptoms were equally divided in number between the action and thought categories were placed in a Mixed group. Following this classification, it was found that premorbid social competence level does predict the relative dominance of Action over Thought symptoms in the expected direction.

Additionally, these findings suggest that the substitution of pathological for normal behavior patterns does not constitute regression in the sense of a blanket primitivization of behavior. That is, the individual in becoming symptomatic does not appear to change his habitual behavior style. The action-oriented, less mature, and less socially competent person tends to remain action-oriented in his new and inappropriate reaction pattern. Antithetically, the more mature and more socially effective person who is predisposed to ideational, indirect, symbolic, or more verbal forms of self–world interaction continues to be so oriented in a period of psychopathology. Thus, the behavior style that characterizes an individual during a phase of disorder appears to reflect a continuation of an enduring life-style.

*Sphere Dominance and Perceptual Development.* As we have just noted, studies of social competence support the proposition that a disposition to respond in thought rather than in action is the developmentally later reaction pattern. We would anticipate, then, that scoring on the Rorschach perceptual indices of psychological development is also related to an increasing tendency for thought to substitute for action. That is, an emphasis on thought symptoms should be associated with a higher degree of perceptual development. Correspondingly, a tendency to express pathological behavior in action rather than in thought should be related to lower levels of perceptual performance. Findings by a number of investigators bear on this formulation.

Hurwitz (13) compared the Rorschach performance of two groups of 50 preadolescent boys, each of whom had had psychiatric referral. The members of one group were referred for hyperactivity, those in the other for underactivity. Hyperactivity includes such deviant behavior as delinquent acts, being disruptive in the classroom, and habitually running about a treatment center rather than staying in an office during a therapy hour. Classification as an underactive child was based on such symptoms as being excessively quiet or always alone, being passive and overly compliant, always staying at home reading or listening to the radio, and never initiating activity. Hurwitz found that the underactive group was characterized by significantly more developmentally high percepts. Thus, the dominance of ideational over motoric activity corresponds to a proportionately higher representation of conceptually advanced responses in the perceptual sphere.

Both Misch (29) and Kruger (24) have examined the Rorschach performance of matched action versus ideationally oriented groups among psychiatrically deviant adults. Misch studied a group of chronically assaultive criminals and a verbal group consisting of psychiatric patients who had a history of threatening assault but had never carried these threats into action.

Kruger examined sets of pathological individuals who expressed contentually different forms of deviant behavior. Her population samples were constituted of (1) individuals who had made a serious suicidal attempt; (2) those who had only threatened to commit suicide but had made no serious attempt to so act; (3) a group of overt sexual deviants, made up primarily of exhibitionists and homosexuals; and (4) psychiatric patients who were obsessed with ideas of being or of acting in a sexually deviant fashion, but who in fact had never done so.

Both of the foregoing investigators found that their ideationally deviant groups performed perceptually at a developmentally higher level on the Rorschach technique than did their action-oriented sample. Subsequent to the completion of these studies, the present writer rescored the test protocols according to the most recent revision of the Rorschach development scoring system (33).[2] The Misch and Kruger samples were then combined, following which they were again divided into an action category composed of the assaultive, suicidal attempt, and overtly sexually deviant groups, and an ideational category that consisted of the threatening assault, threatening suicide, and ideationally sexually deviant groups. In all, 57 subjects were included in the action category and 38 subjects in the ideational category. As anticipated, ideational subjects produced significantly more developmentally high percepts.

---

[2]The writer is indebted to Drs. Robert Misch and Alice Kruger for providing the Rorschach protocols.

These findings with Rorschach developmental level are consonant with those obtained between achieved level of premorbid social competence and the action-thought dimension. Together, all these results support the hypothesis that an individual's behavior style, as expressed in his symptomatology during a period of pathology, represents a continuation of his general style of life. This style molds his behavior prior to the onset of disorder as well as during the period of pathology.

BEHAVIOR STYLE AND OUTCOME IN DISORDER

To the extent that an individual's behavior style within a period of pathology reflects his general style of life, we can expect a correspondence between this behavior style and the degree to which the individual readapts quickly and effectively back into the community following the onset of disorder. Phillips and Zigler (35) have tested this proposition, making use of the indices of Role Orientation and Sphere Dominance as their measures of pathological behavior style. Outcome was measured in terms of length of hospitalization and whether or not the patient was returned to a mental hospital subsequent to his release. The shortcomings of the length of hospitalization criterion as a measure of performance in the community were discussed earlier. This deficiency is balanced somewhat by the read-mission index. This criterion is more directly expressive of the person's ability to adapt within the family setting following discharge from the hospital (8).

These studies on the relation of pathological behavior style to outcome in disorder were conducted on a sample of over 250 patients never previously admitted to a psychiatric hospital. They were about equally divided between men and women. Findings with Role Orientation will be reported first, followed by those with Sphere Dominance.

*Role Orientation and Outcome*

The literature is replete with empirical studies that indicate that a wide variety of symptoms are associated with outcome in disorder (14, 48). Although not completely consistent, the findings suggest that symptoms indicative of guilt, intropunitiveness, self-condemnation, and depression are associated with a favorable prognosis. Thus, Zubin *et al.*, have noted that in 15 studies that considered the prognostic significance of feelings of guilt, all concurred in finding these a positive prognostic omen. Similarly, Albee (1, 2) found that delusions of a self-condemnatory nature and intropunitive behaviors were associated with psychiatric recovery. All these symptoms correspond to the Role Orientation of Turning Against the Self, which we have taken to imply an acceptance of responsibility for one's own destiny. On this basis, Phillips and Zigler (35) presumed that pathological individuals characterized by a Role Orientation predominantly indicative of Turning Against the Self should tend to a more favorable outcome to their disorder than those whose symptoms marked them as Turning Against Others or as Avoidant of Others.

Of approximately 250 patients available for this study, 39 men and 59 women could be clearly classified as Turning Against the Self. Of the others, 46 men and 32 women were classed as Avoidant of Others. Only 6 cases fell into the Turning Against Others category, and because of the small number so classified, these were dropped from consideration in subsequent analyses. The small number of cases in this category reflects the fact that patients manifesting such a symptom picture are rarely committed following an observation period. Those patients who could not be clearly placed within the other two role categories also were dropped from the study.

Analyses of the relationship between role orientation and the two outcome measures were carried out separately for men and women. Role orientation was found to be related to length of hospitalization in the predicted manner for women, and a trend in the same direction was found for men. No significant relationship was found between role orientation and rehospitalization in either the male or female samples.

Since role orientation has been found to be related to social competence (44), which in turn has been found to be related to length of hospitalization (45), a further analysis was conducted in order to assess whether the relationship between role and length of hospitalization was solely attributable to the higher social competence scores of Turning Against the Self patients. Social competence scores were computed for all patients in the two role groups. By means of the analysis of variance technique, it was found that role orientation is significantly related to length of hospitalization, independent of achieved level of social competence. It thus appears that an attitude of acceptance of responsibility for one's destiny, even in a period of pathology, as expressed in the Role Orientation of Turning Against the Self, is indicative of a favorable outcome to psychiatric disorder, independent of the individual's effectiveness in society.

*Sphere Dominance and Outcome*

The relation of Sphere Dominance to outcome has been examined only in terms of the relative dominance of thought to action symptoms in the manifestations of disorder. Of the approximately 250 first-admission patients available for a study on outcome (45), 82 could be classified as Thought dominant, 21 as Action dominant, and 86 as Mixed in their symptomatology. The remaining individuals, whose symptomatology was too ambiguous for classification, were removed from further consideration in subsequent analyses. Because of the small number of subjects assigned to the Action dominant group, further analyses were run on the Thought versus the combined Action and Mixed groups. Thus, comparisons were made between a group of patients manifesting symptoms only in Thought, and a second group who showed at least some of their symptoms in the domain of physical action.

No significant relationships were found between the Thought-Action orientation and length of hospitalization. Further, contrary to expectations, men in the Thought category were more likely to be rehospitalized than those in the Action group, with a trend in this direction found also among women. These findings are incongruent with those found earlier that Thought dominant patients have achieved higher levels of social competence (34) and that social competence is positively related to outcome (44). In order to explore further the perplexing findings, an analysis that included social competence level was undertaken. It was found that high-competence, Thought dominant patients had shorter periods of hospitalization than low-competence Thought patients. Similarly, it was found that high-competence, Thought dominant patients are less likely to be rehospitalized than are low-competence, Thought dominant patients. Among Action dominant patients, competence level did not influence either length of hospitalization or the likelihood of rehospitalization.

The relationship between the Thought-Action orientation and outcome is not, therefore, a simple one. A reexamination of the original data of this study suggested to the investigators a tentative explanation for the observed findings. It was noted that Thought symptoms associated with lower levels of social competence reflected a more profound disorganization of psychological functioning, such as hallucinations and delusions, than did thought symptoms associated with higher levels of competence. Here the symptomatology reflected such disturbances in thought content as suicidal ideas, but not a severe disruption in the formal processes of thought. What appears to be implied is that when the structure of thought remains relatively intact in psychiatric disorder, prognosis is favorable, whereas when formal thought become disorganized, the outlook is ominous. This interpretation is consistent with that reported elsewhere by the present writer (31) and by other investigators (48).

## THE PROCESS-REACTIVE DISTINCTION AND PSYCHOLOGICAL DEVELOPMENT

Various investigators (3, 4, 10, 15, 16, 20, 22, 25, 27, 28, 40, 47) have distinguished between two types of patients, both of which are diagnosed as schizophrenic. These patient types are differentiated by the abruptness with which their disorder appears and the outcome of their pathology. One of these types of disorder has been called "process schizophrenia" and is marked by a social inadequacy, an insidious onset with no indication of a clear precipitating factor, and an unfavorable outcome. The alternative form of disorder has been called "reactive schizophrenia" and is characterized by a relatively high level of premorbid social adequacy, a sudden onset with a specific event precipitating the disorder, and a relatively favorable outcome (17–19). The assumption is frequently made that process schizophrenia mirrors an organic etiology whereas reactive schizophrenia is of psychological origin (5, 6, 12, 22, 25, 28, 47).

The question whether the symptoms manifested in the acute phase by the process schizophrenic differ from those of the reactive schizophrenic has remained ambiguous. Considerable disagreement exists between investigators, who have variously suggested that a difference exists between the two types in the incidence of such symptoms as "massive hallucinatory experience," "ideas of reference," "mild paranoid trends," "cloudy sensorium," "thought disorder," "dull, rigid or inappropriate affect," "tension," "confusion," "somatic delusions," "loss of decency," etc. (3, 7, 10, 15, 16, 25, 40). Yet no clear-cut distinctions between the process and reactive types have been established that are associated with differences in symptomatology. Even Langfeldt, who had been the most adamant in the view that process schizophrenia could be differentiated from reactive schizophrenia (schizophreniform psychosis) on the basis of presenting symptoms, finally shifted to the position that the distinction between the two types must ultimately be made on the basis of premorbid personality, onset of illness, and other factors extraneous to the presenting symptomatology (7). The currently predominant view appears to be that there is little or no difference in the gross psychiatric symptomatology of process and reactive patients.

Implicit in the process-reactive distinction is the view that individuals who vary greatly on certain significant behavioral dimensions, such as premorbid social competence and potential for recovery, regress during the acute phase to a common low level of functioning during which symptomatic behaviors are unrelated to these dimensions. Such a view is contrary in two respects to the developmental approach to psychopathology put forward here. In contrast to the regression hypothesis, we assert that disorder represents a continuous process in which the premorbid, initial, middle, and ultimate stages are meaningfully interrelated. The other point of difference concerns the range of applicability of the process-reactive dimension. The developmental position maintains that the relationship of achieved level of psychological development to certain dimensions of psychopathology is not unique to schizophrenia, but instead cuts across all forms of psychopathology.

Consonant with this formulation, Zigler and Phillips (46) set out to test the hypothesis that within a schizophrenic population the symptom pattern of individuals who have exhibited a relatively good level of premorbid social competence will be characterized by the role orientation of Turning Against the Self, whereas the symptom pattern of individuals who have exhibited poor premorbid social competence will be characterized by either Avoidance of Others, or Self-Indulgence and Turning Against Others. A second hypothesis tested in their study was that this relationship between social competence and symptomatology is not unique to schizophrenia, but instead also obtains in the nonschizophrenic portion of a pathological population.

This study was based on an examination of the case histories of over 800 hospitalized psychiatric patients categorized into four major diagnostic groups: schizophrenics, manic-depressives, psychoneurotics, and personality or character disorders. The six-item index of social competence described in Chapter 4 was used in this study to divide both the schizophrenic and combined nonschizophrenic samples into three numerically equal groups according to achieved level of competence. As predicted for both samples, higher levels of social competence were found associated with Turning Against the Self, lower levels of competence with both Avoidance of Others and Self-Indulgence and Turning Against Others.

Alcoholism has also been dichotomized into essential and reactive forms (21) in a fashion quite similar to the process and reactive forms of schizophrenia. The essential type of alcoholism is the more severe, and includes those who begin drinking early without a clear precipitating factor. These individuals drink anything that provides the desired pharmocological effect. They perform poorly in society and are characteristically unable to support themselves financially except for brief periods. Their prognosis is poor. By contrast, reactive alcoholics are reliable and responsible members of society who are able to hold jobs for long periods. Drinking starts later than with the essential type and clear stresses are often present prior to the onset of the excessive use of alcohol. Prognosis tends to be more favorable than for the reactive type of alcoholic.

Sugerman and his co-workers (39) proposed that essential and reactive alcoholics can be distinguished in terms of their achieved level of social competence. They made use of a quantified case history questionnaire devised to discriminate between these types of alcoholics (37) and related scoring on this instrument to social competence level, as assessed by means of the Zigler and Phillips (46) six-point index. With a sample of over 100 male alcoholics, Sugerman and his co-workers obtained a correlation of .45 between the competence and alcoholic-type variables, with the reactive alcoholics scoring at a higher level of achieved social competence.

Even when the overlapping items of education and employment history were removed, the relationship between the essential-reactive dimension and competence remained highly significant. Thus, these investigators obtained a parallel relationship between social competence and the process-reactive types within the alcoholic syndrome, as Zigler and Phillips had demonstrated within both schizophrenic and nonschizophrenic samples of psychiatric patients.

If the general formulation of a correspondence between psychological development and form of disorder is correct, then psychological development, as measured by Rorschach perceptual indices, should also predict placement on the process-reactive continuum. That is, those patients who function at higher Rorschach developmental levels should tend to be classified as reactive; those who score at lower developmental levels should be classified as process individuals.

To test this hypothesis, Becker (3) devised a six-point developmental level scaling system for Rorschach responses from which he obtained a measure of severity in schizophrenic disorders. He then related placement on this measure to scoring on the Elgin Prognostic Scale (42, 43), taken as a measure of the process-reactive dimension. His subject samples were 24 male and 27 female schizophrenics. Becker predicted that the more processlike schizophrenics would score at a lower Rorschach developmental level than reactive-type schizophrenics. The hypothesis was confirmed for both sexes. Correlation between Rorschach developmental scoring and the Elgin Scale was $-.60$ for the men and $-.68$ for the women. Steffy and Becker (38) replicated the essential findings of this study, substituting the Holtzman Inkblot Test for the Rorschach. In a sample of 36 schizophrenics, developmental level ratings were found to be significantly correlated with Elgin Prognostic Scale scores.

Zimet and Fine (47) also have related Rorschach developmental level scores to the process-reactive distinction among 60 schizophrenics. The process and reactive classifications were based on an examination of case histories. Higher developmental level scoring characterized the reactive in contrast to the process schizophrenics.

The results of this series of studies confirms a consistent relation between psychological development, measured in terms of either social competence or perceptual development, and the process-reactive distinction. That is, the results of these studies imply that the process and reactive forms of disorder reflect some basic continuity in the life-style of the individual patient, a continuity that traverses the premorbid, pathological, and postmorbid periods. The construct of continuity in life-style permits us, then, to conceptualize within a common framework forms of disorder that heretofore have been conceived as deriving from very different etiologies.

A more general thesis as to the nature and significance of psychopathology has also been proposed and demonstrated in this chapter. The findings that have been reviewed here support the hypothesis of a continuity in life-style between an individual's premorbid history, the form of his disorder, and its outcome. Specifically, it has been shown that acceptance of responsibility for one's situation, expressed in symptomatology in the Role Orientation of Turning Against the Self, is related to higher levels of psychological development, as this is measured in terms of either social competence or Rorschach indices of perceptual development. Similarly, a tendency to blame others for one's condition, manifested in symptoms indicative of a Role Orientation of either Turning Against Others or an Avoidance of Others, is associated with lower levels of psychological development. Similar relations between role orientation and outcome in disorder have also been demonstrated, with Turning Against the Self associated with more favorable outcome, the two alternative roles with a more ominous prognosis.

We have seen, too, that Action versus Thought dominance in symptomatology also bears a relation to achieved level of psychological development as well as to outcome in disorder. In accordance with the developmental hypothesis, it has been shown that Thought dominance is associated with higher levels of psychological development. Correspondingly, a relative emphasis on Action symptoms is associated with lower levels of development. Relationships between Action and Thought dominance and outcome in disorder, although present, do not follow any simple or direct relationship.

## REFERENCES

1. Albee, G. Patterns of aggression in psychopathology. *Journal of Consulting Psychology*, 1950, **14**, 465–468.
2. Albee, G. The prognostic importance of delusions in schizophrenia. *Journal of Abnormal and Social Psychology*, 1951, **46**, 208–212.
3. Becker, W. C. A genetic approach to the interpretation and evaluation of the process-reactive distinction in schizophrenia. *Journal of Abnormal and Social Psychology*, 1956. **53**, 229–236.
4. Becker, W. C. The process-reactive distinction: A key to the problem of schizophrenia? *Journal of Nervous and Mental Disease*, 1959, **129**, 442–449.
5. Brackbill, G. Studies of brain dysfunction in schizophrenia. *Psychological Bulletin*, 1956, **53**, 210–226.
6. Brackbill, G., & Fine, H. Schizophrenia and central nervous system pathology, *Journal of Abnormal and Social Psychology*, 1956, **52**, 310–313.
7. Eittinger, L., Laane, C., & Langfeldt, G. The prognostic value of the clinical picture and the therapeutic value of physical treatment in schizophrenia and the schizophreniform states. *Acta Psychiatrica et Neurologica Scandinavica* 1958, **33**, 33–53.
8. Freeman, H. E., & Simmons, O. G. *The mental patient comes home.* New York: Wiley, 1963.

9. Freud A. The mutual influences in the development of ego and id: Introduction to the discussion. *Psychoanalytic Study of the Child*, 1952, **7**, 42–50.
10. Garmezy, N., & Rodnick, E. Premorbid adjustment and performance in schizophrenia. *Journal of Nervous and Mental Disease*, 1959, **129**, 450–466.
11. Hartmann, H. Mutual influences in the development of ego and id. *Psychoanalytic Study of the Child*, 1952, **7**, 9–30.
12. Hoskins, R. *The biology of schizophrenia*. New York: Norton, 1946.
13. Hurwitz, I. A developmental study of the relationship between motor activity and perceptual processes as measured by the Rorschach test. Unpublished doctor dissertation, Clark University, 1954.
14. Huston, P., & Pepernick, M. Prognosis in schizophrenia. In L. Bellak (Ed.), Schizophrenia. New York: Logos Press, 1958. Pp. 531–546.
15. Kantor, R., Wallner, J., & Winder, C. Process and reactive schizophrenia. *Journal of Consulting Psychology*, 1953, **17**, 157–162.
16. Kantor, R., & Winder, C. The process-reactive continuum: A theoretical proposal. *Journal of Nervous and Mental Disease*, 1959, **129**, 429–434.
17. Kety, S. Biochemical theories of schizophrenia. Part I. *Science*, 1959, **129**, 1528–1532 (a)
18. Kety, S. Biochemical theories of schizophrenia. Part II. *Science*, 1959, **129**, 1590–1596. (b)
19. Kety, S. Biochemical theories of schizophrenia. Part III. *Science*, 1959, **129**, 3362–3363. (c)
20. King, G. Research with neuropsychiatric samples. *Journal of Psychology*, 1954, **38**, 383–387.
21. Knight, R. P. Dynamics and treatment of chronic alcohol addiction. *Bulletin of the Menninger Clinic*, 1937, **1**, 233–250.
22. Kretschmer, E. *Physique and character*. New York: Harcourt, Brace, 1925.
23. Kris, E. Notes on the development and on some current problems of psycho-analytic child psychology. *Psychoanalytic Study of the Child*, 1950, **5**, 34–62.
24. Kruger, A. Direct and substitute modes of tension-reduction in terms of developmental level: An experimental analysis of the Roschach test. Unpublished doctor dissertation, Clark University, 1954.
25. Langfeldt. G. *The prognosis in schizophrenia and the factors influencing the course of the disease*. London: Milford, 1937.
26. Lewin, K. *Dynamic theory of personality*. New York: McGraw-Hill, 1936.
27. Lewis, N. *Research in dementia praecox*. New York: National Committee for Mental Hygiene, 1936.
28. Mauz, F. *Die Prognostiz der endogenen Psychosen*. Leipzig: Thieme, 1930.
29. Misch, R. C. The relationship of motoric inhibition to developmental level and ideational functioning: An analysis by means of the Rorschach test. Unpublished doctor dissertation, Clark University, 1954.
30. Piaget, J. Principal factors in determining evolution from childhood to adult life. In D. Rapaport (Ed.), *Organization and pathology of thought*. New York: Columbia University Press, 1951. Pp. 154–175.
31. Phillips, L. Case history data and prognosis in schizophrenia. *Journal of Nervous and Mental Disease*, 1953, **6**, 515–525.
32. Phillips, L. Unpublished manuscript. Worcester State Hospital Psychology Department Library, 1966.
33. Phillips, L., Kaden, S., & Waldman, M. Rorschach indices of developmental level. *Journal of Genetic Psychology*, 1959, **94**, 267–285.
34. Phillips, L., & Zigler, E. Social competence: The action-thought parameter and vicariousness in normal and pathological behaviors. *Journal of Abnormal and Social Psychology*, 1961, **1**, 137–146.
35. Phillips, L., & Zigler, E. Role orientation, the action-thought dimension, and outcome

in psychiatric disorder. *Journal of Abnormal and Social Psychology*, 1964. **4**, 381–389.

36. Rapapport, D. Toward a theory of thinking. In D. Rapapport (Ed.). *Organization and pathology of thought*. New York: Columbia University Press, 1951. Pp. 689–730.

37. Rudie, R. E., & McGaughram, L. S. Differences in developmental experience, defensiveness and personality organization between two classes of problem drinkers. *Journal of Abnormal and Social Psychology*, 1961, **62**, 659–665.

38. Steffy, R. A., & Becker, W. C. Measurement of the severity of disorder in schizophrenia by means of the Holtzman Inkblot test. *Journal of Consulting Psychology*, 1961, **25**, (6), 555.

39. Sugerman, A. A., Reilly, D., & Albahary, R. S. Social competence and essential-reactive distinction in alcoholism. *Archives of General Psychiatry*, 1965, **6**, 552–556.

40. Weiner, H. Diagnosis and symptomatology. In L. Bellak (Ed.), *Schizophrenia*. New York: Logos Press, 1958. Pp. 107–173.

41. Werner, H. *Comparative psychology of mental development*. (Rev. ed.) Chicago: Follett, 1948.

42. Wittman, P. Scale for measuring prognosis in schizophrenic patients. *Elgin State Hospital Papers*, 1941, **4**, 20–33.

43. Wittman P. Follow-up on Elgin prognosis scale results. *Illinois Psychiatric Journal* 1944, **4**, 56–59.

44. Zigler, E., & Phillips, L. Social effectiveness and symptomatic behaviors. *Journal of Abnormal and Social Psychology*, 1960, **2**, 231–238.

45. Zigler, E., & Phillips, L. Social competence and outcome in psychiatric disorder *Journal of Abnormal and Social Psychology*, 1961, **2**, 264–271.

46. Zigler, E., & Phillips, L. Social competence and the process-reactive distinction in psychopathology. *Journal of Abnormal and Social Psychology*. 1962, **4**, 215–222.

47. Zimet, C., & Fine, H. Perceptual differentiation and two dimensions of schizophrenia. *Journal of Nervous and Mental Disease*, 1959, **129**, 435–441.

48. Zubin, J., Sutton, S., Salzinger, K., Salzinger, S., Burdock, E., & Peretz, D. A biometric approach to prognosis in schizophrenia. In P. Hoch & J. Zubin (eds.), *Comparative epidemiology of the mental disorders*. New York: Grune & Stratton, 1961. Pp. 143–203.

# 10/PATHOLOGICAL BEHAVIOR STYLE
# AND LIFE-STYLE

In the preceding chapter it was shown that the form taken by pathology is related to both achieved level of psychological development and outcome of disorder. This set of relationships was taken to indicate a continuity in patterns of behavior as a general style of life. However, the discussion of this relationship was limited to the variables of psychological development (measured in terms of premorbid social competence and achieved level of perceptual development), outcome of disorder, and pathological behavior style. We now want to explore further the comparability in behavior style during periods of normality and pathology.

To maintain that normality and pathology are in any way comparable violates the usual assumption that these are antithetical behavior states. Descriptions of pathological behaviors emphasize their deviation from those to be found in conditions of psychological normality. Thus, symptoms are taken to express a way of life distinctly deviant from that lived during a period of normality. This assumption is shared not alone by those who view psychiatric disorder as an "illness" or "disease" of which the patient is an unwilling victim, but also by those investigators who are committed to the social origins of disorder. For them, pathology is to be defined as a deviation in behavior from that called for by social norms and values. Thus, the deviant and the bizarre are almost universally considered a defining characteristic of psychopathology.

The viewpoint espoused here runs quite counter to this established formulation. An inherent continuity is stressed in both motivational intent and behavior style as the individual moves from a period of normality to one of pathology. Obviously, it would be futile to look for complete correspondence in normal and pathological behavior patterns, for a manifest change in behavior does occur between the normal and pathological phases of life. However, the qualitative characteristics of this deviation are determined by the general style of life that the individual adopted earlier in his career. The similarities we shall look for, therefore, are continuities in the formal, stylistic dimensions of behavior as these have been elaborated in earlier chapters. These include constancy in an individual's dominant Role Orientation and Sphere Dominance despite a shifting from an adaptive to a deviant pattern of response. As an example of what is meant, we should want to investigate whether a person who is self-critical in a period of normality will continue to be self-critical in a period of pathology; in the latter circumstance his self-accusations may lead to thoughts of suicide or to an actual suicidal attempt. In any event, the expression of self-critical attitudes in a period of disorder will be inappropriate and will not lead to a constructive pattern of interpersonal relationships with others. Pathological self-criticism is characteristically marked by its intensity and potential self-destructive quality, in contrast to the relatively more detached, objective, and rational self-evaluation more frequent in normal states.

In this chapter, then, we intend to explore certain possible parallels in normal and pathological behaviors. In principle, this could be undertaken in any of a number of ways. We could compare behavior patterns during adaptive and deviant states of lower- or middle-class individuals, of various ethnic groups, of people at different age levels, of different occupational categories, or of the two sexes. Yet limitations of space alone preclude an extensive review of all the possible comparisons between the ways of life endogenous to these various categories and to their corresponding forms of psychopathology. In practice, it is neither possible nor necessary to run through such a gamut of classifications in comparing normal and deviant behavior styles. It is not possible because the requisite data upon which these comparisons might be made are for the most part simple not available. It is not necessary because the intent here is not to provide comparative data on normal and deviant behaviors within each possible classification of individuals. Rather, we want only to illustrate that a certain consistency in response style across periods of normal adaptation and pathology characterizes individuals no matter how they may be classified in life. To this end, we have chosen two quite different modes for classifying people, occupational type and sex group, as the means for examining consistency in life style. These choices are dictated primarily by availability of the relevant data. They do, however, permit us to explore what is meant by consistency in life-style through two quite divergent groupings of people. In the first section, our account will be limited to results that have emerged from the author's own study of consistency in Sphere Dominance across periods of normality and pathology. We know of no other work that is directly relevant to the issues posed here. By contrast, there is a wealth of material from a variety of sources that bears on the emergence and continuity of sex-typed behaviors. For that reason more space will be devoted to, and a wider range of studies scanned in, our analysis of the data bearing on sex identification and its normal and pathological consequences.

## SPHERE DOMINANCE AND LIFE-STYLE

The proposition that a continuity in life-style will dominate both the normal and pathological behaviors of an individual leads to the expectation that, in becoming symptomatic, the individual does not change his habitual mode of response. This view is supported by findings reported by Phillips and Zigler (27) and presented in the preceding chapter. They noted that the developmentally lower (i.e., less socially competent) persons typically hold jobs that predominantly require physical labor. Further, in terms of their symptom manifestation, they tend to remain action oriented in a period of pathology. In contrast, developmentally higher (i.e., more socially competent) persons are likely to hold positions that require more ideational activity. Such individuals typically develop symptoms that are more ideational than motoric in nature.

Thus, consistency in action or thought dominance across periods of normality and pathology appears to hold for the majority of persons in our society. These findings substantiate the hypothesis that a continuity in life-style is to be expected as a person moves from adaptive patterns of behavior to deviant and pathological forms of response. However, an even more stringent test of this hypothesis suggests itself. As we have noted, developmental theory calls for action dominance in developmentally low individuals and for thought dominance in developmentally high persons. Suppose, however, that contrary to this formulation, we observe persons in a period of normal adaptation who, though developmentally low, are *thought* oriented and others, who thought developmentally high, are *action* oriented? What will happen to these individuals during a period of pathology? Will their developmental level determine the form taken by their pathology? If so, then developmentally low, yet ordinarily thought-oriented individuals, should manifest *action* symptoms; the developmentally high, yet usually action-oriented persons, should manifest *thought* symptoms. However, if consistency in life-style takes precedence over achieved developmental level, contrary findings are to be expected. That is, developmentally low yet thought-oriented persons will, in a period of pathology, manifest thought symptoms. Correspondingly, developmentally high yet action-oriented persons will, in a period of disorder, manifest action symptoms.

On the basis of these formulations, Phillips and Zigler developed two hypotheses: (1) When developmental level and behavior style are consistent, developmentally low individuals will be action oriented and developmentally high individuals will be thought oriented in periods of both normality and pathology; and (2) when achieved developmental level and behavior style are discordant, the individual's characteristic life-style takes precedence over achieved level of development. Thus, those individuals who during a period of normality manifest a behavior orientation that is atypical for their developmental level should continue to show that atypical orientation during a period of pathology.

A test of these hypotheses requires a measure of the individual's developmental level and criteria that indicate the individual's behavior style in both adaptive and deviant states. The 6-item index of social competence devised by Zigler and Phillips (40) was used as the measure of psychological development.

Developmental theory as well as empirical findings in the psychology of occupations (e.g., Roe, 28) were employed to derive criteria of both typical and atypical behavior orientations. Since high social competence individuals should typically have occupations that do not predominantly require physical actions or skills, individuals of relatively high social competence whose positions were predominantly of this variety were classified as atypical. Thus, high social competence persons whose occupations placed them in the action category, whatever the level of job skill involved, would be classified as atypical in their behavior orientation. Analogously, low social competence individuals should typically have occupations requiring physical activity. Therefore, individuals of relatively low social competence whose occupations demanded symbolic activity, such as the keeping of records, were classified as atypical.

Employing the criteria just outlined, Phillips and Zigler subjected the following prediction to test: Individuals who have exhibited a relatively high level of premorbid social competence, but who have occupations in the action category, will more frequently manifest symptoms of the Action variety than will individuals of equally high premorbid social competence whose occupations fall into the symbolic or Thought category.

The sample used in the test of this proposition included over 200 hospitalized psychiatric male patients. Women were not used in this study since the range of their occupations was too restricted for adequate statistical analysis. A modified social competence score was obtained for each of the patients employed in this study in which the occupation variable was deleted as a measure of social competence since occupation was being employed as one of the independent variables. Subjects were placed in either a pure Action or Thought group, according to the type of symptoms that they manifested. Only those individuals who were in the High social competence group, and who were also in either the Action or Thought symptom groups, were employed to test this prediction.

The results of this study supported the hypothesis put forward by Phillips and Zigler and indicated that high-competence individuals in the Thought group tended to hold conceptually oriented positions. High-competence individuals in the Action group tended to be classified in action occupations.

A second and parallel prediction to be tested was that individuals who have exhibited a low level of premorbid social competence, but who have occupations of an ideational nature, will more frequently manifest symptoms of the though variety than will individuals of equally low social competence whose occupations fall into action categories. Only those individuals who were in the Low social competence group, and who were also in either the Action or Thought symptom groups, were employed to test this prediction. As anticipated, it was observed that low-competence individuals in the Action group did tend to hold manually oriented positions, while those in the Thought group tended to hold conceptually oriented positions. These findings also confirm the prediction put forward by Phillips and Zigler that when a discrepancy appears between achieved developmental level and behavior style, the individual's characteristic life-style takes precedence over developmental level in determining the form taken by pathology.

This study does not explain why an individual should employ a behavioral orientation which, from the developmental viewpoint, is an atypical one. One suggestion that may be derived from earlier experimental studies (37) is that the individual functions in a substitutive manner when the external environmental conditions are such that they block the individual's typical behavior. Thus, it may be hypothesized that for individuals who employ a developmentally atypical  orientation in their occupation choice, considerable external pressures influence this choice, whereas no such pressure will be found in the cases of individuals who employ a developmentally typical orientation.

Nevertheless, certain findings of the present study cast considerable doubt that external events alone are responsible for such a substitution in type of job functioning. If, as this hypothesis proposes, an individual is forced to choose a developmentally atypical occupation because of external factors, (e.g., parents' aspiration level, employment possibilities, etc.), it would not be expected that this typical orientation would manifest itself in an area where these factors are inoperative or where their strength has been greatly reduced, namely, in the pathological manifestations of the individual. However, the results of the present study clearly indicate that the individual's atypical behavior orientation remains constant in both the normal and pathological phases of his functioning.

The findings just reported suggest that an individual's style of functioning is not solely the product of either his achieved level of psychological development nor of the environmental conditions to which he is immediately exposed. Rather, it may well mirror a specialization in life-style that originates far back in early life experience. It is in order to illustrate how early environmental conditions may contribute to the formation of an enduring style of life under conditions of both normality and pathology that the following section on the origins of sex identity and its consequences is provided.

## Sex Identity and Life-Style

The preceding section has reviewed a correspondence in behavior style between periods of normality and pathology. Findings confirmed the hypothesis that a parallel in life-style is to be observed from a period of appropriate to one of deviant adaptation. Nevertheless, the test was limited to a brief segment of adult life and concentrated on a relatively narrow aspect of behavior, that of Sphere Dominance in occupational choice and symptom expression.

In casting about for a more comprehensive demonstration of continuity in life-style, the differing destinies of men and women both in periods of normal adaptation and pathology appeared to provide striking evidence in support of the continuity hypothesis. This section, therefore, provides a fairly extended survey of the origins and manifestations of the divergent life-styles that tend to characterize men and women, and of the forms of pathology that predominate in the two sexes.

### Origins of Sex Identity

Possibly the single most potent factor in the definition of self is that of one's sex identity. According to Money (23), establishment of sex identity in the child coincides with language development, and usually occurs between 8 and 24 months of age. By the fourth year, gender is indelibly and irreversibly fixed, so much so as to give the impression that sex role characteristics are inborn.

Money and his associates (24), however, believe that gender identity emerges from the individual's decipherment of a multiplicity of environmental and social cues that identify the person's sex as that of boy or girl. These signs include the language cues of nouns and pronouns that designate the individual's sex, the haircut, dress, personal adornment, as well as the approved modes of behavior.

Biological sex is not defined solely by the morphology of the external genitalia. Other biological criteria include hormone patterns, gonadal type, the form of the internal accessory reproductive organs, and chromosonal structure. These biological criteria of sex do not in all cases agree with each other; in some persons, the physical sex characteristics of both sexes may be present in various degrees of definiteness or completeness. Such cases of sexual ambiguity are called hermaphrodites.

Money *et al.* investigated the gender role of 105 hermaphrodites of all ages. Gender role is defined in terms of those activities which characterize a person as a boy or girl, or as a man or woman. These authors discovered that the sex identification of these individuals is "consistently and conspicuously" more dependent on the sex assigned to the child at birth and within which it was reared than it is upon any combination of the biological indices of sex. The gender role and orientation of only five of their cases was ambiguous or deviant from the sex assigned.

As evidence for the dominant psychological significance of the sex of assignment and rearing over biological sex criteria, Money *et al.* offered the cases of persons of identical physical diagnosis, some of whom were reared as boys and some as girls. They said:

It is indeed startling to see, for example, two children with female hyperadrenocorticism in the company of one another in a hospital playroom, one of them entirely feminine in behavior and conduct, the other entirely masculine, each according to upbringing. As a social observer, one gets no suspicion that the two children are chromosonally and gonadally female, for psychologically they are entirely different.

The attitudinal sets of our culture generally must also be considered in the question of sex role identification. In Western society, the male is more highly valued, and this may tend to weaken the feminine identification of girls, all the more since girls are allowed a greater freedom in sex role learning (6). Thus, "tomboy" girls are accepted and even approved, whereas "sissy" boys are the objects of scorn and derision. Lynn (19) has suggested that, with increasing age, boys become more firmly ensconced in behaviors appropriate to their sex, whereas girls become less so. The consequence is that more females than males prefer and adopt aspects of the role of the opposite sex (5).

*Training for Sex Roles*

Parents tend to use a double standard for the two sexes in dealing with behaviors that they approve or disapprove in their children. By the time children are 5 years of age, boys and girls in our society are disciplined differently. The sharpest difference is in the child's expression of aggression, and here boys are handled with more permissiveness than girls. However, boys more commonly receive physical punishment, and discipline is generally meted out by the father. Those mothers who are convinced that different behavior standards should be observed for each of the sexes are those who are more insistent that girls act in conformity with adult standards (31).

Hubert and Britton (15) found that mothers generally were more attentive to daughters and enjoyed rearing them more than did mothers with sons. The latter were less strict with their boys in matters both of physical activities and observation of rules of conduct. The fathers in these latter families had more responsibility for household chores then did those fathers in families where the child under consideration was a girl. Thus in the households of the male children, the roles of mother and father tended to be more nearly alike in behavior, whereas in the families of the female children, parental roles were more clearly differentiated. These observations may explain why girls tend to identify with the mother, while boys are more likely to identify chiefly with cultural stereotypes of the adult male.

Schooling, which is ostensibly identical for the two sexes, actually fosters different self concepts for boys and girls. A report on children's readers, for example, revealed sharp differences in the way male and female characters are delineated (9). This study showed that female characters are more frequently described as sociable and kind, yet are timid, inactive, unambitious, and uncreative. The central character more frequently nurtures a female, suggesting the helplessness of the female, while males are more often depicted as being the ones who supply vital information to central characters. Females are portrayed as lazy in twice as many instances as males, while males are much more frequently shown as achieving their goals by the socially approved route of work and effort. Most striking of all is the relative absence of females in children's readers; male central characters are more than two-and-a-half times more frequent than female ones.

### Social Training

In the training of boys and girls, certain universals correspond to pervasive differences in adult male and female roles throughout the world. In almost all societies, girls are taught obedience and responsibility for routine chores, while there is much more emphasis on the training of boys in physical skill and achievement. This discrimination between the sexes had been found to be valid in the United States. Sears, Maccoby and Levin (31) have reported that those mothers who emphasize the greatest sex role differentiation place the highest demands on girls for instant obedience.

The different upbringing of the sexes stresses an active and autonomous orientation for boys, but for girls a more passive obedience to family rules.

### The Psychology of Men and Women

Differences in the early experience and training of boys and girls result in remarkably different sets of aptitudes, traits, values, and behavior between the sexes. We shall discuss these within the framework of Sphere Dominance, the development of morality, social role and morality, and self-concept.

*Sphere Dominance.* In considering the differential reinforcement of particular traits between boys and girls, certain quite divergent physical and intellectual orientations can be expected, and, in fact, do emerge between the sexes. Boys become more physically skilled and active than girls; alternatively, the educational process for girls tends to inhibit them in physical activity. The theoretical construct of vicariousness (37) permits us to predict what, as a consequence, will be the preferred mode of self-expression in girls. Vicariousness posits the functional equivalence of action and thought. A person who is thwarted in physical expression will turn toward an ideational emphasis in behavior, and since this holds true for girls, we would expect them to be more skilled than boys in the verbal and ideational spheres.

A wide range of differences in aptitudes and interests has been found among children and adults of both sexes. Males demonstrate a greater physical mastery of self-world relationships, a more precise articulation of space, and a greater knowledgeability about physical objects. Anastasi (1) has reported that males tend to surpass females in motor speed, coordination of gross bodily activity, spatial orientation, other spatial aptitudes, and the understanding of mechanics. On the other hand, girls are more adept in most school subjects, particularly those involving verbal skills. They tend to excel in verbal fluency, other language skills, memory, perceptual speed and accuracy, and fine manual dexterity. In line with the greater conformity and symbolic sophistication of girls, it is noteworthy that they surpass boys in routine arithmetic calculation and yet are relatively deficient in arithmetic reasoning.

*The Development of Morality.* Brun-Gulbrandsen (7) posited that the social pressures directed at the two sexes differ markedly. Social pressure on men is exerted toward carrying out activities that are socially approved for the male sex, with less pressure on women for engaging in the same activities. Indeed, the pressure for *not* carrying out these activities is, of course, much less for men and much greater for women. For performances assigned to the female role, the opposite relationships occur. Thus, an activity is considered "good" or "bad" depending on whether the person is male or female. There is positive social reinforcement for the man carrying out a typically male activity, but for a woman so engaged, only social disapproval. Conversely, this holds true in the case of men assuming activities that are considered typically female. Since men are overwhelmingly represented in most criminal categories, Brun-Gulbrandsen hypothesized that most criminal activities are assigned to the male sex role. Further, he proposed that this relationship holds for other antisocial activities, those behaviors that elicit negative social although not legal sanctions.

This formulation is consistent with the differences that characterize child-rearing practices for boys and girls. Boys, for the most part, are brought up to behave in freer, more physically active ways than are girls; for girls a passive subordination to the group and its value system is culturally reinforced. Whatever rewards girls seek are usually obtained in conformity with the social mores.

*Social Role and Morality.* Differences in self-world orientations coincide with different male–female standards for what is morally permissible in the behavior of boys and girls, and subsequently, of men and women. Brun-Gulbrandsen conducted a study in Norway on the different social pressures to which boys and girls are exposed and the consequent differential effects on their respective attitudes and behavior. He distinguished between sex and sex ideal. Sex role may include criminal acts but the sex ideal is best described in terms of more positive traits. Courage, for example, can be demonstrated in many positively rewarded behaviors, but an inverted kind of "courage" can be seen in criminal activities, such as car stealing or reckless driving. Many criminal acts demonstrate the possession of masculine traits such as independence, physical strength, technical ability, and so on. In contrast, few criminal behaviors conform to any femine ideal.

Brun-Gulbrandsen tested these propositins in western Norway by the questionnnaire method among boy and girl subjects, 14 and 15 years of age. None of the respondents was known to be a delinquent. Boys and girls agreed highly on the sex role assignment of a wide variety of work, leisure, criminal, and other asocial activities. They reported that they were exposed to the strongest parental pressure to perform the more acceptable activities ascribed to their own sex role.

They were also asked what they would think of a friend of theirs who engaged in any one of 16 asocial acts. Answers on a five-point scale could range from highly approving to severely disapproving. The social sanction indices were consistently more negative for girls than for boys. Parenthetically, the more an act was judged to be seriously criminal by these respondents, the more they tended to assign it to the male sex role. Further, the girl subjects, more than the boy subjects, rated their parents as disapproving if they themselves performed any of the 16 delinquent acts.

This study by Brun-Gulbrandsen supports the assumption that training in what is morally acceptable differs considerably between the sexes.

*Self Concept.* The self concept of men and women has been compared in a number of studies. McKee and Sheriffs (22) undertook studies in the field of male and female sterotypes. By use of a rating scale technique they discovered that both men and women college students place males as superior to females. This bias, however, appeared to be stronger among women. Similarly, in the study by Brun-Gulbrandsen noted above, a fair proportion of girls opposed their own sex role, whereas the boys showed no such trend. More boys than girls chose their own sex when asked which they would prefer if given a choice. Again, when asked to choose among sex-linked occupations, some girls chose a masculine job whereas no boy chose a typically feminine type of work. Finally, when asked whom they would most wish to be like, more than 10% of the girl subjects mentioned a man, whereas none of the boys chose a female ideal.

Boys are urged toward physical activity and physical skill and the achievement of goals through their own work, effort, and aggressiveness. In contrast, girls are educated in ways that implicitly reward timidity, helplessness, and lack of ambition; they are trained for obedience, conformity, lack of creativity, and to responsiblity for routine chores.

In line with these patterns of indoctrination, males consistently express themselves as more self-reliant and achievement oriented, more self-assertive and aggressive, and more hardy and fearless than females. Females see themselves as more timid and given to loss of emotional control. On the other hand, men exceed women in rating themselves as resourceful, efficient, adventurous, realistic, logical, deliberate, and mature (29).

In the vocational choices of high school students, boys indicate a preference for jobs offering power, profit, and independence; girls desire opportunities for social service and interesting job experiences (32). As might be expected, desire for prestige, power over others, and practical success are more important to men and to women. Thus, despite the generally higher school achievement of females, far more men than women achieve distinction in the sphere of occupations.

Males are also generally reported as more dominant in social interaction than are females (4, 12, 13). Females, on the other hand, are seen as more obedient (2), as well as more passive and dependent (17).

In general, females are much more socially oriented than are males, and this commitment to social participation is expressed throughout the life-span, from the nursery school years to old age. Young girls show more interest, concern, and "motherly" behavior than do boys. Girls generally express more interest in people and this can be seen in the type of games they play, the books they read, and the questions they ask. They do not generally maintain an objectivity in their dealings with people and are consequently more sensitive in their relations with them and more prone to be overconcerned with what people may think about them. They are more likely to be angered by threats to their social prestige and more often experience jealousy.

Adult women more frequently than men see themselves as affectionate and pleasant to others, and as more compassionate and sympathetic. Women have a greater commitment to the welfare of others (8), and more than men they choose social service occupations that minister to the young, helpless, and distressed (33, 35, 36). Even in old age, sociability is highly correlated with happiness in women, but these factors are essentially unrelated in old men (16). Perhaps it is the greater sense of dependency characteristic of women that makes them particularly concerned about their relations with other people.

*Psychopathology and Deviant Behaviors*

Fairly consistent sex differences in pathological reactions have been observed within child and adult populations. In general, males tend to manifest considerably more destructive behaviors, whereas females are inhibited and self-critical. We shall review studies on child behavior problems first, and then turn to reports on the adult deviations.

*Child Disturbances.* More boys than girls are referred for treatment to child guidance clinics (11, 26, 39). The overall ratio in referrals of boys to girls to these clinics approximates $2\frac{1}{2}$ to 1. In the sphere of aggressive or antisocial behavior the ratio rises to 4 to 1. It is obvious that the predominance of male referrals is based largely on a higher incidence of aggressive or delinquent behaviors.

It has been noted that boys, more often than girls, manifest "behavior" or "conduct" problems (3, 14, 20, 25, 34, 38). Their symptoms typically include overactivity, competitiveness, lying, temper tantrums, stealing, truancy, rudeness, and the like.

Girls, on the other hand, predominantly show "personality" rather than conduct problems (20, 25, 34). For example, girls more frequently report fears and worries; are shy, timid, overly sensitive, somber, or excessively reserved; feel inferior or lack self-confidence; suck their thumb, bite their nails, or are fussy about food. Girls, then, characteristically express their difficulties in adjustment in a milder and less violent fashion than do boys.

*Adult Deviations.* Freud (10) posited that differences in superego formation are the basis for those "character traits for which women have always been criticized and reproached, that they have less sense of justice than men, less tendency to submit to the great necessities of life, and frequently permit themselves to be guided in their decisions by their affections or enmities."

Empirical data on the occurrence of the various types of pathological behaviors contradicts Freud's assumptions as to a deficient superego formation in women. In general, women show higher rates of first admissions per 100,000 population for manic-depressive disorders. In contrast, men have far higher rates of arrests for criminal activity. The ratio of arrests for criminal activity has been reported as 19 to 1 for men as compared to women (30).

The sexes also differ markedly in type of symptom manifested. Deviant reactions in men are more frequently expressed in action, whereas in women they are more commonly expressed in thought. The symptoms of men are much more likely to reflect a destructive hostility against others, as well as a pathological self-indulgence. Predominant male delinquencies include the illegal taking of others' property (burglary, larceny, embezzlement, etc.), as well as forms of pathological self-gratifications, including drunkenness, drug usage, gambling, and various types of sex offenses (18). Women, on the other hand, express in their symptoms a harsh, self-critical, self-depriving, and often self-destructive set of attitudes (21).

A study conducted by Zigler and Phillips (40) reported results consistent with the findings above. A comparison of symptom manifestation by male and female mental hospital patients revealed the following differences. Male patients significantly more than female were found to be assaultive or to threaten assault, and to indulge their impulses in such socially deviant ways as in robbery, rape, drinking, homosexuality and other perversions. Female patients, on the other hand, were more often rated as self-depreciatory, depressed, perplexed, withdrawn, as refusing to eat, suffering from thoughts of suicide, and making actual suicidal attempts.

SUMMARY

A clear continuity appears for both men and women between their early experiences and training, their self concept and behavior in adulthood, and the forms of pathology that characterize the two sexes.

For males, child-rearing practices are directed at encouraging initiative and independence. Aggressiveness is applauded and boys are expected to be physically active and skilled, strong and dominant. Hard work, striving, and achievement are ambitions persistently and repetitively imposed on boys during their maturing years.

In adulthood, men more often than women see themselves as mature and self-reliant, as resourceful, efficient, and realistic, and as hardy, fearless, and adventurous. They more often describe themselves as self-assertive and dominant and seek in their careers power and practical success.

Even in childhood, the emotional and behavior disturbances of boys reflect in an exaggerated and distorted fashion the motives of the male world. Their symptoms include an excessive aggressiveness, overactivity, and competitiveness, as well as rudeness, lying, truancy, temper tantrums, stealing, and destructiveness. In adulthood, male psychopathology is marked on the one hand by its self-indulgence, and on the other by its open and active destructiveness toward others. Far more often than women, men are given to excessive drinking, drug usage, sexual adventures, and gambling. They are also more prone to criminal activities, to robbery, rape, and assault.

The history and fate of women is quite different. From early childhood, they are taught to be obedient, conforming, and subordinate, and to be responsible for routine chores. Girls are likely to be more verbal and less physically active than boys throughout their years of growth. They hear their sex described as timid, helpless, and dependent, and yet as kind and sociable. They come to view themselves in adulthood as inhibited and timid, and as more obedient, passive, and dependent than men. They describe themselves as given to jealousy and to loss of emotional control. They are particularly sensitive to potential criticism. Yet, they see themselves as pleasant, affectionate and compassionate. They are interested and concerned with the welfare of others and more often than men commit themselves to careers in social services.

Both the childhood and adult disorders of females reflect their upbringing, experiences, and self concept. In childhood, their symptoms are predominantly those of excessive inhibition, reserve, shyness, and timidity. They lack self-confidence and feel inferior, are self-critical, and suffer from excessive sensitivity, fears, and worries.

In adulthood also, the symptoms of women reflect a self-critical bent. They often express themselves as perplexed, depressed, and withdrawn. More often than men, they are excessively self-critical and depreciatory, often turning toward self-destruction by refusing to eat or by harboring thoughts of suicide.

This completes the review of the origins and characteristics of the life-styles of men and women and their consequences for the forms of pathology predominant in the two sexes. Early experiences mold the self concept and behaviors of adults and give a unique cast to pathological reactions when these appear.

Earlier chapters have indicated the important role that achieved level of psychological development plays in determining the individual's habitual adaptive pattern, as well as the liklihood, form, and outcome of disorder. The present chapter has suggested that nondevelopmental and experiential factors also influence a person's behavior style both in periods of normality and deviance. The next chapter will expand our inquiries into the determinants of patterns of adaptation and deviance through studies carried out in cultures other than our own.

## REFERENCES

1. Anastasi, A. and Foley, J. P., Jr. *Differential psychology.* New York: Macmillan, 1949.
2. Barry, H., Bacon, M. K., & Child, I. L. A cross-cultural survey of some sex Differences in socialization. *Journal of Abnormal and Social Psychology*, 1957, **55**, 327–332.
3. Beller, E. K., & Neubauer, P. B. Patterning of symptoms in early childhood. Paper presented at the 115th annual meeting of the American Psychiatric Association in Philadelphia, 1959.
4. Bernreuter, R. G. *The personality inventory: Tentative percentile norms.* Stanford University, Calif: Stanford University Press, 1938.
5. Brown, D. G. Masculinity-femininity development in children. *Journal of Consulting Psychology*, 1957, **21**, 197–202.
6. Brown, D. G. Sex role development in a changing culture. *Psychological Bulletin*, 1958, **55**, 232–242.
7. Brun-Gulbrandsen, S. *Kinnsrolle og ungdomskriminalitet.* Universitetsforlaget: Oslo, 1958.
8. Cantril, H., & Allport, G. W. Recent applications of the study of values. *Journal of Abnormal Psychology*, 1933, **28**, 259–273.
9. Child, I. L., Potter, E. H., and Levine, E. M. Children's textbooks and personality development: An exploration in the social psychology of education. *Psychological Monographs*, 1946, **60**, 1–54
10. Freud, S. Some psychological consequences of the anatomical distinction between the sexes. *International Journal of Psychoanalysis*, 1927, VIII. (2), 133–142.
11. Gilbert, G. M. A survey of 'referral problems' in metropolitan child guidance centers. *Journal of Clinical Psychology*, 1957, **13**, 37–42.
12. Gordon, L. Some interrelationships among personality item characteristics. *Educational and Psychological Measurement*, 1953, **13**, 264–272.
13. Guilford, J. P., Shneidman, E. S., & Zimmerman, W. S. The Guilford-Shneidman-Simmerman Interest Survey. *Journal of Consulting Psychology*, 1949, **13**, 302–306.
14. Hattwick, L. A. Sex differences in behavior of nursery school children. *Child Development*, 1937, **8**, 343–355.
15. Hubert, M. A. G., and Britton, J. H. Attitudes and practices of mothers rearing their children from birth to the age of two years. *Journal of Home Economics*, 1957, **49**, 208–223.
16. Johnson, W. B., & Terman, L. M. Some highlights in the literature of psychological sex differences published since 1920. *Journal of Psychology*, 1940, **9**, 327–336.
17. Kagan, J., & Moss, H. A. The stability of passive and dependent behavior from childhood through adulthood. *Child Development*, 1960, **31**, 557–591.
18. Long, L. H. (Ed.) *World Almanac.* New York: Newspaper Enterprise Association, World Almanac Division, 1965.
19. Lynn, D. B. A note on sex differences in the development of masculine and feminine identification. *Psychological Review*, 1959, **66**, 126–135.
20. MacFarlane, J. W., Allen, L, and Honzik, M. P. *A developmental study of the behavior problems of normal children between twenty-one months and fourteen years.* Berkeley, Calif: University of California Press, 1954.
21. Malzberg, G. Important statistical data about mental illness. In S. Arieti (Ed.), *American Handbook of Psychiatry.* New York: Basic Books, 1959. Pp. 161–174.
22. McKee, J. P., & Sherriffs, A. C. The differential evaluation of males and females. *Journal of Personality*, 1957, **25**, 356–371.
23. Money, J. Hemaphroditism. In A. Ellis and A. Abarbanel (Eds.), *The Encyclopedia of sexual behavior.* New York: Hawthorn Books, 1961 Pp. 472–485.
24. Money, J., Hampson, J. G., & Hampson, J. L. Imprinting and the establishment of gender role. *A.M.A. Archives of Neurology and Psychiatry*, 1957, **77**, 333–336.

25. Peterson, D. R. Behavior problems of middle childhood. *Journal of Consulting Psychology*, 1961, **25**, 205–209.
26. Phillips, L. Cultural versus intrapsychic factors in childhood behavior problem referrals. *Journal of Clinical Psychology*, 1956, **12**, 400–401.
27. Phillips, L., & Zigler, E. Social competence: The action-thought parameter and vicariousnes in normal and pathological behaviors. *Journal of Abnormal and Social Psychology*, 1961, **63**, 137–146.
28. Roe, Anne. *The psychology of occupations.* New York: Wiley, 1956.
29. Sarbin, T. R., & Rosenberg, B. G. Contributions to role-taking theory: IV. A method for obtaining a qualitative estimate of the self. *Journal of Social Psychology*, 1955, **42**. 71–81.
30. Scheinfeld, A. *Women and men.* New York: Harcourt, Brace, 1943.
31. Sears, R. R., Maccoby, E. E., and Levin, H. Patterns of child rearing. New York: Harper & Row, 1957.
32. Singer, J. L. Projected familial attitudes as a function of socioeconomic status and psychopathology. *Journal of Consulting Psychology* 1954, **18**, 99–104.
33. Strong, E. K., Jr. *Vocational interests of men and women.* Stanford University, Calif.: Stanford University Press, 1943.
34. Terman, L. M., & Tyler, L. E. Psychological sex differences. In L. Carmichael (Ed.) *Manual of child psychology.* (2nd ed.) New York: Wiley, 1954. Pp. 1064–1115.
35. Traxler, A. E., & McCall, W. C. Some data on the Kuder Preference Record. *Educational and Psychological Measurement*, 1941, **1** 253–268.
36. Triggs, F. O. A study of the relation of the Kuder Preference Record scores to various other measures. *Educational and Psychological Measurement*, 1943, **3**, 341–354.
37. Werner, H., & Wapner, S. Toward a general theory of perception. *Psychological Review*, 1952, **59**, 324–338.
38. Wickman, E. K. *Children's behavior and teachers' attitudes.* New York: Commonwealth Fund, 1928.
39. Williams, H. D. A survey of predilinquent children in ten midwestern cities. *Journal of Juvenile Research*, 1933, **17**, 163–174.
40. Zigler, E., and Phillips, L. Social effectiveness and symptomatic behaviors *Journal of Abnormal and Social Psychology*, 1960 **2** 231–238.

# 11/CULTURE, LIFE-STYLE,

# AND PATHOLOGY

Previous chapters have been devoted to a demonstration that individual patterns of adaptation and pathology are complementary facets of a person's style of life. In those chapters the developmental and nondevelopmental aspects of individual psychology and early life experiences associated with different styles of life have been discussed. Here we want to explore a number of related issues that arise out of the findings we have reported earlier. (1) How universal is the observed relation between psychological development and the form taken by an individual's psychopathology? (2) To what extent are the various forms of pathology fixed entities, and to what extent are they modified by the cultural setting in which they occur? And (3) as the dominant life-styles of a culture change, can we observe corresponding changes in its dominant forms of psychopathology?

In earlier chapters substantial evidence has been brought together in support of the proposition that consistent relatonships exist between achieved level of psychological development and the form that pathology takes in the individual. We have also shown that pathological forms differ according to the "culture" in which the individual is immersed, specifically, the differing cultures of occupational types and of the two sexes. One set of findings argues for constancy in the pattern of relations between psychological development and pathological forms, independent of the cultural context. The other supports the position that the manifestations of pathology are substantially molded by the dominant forms of the culture in which they appear.

We want to test the stability of both these two rather paradoxical propositions. In order to do so we have made use of data from culturally quite divergent societies, Argentina and Japan. Within samples of psychiatric patients drawn from each of these cultures we have tested the constancy of the previously observed relation between psychological development and pathological forms. Results of these studies are reported in the first section of this chapter. In the second section we shall report on the different patterns of pathology to be found within these samples, using North American psychiatric data as a base, when controls are instituted for achieved level of psychological development. The intent is to support the proposition that certain universals are to be expected from one society to another in the relation of psychological development to forms of pathology, and yet that the dominant forms of pathology are uniquely characteristic of the cultures in which they emerge.

PSYCHOLOGICAL DEVELOPMENT, BEHAVIOR STYLE, AND CULTURE

The findings reviewed in earlier chapters are largely limited to one cultural milieu, that of the United States. The question arises whether the observed relationship between psychological development and behavior style, as expressed in symptomatology, holds also under different cultural conditions. A test of its more general validity requires that individual level of psychological development be examined in relaton to symptom manifestation within societies that differ culturally from our own. Some preliminary work in this direction has been carried out by the writer and his co-workers on a small sample of Argentine psychiatric patients and within a larger pool of Japanese patients. These studies will be reported first, followed by a brief review of the relevant findings drawn from the general literature on crosscultural psychiatric investigations.

*Psychological Development and Pathology in Other Cultures*

The earlier of two studies carried out by the writer and colleagues (8,9) outside the United States made use of a group of 33 Argentine patients drawn from Buenos Aires and its vicinity. Psychological development was measured in terms of a brief social competence index. This index was scored for each of these subjects based on the 6-item Social Competence measure (19). Role Orientation scores also were computed to indicate whether the patient's symptoms predominantly expressed a Turning Against the Self, a Turning Against Others, or Avoidance of Others. It was found that the role orientation of Turning Against the Self was more frequently encountered among Argentine patients high in social competence than among those low in the same characteristic. The specific symptoms prevalent among the high social competence patients expressed a relatively high emphasis on self-abnegation and self-blame, and thus provided further evidence of the preeminence of self-directed pathology in this group.

The same measures were used in a second study, carried out on a sample of well over 200 male Japanese patients drawn from four psychiatric hospitals located in and around Tokyo. As within the Argentine sample, Turning Against the Self was the predominat role orientation among the high social competence Japanese subjects, while the remaining two roles, Turning Against Others and Avoidance of Others, were encountered at a disproportionately high rate among the low social competence Japanese.

These results were corroborated and extended through an analysis of discrete symptom differences. High social competence patients among the Japanese tended to develop symptoms indicative of self-deprivation and self-abnegation, as had their North American and Argentine counterparts. On the other hand, lower social competence patients tended toward explosive outbursts or retreat from the world of personal relationships.

It is of interest to note that there is a degree of corresopondence between the findings in low and high social competence subgroups within the Japanese psychiatric population and the results of a major empirical investigation of the normal Japanese personality directed by Muramatsu (16). This author and his associates noted a more withdrawn way of life among the Japanese of low socioeconomic status and a greater tendency toward acceptance of responsibility for oneself and others among Japanese subjects at higher levels of socioeconomic scale, trends that appear in an exaggerated and inappropriate form in our clinical sample. Thus, it appears that among the Japanese a suggestive degree of continuity in behavior style obtains between normal and pathological individuals drawn from similar socioeconomic levels.

### Supporting Evidence from Other Crosscultural Studies

The body of work reviewed in earlier chapters has supported the proposition that the form taken by psychopathology is influenced by the level of psychological development achieved by the individual who manifests that pathology. The studies cited so far in this chapter suggest that this relationship holds independently of qualitative differences in culture. Does the wider psychiatric literature support this assumption? Unfortunately, almost nothing has been written that relates personality development to the types of pathology that characterize different societies. There are available, however, some studies, that have examined the relation of the socioeconomic development of a society to its dominant pathological forms. Here we want to examine whether the findings of such studies help to confirm or disconfirm our own results with Argentine and Japanese psychiatric samples.

In order to make use of the available literature, we need to assume first that socioeconomic development within a society brings about a shift in its dominat personality types, specifically, that economic development is paralleled by a corresponding enhancement in psychological development among members of that society. This formulation is similar to that put forward in the context of a theoretical reconstruction of the personality patterns associated with several historical periods by Barbu (1). He proposed that changes in cultural forms tend to show a certain regularity or sequence, and that these are to some extent analogous to that growth in morality, increased emphasis on thought and planning, and increased sense of self-awareness that characterize the normal psychological development of an individual.

Second, we need to devise some method for rating the level of socio-economic development achieved by a society. If a method for assessing the advance of a society is to correspond to that which we have proposed for rating individuals, then it should indicate the relative emphasis on conceptual thought within a society and the degree of reciprocal concern for the welfare of oneself and others. Such measures are not easy to achieve, but as a very rough approximation for the first of these variables the writer proposes two indices, degree of literacy and technological development. These are both accessible to relatively direct measurement. Reciprocity, unfortunately, is not so open to objective assessment.

Following this line of reasoning, we should expect that the relationship between the educational and socioeconomic level of societies and their dominant behavior styles in pathology should correspond to those observed between individual psychological development and pathological behavior style. Studies conducted within other cultures suggest that there is indeed some relation between the literacy and technological level of a society and its dominant pathological forms. Thus, Benedict and Jacks (3) have proposed that the high incidence in nonliterate societies of pathology marked by confused excitement, often combined with homicidal behaviors, and the contrasting rarity of depressive states, implies that in these societies the psychotic's hostility is directed outward, whereas in advanced Western societies this hostility is more often directed inward.

As these authors have noted, Western culture presents a significant contrast to many nonliterate cultures in the mechanisms of conscience and self-control. In backward societies responsibility for one's fate tends to be shifted to supernatural powers, to the virtual exclusion of ideas of free will and personal responsibility, so that the individual suffers from a minimum of self-reproach or feelings of guilt. From the historical perspective, Barbu (1) likewise has observed that in advanced societies "the external function of society in preventing crime is partly handed over to the inner processes of guilt and atonement." It appears, then, that in a technologically backward society, pathology is likely to be expressed in a self-centered tendency to blame others for one's difficulties. In contrast, in technologically more advanced societies, the patient's preoccupations are more often apt to center on a feeling of personal guilt indicative of a pathologically exaggerated sense of moral responsibility for the welfare of others.

As we might also expect from the theoretical position just outlined, we find that in technologically less advanced societies, psychopathology tends to be action oriented, affect is either explosive or apathetic, and thought typically is extremely disordered. In more advanced societies, psychopathology is more often expressed in thought rather than in action, and the person is often depressed emotionally, while thought is often relatively rational. For example, the psychoneuroses, which comprise the milder forms of psychopathology, have rarely been observed in nonliterate societies, although they are relatively common in more advanced cultures (24).

In summary, we provided evidence in earlier chapters that in the pathological individual achieved level of psychological development substantially influences the form taken by disorder. The burden of the present section was to show that this same relationship holds also within a number of divergent cultures. We do not claim, however, that the same forms of pathology are dominat within all societies. On the contrary, it is proposed that the pathological forms dominant in a society will reflect the characteristic ways that individuals in that culture adopt in attempting to fulfill the expectations with which their society confronts its members according to their place in society. The next section is devoted to an examination of evidence that bears on this proposition.

## CROSSCULTURAL DIFFERENCES IN PATHOLOGY

In this section we want to examine differences in psychopathology from one society to another. Unfortunately, this is not an easy task, in part because of technical difficulties that beset collection of the necessary data. First, psychiatric facilities are unevenly distributed across the world and where facilities do not exist, cases cannot be reported. Consequently, prevalence figures from one society to another must be viewed skeptically. Second, the European and American system of diagnosis has been the dominant method of classification of disorder. While this provides a rough comparability of data collected in many studies, the behavior deviations in cultures that differ widely from a European model do not fall happily into the slots provided by the standard method of classification. Thus, in nonliterate societies, one of the problems in the detection of schizophrenia and other psychiatric disorders that are marked by severe disturbances in thought is the degree to which these societies fail to distinguish between logical and alogical thought. In this regard, Benedict (2) has observed that technologically backward cultures are suffused with magical devices and supernaturalism whereby the deluded thought content of the psychotic may be reinforced. In this magico-religious world the schizophrenic is often able to escape detection. For example, in Brazilian rural society it is considered possible to talk to God, but probably only schizophrenic individuals do so in the form of visual or auditory hallucinations. The contrasting emphasis in Western society on rational and objective thought makes it considerably more difficult for the psychotic individual to adjust and escape detection. Even in Western societies schizophrenics drawn from different ethnic groups often manifest widely divergent symptom pictures. For example, Opler and Singer (17) have described a group of schizophrenic patients of Irish ancestry as latent homosexuals and as being dominated by fixed delusions revolving about sin and guilt. In contrast, they characterized a group of schizophrenics of Italian ancestry as often overtly homosexual, frequently hypochondriacal, and marked by violent acting-out behavior with only slight, scattered, and changeable delusions.

Conceivably, ethnic diversity in symptomatology might be hypothesized as corresponding to genetic differences, but this assumption is not easily maintained for other observations of symptom differences. For example, Japanese schizophrenics in Japan are described as physically assaultive whereas Japanese schizophrenics in Hawaii are described as suspicious and suffering from ideas of being controlled or influenced. Thus, persons of the same racial stock who are assigned the same diagnosis develop different kinds of symptoms, depending on the society in which they live.

An alternative to the use of traditional diagnostic categories in intercultural research on psychopathology is to base case classifications on the more objective criterion of specific symptom manifestation. Our own intercultural studies (8–11), as well as those by several other authors, are based upon the symptom as a discrete unit of comparison. Elsewhere (18) we have outlined at length some of the advantages that attend the choice of symptom as the basis of intercultural comparison. Most important, tabulation of explicit symptoms is expected to interpose less of observer and cultural bias than would global diagnostic statements.

Whether symptoms, diagnostic labels, or other descriptive statements are used, problems of finding comparable or matched psychopathological samples inevitably arise. In our own work, we have tried to cope with these issues by equating subjects from several culturally and geographically distinct sites on several social and biographical variables: sex, age, education, occupational level, and a composite estimate of social competence. Moreover, since we were unable to perform major epidemiological studies that would encompass all the identified manifestations of psychopathology at two or more points of the globe, we settled for the expedient of matching the limited available samples of our studies in diagnostic characteristics. In this way, we made our samples less representative of the populations from which they were drawn. But at the same time, we slanted the composition of our samples in the direction of the null hypothesis and therefore could legitimately place a higher degree of confidence in any differences obtained.

Earlier in this chapter we were concerned with a test of the universality of a set of psychological and behavioral relationships. By contrast, the comparison of symptomatology across culture lines, to which the present section is addressed, has been undertaken without the benefit of theoretical preconceptions or hypotheses that were formulated in advance. In keeping with this exploratory orientation, our attention was first directed to the relative frequencies of discrete symptoms among Argentine and North American psychiatric patients. For the purpose of this study a psychiatric sample in the United States was carefully matched with the 33 Argentine patients described in the previous section. Symptom differences between these groups may be described in terms of several conceptually coherent clusters. Pathology in Argentina is frequently expressed through reactions of estrangement, withdrawal, loss of interest in interpersonal relationships and reality-oriented pursuits, as well as through a qualitative impoverishment of behavior. North American patients, on the other hand, manifest a constellation of behaviors expressive of conspicuous disorganization and behavioral explosiveness. The results of comparing the number of symptoms in the more formal categories of Role Orientation and modality supplement and confirm the foregoing impressions. The role orientation of Turning Against Others is encountered significantly more frequently among North American patients. Further, more individuals among our North American sample are affect dominant and there is a significant tendency among Argentines to rely upon somatization as a predominant mode of symptom expression.

A second study (11) carried out by the writer and his collaborators explored contrasts in symptomatology between Japanese and North American patients. From the sample of Japanese psychiatric patients described in the previous section we undertook to match patients individually with a sample of patients drawn from out North American psychiatric population. Two carefully equated samples were constructed that consisted of 50 male subjects each whose demographic, social, and diagnostic characteristics did not significantly differ from each other. A comparison of symptom manifestation in these two groups indicates that they do not differ in Role Orientation and there is only suggestive evidence pointing to a disproportionately high representation of the Thought sphere among North American patients. For individual symptoms, the picture is quite different. A high proportion of the symptoms of the Japanese psychiatric patients tend to express an impulsive emotional lability that may eventuate in phsysical assault, and yet a brooding withdrawal from the company of one's fellowman. In contrast, a major share of the symptomatology of North American psychiatric patients appears to be given to self-destructive thoughts, and yet alternatively, there is also a high representation of sexual perversions. Whether this last finding represents some true difference in behavior between Japanese and American patients, or simply expresses differences in the forms of deviant behavior to which psychiatrists in these countries are differentially sensitized, is unknown.

What is the import of these two studies? First, they provide another demonstration that diagnostic statements do not adequately describe the differences in the expression of psychopathology from one culture to another. Thus, Argentines, Japanese, and North Americans of the same diagnostic description appear to differ in behavior in ways responsive to the attitudes and values that inhere in their cultural milieu. The challenge to the investigator of intercultural diversity in psychopathology is to relate this panorama of human maladaptiveness to the corresponding more adequate and appropriate modes of behavior that predominate in the same milieu. To date, this task has barely been initiated. In this regard, we know of no systematic data that reflect the parallels of divergences in behavior patterns that exist between the healthy and pathological members of the three societies that we have compared in this paper. Our own results, however, may be useful in delineating axes of intercultural difference that should be further explored in crosscultural investigations concerned with the behavior of modal, as well as deviant, members of the two cultures. Along these lines, the comparative investigation of Argentine and North American patients yielded a number of symptom differences that could easily be placed along the axis of passivity to activity, a dimension that, as Diaz Guerrero (7) maintains, may be descriptive of the culture contrast between the two Americas. In reference to the culture groups compared in the Japanese-American study, we are struck by the global, diffuse, and unmodulated character of Japanese symptomatology, in contrast to the equally maladaptive, but more highly focused and crystallized behavior patterns of the psychiatrically hospitalized residents of the United States. This difference appears particularly marked in the realm of aggressive expression and, in this respect, echoes the findings obtained earlier with an overlapping, but not identical, sample of Japanese patients (20). It would seem that aggression is likely to remain suppressed in an undifferentiated, unmodulated state in a society such as that of Japan, in which interpersonal decorum and propriety are greatly stressed. When expressed during the states of clinical disturbances, aggression comes to the surface in an all-or-none, diffuse manner.

Another explanation is possible for the more frequent incidence of physical aggression among Japanese schizophrenics than their American counterparts. Japanese society is in a period of rapid change ("Americanization"), with a breaking down of old family patterns. There are indications that as family ties loosen, a concurrent moral laxness also becomes manifest with a lessened sense of responsibility for others and an increased self-centeredness. Ideally, these findings should be brought into correspondence with empirically established knowledge of culture and personality characteristics in Argentina, Japan, and the United States, for the conceptual position espoused here proposes that psychopathology does not represent a behavioral aberration *sui generis*, but relates in some lawful manner to the cultural characteristics of the milieu in which it appears. That is, we propose there is a correspondence, or perhaps complementarity, between the typical behavior patterns of the normal and deviant members of a society. The task of the intercultural investigator is to articulate these correspondences. Yet we find that this task has rarely, if ever, been attempted. Rather, we are impressed by the fact that intercultural studies of psychopathology, on the one hand, and of normal personality and behavior, on the other, have been carried on in airtight isolation from each other.

If this isolation were broken down, exploration of a number of conceptual issues might proceed. Thus, we could ask if the maladaptive responses found within a given society represent a contrast to, or an exaggeration of, its modal behavior patterns. Some investigators, for example Schooler and Caudill (20), favor a contrast interpretation. On the other hand, our own data from Argentina suggest that psychopathology expresses an exaggeration of the prevailing cultural behavior pattern. We must wait for future studies to resolve this issue.

To this point we have provided evidence that pathological expression is substantially influenced by the cultural context in which it appears. A logical corollary to this observation is that changes in the values and expectations of a society should bring about corresponding shifts in its common forms of pathology. The final section of this chapter is concerned with the validity of this proposition.

Culture Change and Pathology

It is widely recognized that the nature of American society and its value system have changed markedly since the turn of the century. As May (15) has written: "Everybody knows that at some point in the twentieth century America went through a cultural revolution. One has only to glance at the family photograph album, or to pick up a book or magazine dated, say,

1907, to find oneself in a completely vanished world.... At some point, if not an instantaneous upheaval, there must have been a notable quickening of the pace of change, a period when things began to move so fast that the past, from then on, looked static...." And Marshal Fishwick (12) goes on to elaborate this concept: "Descartes was being supplanted by Einstein; the static by the fluid; causality by purpose; harmony by dissonance; product by process. The single-mindedness of Victorian days gave way to ambivalence and a plurality of feeling. Soldiers died in the Spanish-American War quoting the Founding Fathers. The G.I. Joes of World War II went out quoting Ernest Hemingway." Or as Wheelis (23) has put it: "The key words of our time are flexibility, adjustment, and warmth—as, for our grandfather, they were work, thrift, and will."

The pattern of living has shifted from an adherence to fixed standards for behavior to an acceptance of rules as relative, flexible, and multiple. Wheelis has said that today we tend to conduct ourselves according to the mores of society, not according to internalized moral standards of conduct. Mores refer to prevailing practice, to what is customary in the present, and therefore temporary and relative, whereas morals refer to what is transcendent, permanent, and absolute. They concern matters of principle, not of practice.

Formerly, morality was instilled predominantly by parental figures; today, it is apt to be absorbed from one's contemporaries. Presumably this is the result of the accelerated rate of cultural change. If changes in social values occur with rapidity, the cues will more likely derive from one's peers rather than one's parents. Thus, the peer group has gained in power and dominance while the internalized sources of conscience have withered in significance. Adjustment to the present has become preeminent over coming to terms with conscience, which found its source in early experience: "morality has changed in content. Many things at which our grandparents would have drawn the line now pass muster; and we balk at some things which caused them no compunction" (23).

Two interrelated changes in the nature of conscience distinguish our present culture from that of even the recent past. The first is a more general tolerance in the social mores for the expression of previously tabooed sexual and aggressive behaviors. In particular, parents are generally more permissive of these behaviors in their children. The second change is a heightened awareness of moral relativism; for instance, that which may be unacceptable behavior within one's own group may well become accepted in the near future, since approval of conduct once disapproved has occurred within the span of only a few years. A typical example of such increased permissiveness is in the range of sexual experiences now portrayed on the movie screens of neighborhood theaters. The theme of homosexuality has become commonplace, and significantly the message conveyed is a disapproval of those who act against the homosexual, by either gossip or blackmail.

The very recognition of moral relativism tends to speed the rate of change of moral standards. As we realize that the conventions we live by *are* arbitrary conventions and not the inevitables of human experience, they are to that extent already exposed to attrition by the tests of their appropriateness to the present and the satisfactions to be derived from social conformity.

A major consequence of a rapidly evolving and flexible morality is the expanded range of feelings, fantasies, and actions that have become socially acceptable, and therefore accessible to individual awareness. It is no longer forbidden to feel afraid in battle, to recognize in oneself extramarital sexual interests, to be angry with one's parents. As Wheelis observed, "there has occurred in society as a whole during the past two generations a development analogous to that which occurs in an individual during psychoanalysis, an expression of awareness at the expense of the unconcious."

Wheelis has also described the growing emphasis on individuality in our present era. He wrote that "modern man has become more perceptive of covert motivations, in both himself and others. Areas of experience formerly dissociated from consciousness have become commonplace knowledge. Passivity, anxiety, disguised hostility, masochism, latent homosexuality—these are not new with the present generation; what is new is the greater awareness of them." But Wheelis believes that individualism also means "self-reliance, productive self-sufficiency, following one's chosen course despite social criticism, and bearing personally the risks of one's undertakings; and all of these are on the wane. Ours is an age of reliance on experts, of specialized production, of deference to public opinion, and of collective security." He has said:

Identity is a coherent sense of self. It depends upon the awareness that one's endeavors and one's life make sense, that they are meaningful in the context in which life is lived. It depends also upon stable values, and upon the conviction that one's actions and values are harmoniously related. It is a sense of wholeness, of integration, of knowing what is right and what is wrong and of being able to choose.

During the past fifty years there has been a change in the experienced quality of life, with the result that identity is now harder to achieve and harder to maintain. The formerly dedicated Marxist who now is unsure of everything; the Christian who loses his faith; the workman who comes to feel that his work is piecemeal and meaningless; the scientist who decides that science is futile, that the fate of the world will be determined by power politics—such persons are of out time, and they suffer the loss or impairment of identity.

If our basic premise is valid, that pathological behavior style is a facet of an enduring life-style, then these recent dramatic changes in the American world view should have influenced the forms of pathology dominant in

American society. To test this proposition it is necessary to ask if indeed pathological types have changed drastically over the last half century, and further, whether such possible changes are in accordance with these reputed shifts in American life-style. Let us turn to the hard evidence that bears on these issues.

### Changes Over Time in Types of American Pathology

Various investigators have noted changes in the dominant forms of psychiatric disorder in American society. Thus, Malzberg (14) has reported a continuous decrease in first-admission rates to New York State hospitals for manic-depressive psychoses in the period 1909–1951. Women are consistently more prone to this disorder, yet for both sexes the drop in rates is quite dramatic. During this period of 42 years, the rate per 100,000 population decreased from 4.5 to 1.9 for men and for women from 7.4 to 3.1. During the period 1917–1933, however, a time that included both a major war and depression for the United States, this general trend for the manic-depressive disorders was reversed and their incidence increased. This specific finding conforms to data on the 1917–1933 first-admission rates in Massachusetts for manic-depressive psychoses provided by Dayton (6).

Hysterical neuroses are another form of disorder that is reported as becoming less frequent. Exact statistics are not generally available on the prevalence of the milder forms of psychopathology, but there is general consensus that cases of hysteria, once the prime example of neurotic repression, are now rare. Wheelis (23), Chodoff (5), von Bertalanffy (4), and Jackson (13) concur in this observation.

In contrast, criminal and delinquent behaviors appear to have become more common. Juvenile delinquency, for instance, rose approximately 230% between 1940 and 1959, at a time when the number of 10- to 17-year-olds rose only 25%. During the years of World War II, a particularly striking rise in delinquency rates took place that diminished in the postwar period (21). Total crime rates per 100,000 also showed a significant rise of 70% in the years 1940–1959, with a slight decrease during the war years. The number of arrests correspondingly has risen, during the period from 1940 to 1960, 102% for those under 18 and 53% for those 18 years old and over. World War II brought about a definite upsurge in arrests within the younger group and a decline in the older group (22). These discrepant shifts in arrests for crime may, in the case of older men, reflect their withdrawal from the home into the armed services, and for younger persons, the loss of a controlling father or older brothers. Other factors that must be considered are the inevitable disruption of home life when there is an absence of key family figures, a high proportion of working mothers, and a growing trend for families to become migratory.

While the population of the United States rose approximately 18.5% from the 1950 to 1960 censuses, crimes for which directly comparable data are available rose between 60 and 90%, and this includes crimes of theft and violence (22). A similar increase in violations of the narcotic drug laws has taken place. In contrast, arrests for prostitution and rape have tended to decrease (22). The indications are that violence and self-indulgent transgressions of traditional morality are on the increase, and are expressed in the increased rates of theft and narcotic addiction. The decreased frequency of reported rape and arrests for prostitution suggest a widened range of sexual freedom among females, rather than a stricter observance of a moral code. In support of this assumption, it will be noted that other sexual offenses, including sexual relations with girls below the legal age of consent, show no such drop in rate.

Malzberg (14) has provided data on first admissions for dementia praecox (schizophrenia) to the New York State Hospital system for the years 1909–1951 inclusive. During this period there was a consistent rise in first-admission rates for both men and women suffering with this disorder. The increase was 10.8 to 31.5 per population, for men, and 10.0 to 31.0 for women. Further, a marked shift has occurred recently in the proportion of cases that fall into the various subcategories of schizophrenia, such as the hebephrenic, catatonic, and simple subtypes, all of which have almost disappeared. For instance, of 500 first-admission cases of mental disorder admitted to Worcester State Hospital during 1962–1965, there were no cases of hebephrenic or catatonic schizophrenia and only a single case of simple schizophrenia.

It is conceivable that all these apparent changes in the incidence of psychiatric disorder are the consequence of changes in diagnostic style or shifts in dominant attitudes within American society. It may be that the true incidence of the various forms of psychological and social disorder has remained static. It has been suggested, for example, that cases of manic-depressive reaction are now treated in the community and frequently never reach the mental hospital, or alternatively that many cases that would previously have been included among the manic-depressive disorders are now diagnosed as schizophrenia or neurosis. It has also been pointed out that crime reports are notoriously unreliable, fluctuating with the budgetary or political needs of individual police forces. Further, popular attitudes have relented toward certain forms of atypical behavior, such as homosexuality, and the legal status of drug addicts and alcoholics has likewise changed under the impact of recent Supreme Court decisions. Similarly, police officers may tend to adopt a somewhat greater skepticism than previously in cases where rape is claimed, expressing in this way the increased psychological sophistication of our times.

For all these reasons, changes in the reported incidence of disorder are suspect. There is no easy or obvious way to overcome this barrier to establishing the true rates of disorder. Certain comments, however, are in order. First, some of the limitations on the reliability of classification are random in nature and should even out over time. Some of the pressures that modify crime reports, for example, wax and wane according to local conditions and should average out in national statistics. Second, it is quite understandable that influences in society that tend to shift the frequency of deviant behaviors will also affect the attitudes of those who classify these behaviors. To claim that reported incidence rates reflect attitude modification in those who do the reporting is not to gainsay corresponding true changes in deviant behaviors. Third, and most important, the only proposition made here is that change in the values and attitudes dominant in a society does influence the true rate of occurrence in a wide variety of pathological responses. It is not essential to the validity of this hypothesis that culture variables be the sole source of this fluctuation in incidence levels. In contrast, to propose that no true change has taken place over the last half century in the frequency of various forms of disorder is to deny that profound shifts in cultural forms, attitudes, and values have had any influence on deviant modes of response to the conditions of life in our society. This denial requires a heterogeneous array of reasons to explain away the manifest changes over time in the observed rates of different pathological response patterns.

Specifically, it is suggested that shifts in the reported rate of the various types of deviance are approximations to true changes in their incidence, and reflect extensive changes in personal values and attitudes in American life. They represent an increased awareness and toleration of personal motives that, as little as half a century ago, would have been most severely disapproved. Extension in the range of experience that is permissible corresponds in time to a decrease in those disorders that are manifestations of repression (hysteria) or of self-depreciatory attitudes toward one's achievements and in a sense of moral rectitude (manic-depressive disorders). The decrease in hysterical neuroses, which are considered in psychoanalytic theory to represent defensive measures against the overt expression of sexual wishes, may be indicative of an increased societal and personal tolerance of sexual feelings, fantasies, and behaviors that previously were taboo. In contrast, this century has witnessed both a general increase in violent and self-indulgent pathologies expressed in rising rates of delinquency, crime, and addictions.

Wheelis also has commented that psychoanalysts are increasingly faced with disorders that do not conform to the traditional syndromes. Most common today in the practice of psychoanalysis, he believes, are patients who suffer from vague states of discomfort, a sense of isolation, and a lack of goals and direction. They come to the therapist complaining of loneliness, doubts, insecurity, unhappiness, lack of fulfillment, boredom, and restlessness. Perhaps the reported increase in the incidence of schizophrenic disorders is associated with a generalized increase in a sense of isolation pervasive in American society.

As noted in Chapter 8, the diagnoses of personality and character disorders are most closely associated with symptoms of turning against others; a diagnosis of schizophrenia with symptoms indicative of withdrawal from others, and of the manic-depressive disorders with symptoms of turning against the self. Recent changes in the incidence of the various diagnostic groups may reflect changes in role emphasis in our society. This century has witnessed both a general increase in violence, theft, and self-indulgent pathologies and an increased sense of isolation and alienation. At the same time, the decrease in manic-depressive disorders suggests a lessened tendency to blame oneself or wrongdoing and a decreased harshness in the moral tone of society.

## REFERENCES

1.  Barbu, Z. *Problems of historical psychology*. New York: Grove Press, 1960.
2.  Benedict, P. K. Socio-cultural factors in schizophrenia. In L. Bellak (Ed.), *Schizophrenia*. New York: Logos Press, 1958. Pp. 694–729.
3.  Benedict, P. K., & Jacks, L. Mental illness in primitive societies. *Psychiatry*, 1954, **17**, 377–389.
4.  Bertalanffy, L. von. Some biological considerations sof the problem of mental illness. In L. Appleby, J. M. Scher, and J. Cumming (Eds.), *Chronic schizophrenia*. Glencoe, Ill.: Free Press, 1960. Pp. 36–53.
5.  Chodoff, P. A reexamination of some aspects of conversion hysteria. *Psychiatry*, 1954, **17**, 75–81.
6.  Dayton, M. A. *New facts on mental disorders*. Springfield, Ill.: Charles C. Thomas, 1940.
7.  Diaz Guerrero, R. La dicotomía activo-pasiva en la investigación transcultural. In M. B. Jones (Ed.), *Proceedings of the Ninth Congress of the Interamerican Society of Psychology*. Miami: Interamerican Society of Psychology, 1964. Pp. 144–149.
8.  Draguns, J. G., Knobel, M., Fundia Toba A. de, Broverman, Inge K., & Phillips, L. Social competence, psychiatric symptomatology and culture. In M. B. Jones (Ed.), *Proceedings of the Ninth Interamerican Congress of Psychology*. Miami: Interamerican Society of Psychology, 1964. Pp. 610–615.
9.  Draguns, J. G., Knobel, M., Fundia, Toba A. de, Broverman, Inge K., & Phillips, L. Sintomatología psiquiátrica y cultura: Investigación intercultural. *Acta Psiquiatrica y Psicologica de la American Latina*, 1966, **12**, 77–83.
10. Draguns, J. G., Nachshon, I., Broverman, I. K., & Phillips, L, Ethnic differences in psychiatric symptomatology: study of an Israeli child guidance clinic population. Paper presented at the Eastern Psychological Association, Boston, April 1967.
11. Draguns, J. G., Phillips, L., Broverman, I. K., Caudill, W., and Nishimae, S. Psychiatric symptoms in relation to social competence and culture: A study of Japanese patients. In C. E. Hereford (Ed.), *Proceedings of the Tenth Interamerican Congress of Psychology*. Austin, Tex.: University of Texas Press, 1967, p. 462.
12. Fishwick, M. The twist: Brave new whirl. *Saturday Review*, 1962, March 3, 8–10.

13. Jackson, D. D. A critique of the literature on the genetics of schizophrenia. In D. D. Jackson (Ed.), *The etiology of schizophrenia*. New York: Basic Books, 1960. Pp. 37–87.
14. Malzberg, B. Important statistical data about mental illness. In S. Arieti (Ed.), *American handbook of psychiatry*. New York: Basic Books, 1959. Pp. 161–174.
15. May, H. F. *The end of American innocence*. New York: Knopf, 1959.
16. Muramatsu, T. (Ed.) Nihonjin: Bunka to pasonarity no jissho-taki kenkyu. (The Japanese: Study in culture and personality). Nagoya: Reimei Shobo, 1962. (Reviewed by T. Sofue, in *Transcultural Psychiatric Research*, 1964. **1**, 100–102).
17. Opler, M. K., & Singer, J. L. Ethnic differences in behavior and psychopathology: Italian and Irish. *International Journal of Social Psychiatry*. 1956, **2**, 11–23.
18. Phillips, L. & Draguns, J. G. Some issues in intercultural research on psychopathology. In W. Caudill & T. Y. Lin (Eds.), *Mental health in Asia and the Pacific*. Honolulu: East-West Center Press, in press.
19. Phillips, L., & Zigler, E. Social competence: The action-thought parameter and vicariousness in normal and pathological behvariors. *Journal of Abnormal and Social Psychology*, 1961, **63**, 137–146.
20. Schooler, C., & Caudill, W. Symptomatology in Japanese and American schizophrenics. *Ethnology*, 1964, **3**, 172–177.
21. Uniform Crime Reports for the United States, J. Edgar Hoover, Director, Federal Bureau of Investigation, U. S. Department of Justive, Washington, D. C., 1959.
22. Uniform Crime Reports for the United States, J. Edgar Hoover, Director, Federal Bureau of Investigation, U. S. Department of Justice, Washington, D. C., 1960.
23. Wheelis, A. *The quest for identity*. New York: Norton, 1958.
24. Wittkower, E. D., & Fried, J. Some problems of transcultural psychiatry. In M. K. Opler (Ed.), *Culture and mental health*. New York: Macmillan, 1959. Pp. 489–500.

# 12 / THE SOCIAL BASES OF

# ADAPTATION AND FAILURE

To this point we have been concerned with the role played by psychological variables in social adaptation and pathology. In particular, we have discussed psychological development and behavior style as determinants of adaptive and deviant patterns of behavior. We have also reviewed the influence of sociocultural factors on the form taken by psychopathology. We have not, however, yet considered the way in which environmental variables play a role in determining success in adaptation and in the emergence of pathological forms of behavior.

A tendency to minimize the role of environment is pervasive in the clinical disciplines. Perhaps this deficit is a consequence of the insights that have been achieved in the last three fourths of a century into personality mechanisms and their deviations. It was Freud who succeeded in articulating the latent rationality in the ostensibly irrational acts of the psychiatrically deviant individual. Freud's great contribution to the understanding of human behavior was the concept of the unconscious. Its general theme is that a person's behavior is guided not alone by intentions of which he is aware, but also in significant yet unrealistic ways by psychic factors that lie outside conscious experience. After Freud it was impossible to maintain that the meaning of human behavior could be apprehended by direct observation alone. Any sophisticated understanding required the classification and interpretation of behaviors in terms of a covert intrapsychic dimension of human function.

Investigators of a psychodynamic persuasion stress individual differences in stimulus sensitization and response potential. They are concerned, for example, with the oral fixation of the alcoholic and its translation into drinking behavior, or with the exquisite sensitivity of the paranoid to slight with its consequence in delusions of persecution. The concern of these investigators is primarily with those characteristics of the person that lead him to act in one rather than another clinically meaningful way. Interest in specifying the conditions that will precipitate the type of pathological behavior to which an individual may be predisposed is minimal. It seems sufficient for these writers to recognize that under conditions of an "average expectable environment" (16) people can diverge substantially in their ways of behavior. The proponents of the intrapsychic position have done little to elaborate our knowledge of precisely what constitutes an environment, or of the trigger mechanisms that elicit deviant behaviors in predisposed people.

The interactionist position advanced here proposes that prediction in psychology requires us to focus on the determinants of behavior that lie both within and outside the person, for behavior is not simply an expression of individuality, but a transaction between the subject and his environment. That is, we cannot predict an act solely on the basis of knowledge of a person, no matter how complete or theoretically precise this information may be. Prediction requires equally a congruent insight into those determinants of behavior that reside in the environment. Behavior is conceptualized as an interaction between predisposing factors within the person and precipitating circumstances in the environment.

It follows that in order to develop an adequately predictive science of behavior we need to develop as thorough a theoretical understanding of environment as of personality. In principle, we should be as able to predict behavior, having knowledge only of environmental factors and assuming an "average expectable personality," as we now may do based on an understanding of personality variables alone. Indeed, much of prediction in economics, such as future stock market performance or anticipated demand for housing, is based on precisely this method of analysis. Hence, prediction should be enhanced when personality and environmental factors are both taken into account.

Two facets of contemporary theorizing and research shed light on the role that environment plays in determining behavior. One of these capitalizes on the ubiquitous and insistent nature of information seeking in both humans (4, 17, 19, 27) and animals (31). It appears that all species strive toward an optimal level of stimulus input. On the one hand, a low level of information input is eschewed in order to avoid boredom; on the other, a high level is avoided to escape an excessive variety of intensity of stimulation. This interpretation of organismic–environment interrelations may help us understand the role of the social and interpersonal milieu in human behavior. The social environment is of major significance as a source of stimulation and of information relevant to survival in a world of uniquely human significance. The stimulating and organizing properties of the social environment play significant roles in the efficacy of the individual's adaptive pattern.

## THE GROUP

The interpersonal environment of which the individual is a part provides stimulation and cues to guide his behavior. When the information input corresponds to the level and type of adaptive resources at the person's command, he is able to live in harmony with the social setting in which he takes part.

A particularly striking example of the group fulfilling its enveloping and protective function is to be found within the religious sect of the Hutterites. This order has been studied intensively from both the psychiatric and the sociological points of view. The Hutterites originated in Germany during the Protestant Reformation, transferred to Russia under the duress of religious persecution, and eventually settled in South Dakota in 1874. They now number nearly 5000 members, gathered into a number of closely knit communistic farming communities distributed over several north central states and Canadian provinces.

Several principles of living characterize these Hutterite communities. All property is owned by the group. The members are dedicated to a life of austere simplicity and of self-sufficiency, as nearly as this can be approximated. The leadership in each community frowns on education beyond that modest degree required for practical affairs and attempts to isolate the community from the outside world, modifying their way of life only very slowly as the changing values of the group make necessary. There is much stress on duty both to God and to one's fellow man and there is much social pressure to restrict the expression of hostile attitudes. Children as well as adults are taught to look for guilt within themselves rather than in others. Although people with various forms of psychopathology exist in this sect, they are well cared for within the community, if possible at home. No stigma attaches to mental disorder and the entire community is aroused to demonstrate love and support for these unfortunates. The only forms of deviant behavior that are frowned upon are antisocial acts and self-destruction. Suicide is considered a profound transgression of God's laws and a depressed patient is carefully guarded to prevent suicidal acts. The Hutterite patient himself will consider suicidal ideas a temptation of the devil and will struggle desperately against carrying out the act. The success of religious teaching and of community response to the danger of suicide is shown in that only two cases of successful attempts at suicide are known among the Hutterites since their arrival in America in 1874, and one of these was carried out by a man several years after he left the sect.

Eaton and Weil (13) report the Hutterite lifetime morbidity rate for psychosis as third among ten communities studied across the world. Their true rank, however, is probably much lower, for these authors systematically sought out each case within the community, whereas the case-finding method was much less direct among the other groups reported. Perhaps most dependable is the relative occurrence of the various types of disorder. Cases of schizophrenia were rare and Eaton and Weil also reported the virtual absence of severe personality disorders, obsessive-compulsive neuroses, psychopathic conditions, and psychoses associated with syphilis, alcoholism, and drug addiction. They did not find a single case of murder, assault, or rape, and physical aggressiveness of any sort was quite rare. No Hutterite had been involved in a sex crime that came to the attention of the authorities and there were no known acts of overt homosexuality. The form of disorder most frequently observed were depressed states at both a psychotic and neurotic level of severity. It is of interest to note that this most common form of pathology reflects the Hutterite demand that each individual live up to the strict sense of obligation imposed by the group's value system. Virtually absent are those antisocial pathologies not tolerated by group norms as well as the schizophrenic reactions that tend to express an alienation from group life.

This study by Eaton and Weil suggests that a closely knit and highly structured community tends to reduce, although not to eliminate, the prevalence of palpable psychiatric disturbance. Most striking is the influence of the Hutterite form of community life on the dominant forms of pathology. Research on the Hutterite sect indicates the predominance of depressive affect and ideation at both clinical and subclinical levels within their self-contained community. Remarkable is the dearth of cases classifiable as schizophrenic disorders or personality and character deviations. These observations are consistent with the formulation put forward by Arieti (2), who maintained that depression is the psychopathology of social overintegration, and schizophrenia that of social disintegration. Empirical support for this hypothesis comes from a recent report by Chance (5), who observed a high degree of correspondence between the occurrence of self-depreciative symptomatology and the cohesive nature of the social environment. This interpretation is based upon the study of depressive manifestations in 39 cultures representing a wide range of social structures and controls.

## PRESSURES FOR CONFORMITY

So far, our concern has been with the forces at work within a group that give it cohesion, and their consequences in the prevalence and form of psychopathology. At this point, we want to examine more closely the way these social forces operate to mold and constrain the behaviors of group members. What precisely are the social pressures that keep people in line, and what is the source of their obvious great strength? After all, most people feel the strain of continuously behaving as they are expected to and at one time or another would love to "break out." Yet, relatively few people ever do. Cohen (7) has proposed that there exist three sets of factors that press for conformity. These are: (a) the objective consequences of action in either satisfaction or deprivation; (b) role definitions that tend to set limits to action; and (c) moral imperatives. Both (b) and (c) generally support conformity to the mores of the group.

We shall discuss first the objective consequences of action. These are of two types. One consists of satisfaction or deprivation of goods or services, including food, clothing, shelter, money, medical care, entertainment, and so on. The other involves fulfillment or loss of social-emotional needs based on relationships with other persons or groups. Goods and services are distributed through an array of social structures including the family, the work setting, fraternal organization, and the church. To obtain the goods and services desired, the individual must participate in these organizations on their own terms.

Satisfaction of social-emotional needs is dependent on the expression of gratifying emotional responses by others with whom we value such relationships. These responses by the relevant others are dependent on the criteria by which they judge the individual's personal qualities and conduct. To the extent that a person's reference groups are themselves integrated into the general social order, his social-emotional security is dependent on his conformity to societal expectations. Institutions and social systems typically fulfill not one but many wants, both social and nonsocial, and isolation from any of these, the family, neighborhood, or work, will deprive the person of a wide range of satisfactions. These contingencies will act as a strong deterrent to deviant behavior, even under conditions of severe strain.

Role consistency and a sense of moral integrity are also sources of impelling human satisfactions. These two factors are easier to differentiate in theory than they are in practice; that is, role expectations for the behavior of different age and sex groups vary and, presumably, internal constraints on behavior will also vary in a corresponding fashion. For example, there are certain moral universals in our culture (e.g., it is wrong to steal), but there are relaxation of these prohibitions for particular groups. Thus, if an adolescent boy steals a car and goes for a joyride, this may be accepted simply as "high spirits," or in terms of a folk attitude of "boys will be boys." Expectations of behavior come to be implicitly reached between the actor and his "normative reference groups," those groups of people who set the limits of acceptable behavior. Violations of these standards are internalized as transgressions of the moral code. When all reference groups set parallel limits to action, transgression of these boundaries becomes virtually impossible, for such behavior raises the danger of being cut off from all forms of emotional support and from all gratification of needs and wants. However, for those who live in a subsociety, such as a slum area, for which the role expectations of society at large are remote and hazy and in which deviant standards are viewed as appropriate by the immediately present adults and peers, violations of general societal expectations are common. This is particularly true when violation is reinforced by direct gratifications, whereas conformity to the standards set by a remote wider society leads only to deprivation.

If a person is a member of a group whose values deviate from those of the larger society, and in which he enjoys a reasonable degree of status, it will be extremely difficult to modify his behavior in the direction set by societal standards, for he possesses neither membership nor status in the general community. Lewin (24), in fact, came to the conclusion that it would be easier to change the behavior of deviant individuals as a group, rather than as social isolates. That is, when the behavior of individuals manifesting a particular form of pathology is to be changed, as for example that of adolescent delinquents or chronic alcoholics, it may be easier to isolate a small group of such persons from their usual social contacts in order to free them from the pressures toward conformity with socially deviant norms. This isolation may then make possible a change in the behavioral expectations of the small subgroup chosen for therapeutic work. A change in individual behavior toward a conformity with the values of society at large, and toward which the values of the small subgroup are moving, will then bring the individual a greater degree of social participation and status in his group, rather than less. In these circumstances therapeutic change becomes possible. This type of reasoning led Lewin (24) to propose the concept of a "cultural island" to describe the activities of summer camps, workshops, and similar techniques for isolating the person from his usual social environment, thus freeing him from fixed standards of thought and behavior. The paradox is that, should he return to his former social group, the pressures toward conformity with previous deviant standards come into play and there is every likelihood that he will relapse into his more firmly established pattern of activities. Without specific reference to Lewin's formulations, analogous principles have been used to achieve dramatic attitude changes based on the techniques of "thought reform" and "brain washing" (18, 25).

## THE BEHAVIOR DEVIATIONS

Theories on the social causation of deviant and pathological behavior patterns have often implied some notion of isolation and breakdown in interpersonal relationships. Why should isolation from the life of the community result in mental disorder or other forms of deviant behavior? Merton (28) has provided probably the most systematic and theoretically most sophisticated analysis of the isolation of the individual from society generally and of why its possible consequences should increase the likelihood of deviant behavior. He attmpts to explain "how some *social structures exert a definite pressure upon certain persons in the society to engage in non-conforming rather than conforming conduct.* If we can locate groups peculiarly subject to such pressures, we should expect to find fairly high rates of deviant behavior in these groups, not because the human beings comprising them are compounded of distinctive biological tendencies but because they are responding normally to the social situation in which they find themselves. . . . Should our quest be at all successful, some forms of deviant behavior will be found to be as psychologically normal as conformist behavior, and the equation of deviation and psychological abnormality will be put in question" (italics in original).

Merton distinguishes two social and cultural structures as important in the determination of conformity or deviance in social behaviors. The first of these are the goals, purposes, or interests set out as legitimate objectives for all or for specific segments of the society. This network of goals he designates as the frame of aspirational reference. The second pertinent facet of the social structure is the set of regulations or acceptable modes of institutionalized norms for reaching these goals. Merton has provided a list of modes of individual adaptation based on acceptance or rejection of either the societally dominant goals or the acceptable means for their achievement. These are listed in Table 12–1.

TABLE 12–1
A TYPOLOGY OF MODELS OF INDIVIDUAL ADAPTATION

| Modes of adaptation | Culture goals | Institutionalized means |
|---|---|---|
| I. Conformity | $+^a$ | $+$ |
| II. Innovation | $+$ | $-$ |
| III. Ritualism | $-$ | $+$ |
| IV. Retreatism | $-$ | $-$ |
| V. Rebellion | $\pm$ | $\pm$ |

[a]The plus sign signifies "acceptancy," the minus sign, "rejection," and plus over minus, "rejection of prevailing values and substitution of new values."

The first mode of adaptation enumerated by Merton is conformity. As he notes and as we have commented earlier, the path of least resistance in a viable society, and the one therefore adopted by most individuals, is simple conformity to societal expectations. The remaining four modes of adaptation described by Merton will be discussed in turn.

## Innovation

When the dominant cultural values extol a set of universal success-goals, while certain classes in the society are systematically denied access to these goals, a high level of deviant behavior is insured. Innovation occurs when the individual does not relinquish the societally structured goals, but nevertheless accepts alternative and socially disapproved means for achieving them.

It is generally true, for example, that people aspire to high-level occupational goals for themselves or their children even if they despair of achieving them. Merton observed that many Negroes and whites of lower occupational levels want professional careers for their children, yet these people are unable to help in the fulfillment of these aspirations. Such a combination of introjected, unrealistically high goals and severely limited opportunities is a likely breeding ground for deviant behaviors. As Merton observed: "it is the *disjunction* between culturally induced high aspirations and socially structured obstacles to realization of these aspirations which is held to exert distinct pressure for deviant behavior" (italics in original). In this situation, delinquent or criminal behavior is a possible outcome.

## Ritualism

This form of adaptation implies the elevation of conformity to the level of a moral mandate and of living according to institutionalized regulations as a preferred way of life. It is the retreat of fusty, bureaucratic minds for which hope is gone of ever achieving meaningful goals, so that the very existence of these is denied as a self-protective mechanism. This should occur most commonly among lower middle-class individuals, for it is the parents of this class who demand that their children live by the moral mandates of society and yet for whom the achievement of high social status is unlikely. The severe and arbitrary morality of this class tends to inculcate an unremitting self-criticism that makes unlikely any deviation from a restrictive and highly conventional morality. Obsessive-compulsive neuroses or depressive states would appear likely pathological forms for such a personality type.

## Retreatism

Retreatism is the consequence of giving up practical efforts for reaching the supreme value of the success-goal, although the wish to achieve success has not yet been renounced. People who adapt in this manner do not participate in society because they have interiorized a twofold conflict: (1) they have accepted the moral obligation to adopt institutionalized means but accessible avenues for effort have not produced success; and (2) they cannot resort to illicit or antisocial means for achieving the thoroughly assimilated general culture goals. Dunham's (11) description of the typical catatonic schizophrenic as the alienated "quiet one" of slum society who accepts the values of the larger community is consistent with the formulation presented here. Because of membership in the lower class they do not have access to those effective means of achieving success, nor can they bring themselves to adopt illegal and generally disapproved means for reaching success and status. People who use this form of adaptation are the nonparticipants of our society, the withdrawn psychotics, vagrants, tramps, chronic alcoholics, and drug addicts. These types are marked by defeatism, quietism, and resignation, mechanisms that eliminate conflict but serve to alienate the individual from society.

### Rebellion

Rebellion encompasses the rejection of both conventional means and ends, both of which have come to be regarded as completely arbitrary. This fifth form of adaptation is qualitatively different from the others. It represents efforts to change the existing social structure and thus moves the realm of behavior into the sphere of political action. The other modes of adaptation correspond to various ways of coming to terms with society as it is, for they all imply an acceptance of its fundamental values. Deviations in behavior expressed by other adaptive typologies are the result of failures or anticipated failures in achieving these goals by legitimate means. The behavior response patterns adopted (Types II, III, IV) are inappropriate in this society and are commonly taken to imply some form of individual psychopathology. In contrast, Merton has suggested that they can more parsimoniously be seen as normal response patterns to socially deviant conditions.

### RESEARCH ON ISOLATION AND PATHOLOGY

A good deal of evidence can be advanced to support Merton's hypothesis that cultural and social isolation or conflict can act to precipitate a variety of pathological reactions. We shall review in turn studies that relate cultural and social isolation to psychiatric disorders, to antisocial behaviors and addictions, and to somatic diseases.

### Isolation and Mental Disorder

Available evidence indicates that individuals who have become isolated from their cultural origins and who at the same time have failed to identify with the society in which they live are the more prone to develop pathological reactions. Thus, Dunham (12) has reported that persons residing in areas not primarily populated by members of their own ethnic group tend to show considerably higher rates of mental disorder than do those of the numerically dominant ethnic group. Similarly, Dayton (8), studying the hospitalization rates of the foreign born in Massachusetts from 1920 to 1930, found a higher rate of mental disorder among those who failed to become naturalized than among those who did.

Parallel conclusions may be derived from a study reported by Srole *et al.* (34). On the basis of responses to a brief questionnaire, these investigators classified their respondents as "attached" or "detached" from their cultural origins. The content of this questionnaire concerned attitudes in the following areas: relative preference for American versus one's native style of cooking; celebration of ethnic get-togethers; and attitudes toward a child marrying outside one's ethnic group. Similarity in language, customs, and religion to those dominant in the United States increased the ethnic detachment score. It was noted that ethnic affiliation, as indicated by scoring on these indices, decreased with increasing number of generations in America. Equating for age and for generation in America, a significant relation emerged between the attached-detached index and mental health scoring. Findings were consistent with the data provided by Dayton in that those individuals who have become acculturated to the American scene show a lesser degree of psychiatric impairment. There are reports (9, 10) that indicate that it is partially acculturated groups, who are in transition somewhere midway between the culture of descent and that of adoption, that are particularly prone to disruption, with their members given to moods of depression and anxiety.

The impact of acculturation is often reported as being expressed in what is known as second generation conflict. Lemert (22), Thomas and Zaniecki (36), and Stonequist (35) have all stressed the intergeneration conflicts between immigrant parents and their children. The latter reject the old-fashioned practices of their parents, and often become what Stonequist has called *marginal people* without secure roots or values. Malzberg (26) has reported that the second generation of mixed parents, one foreign born and one native American, has more commonly developed the socially determined psychoses of alcoholism and general paresis, as well as the psychoses of old age. In general, the children of mixed parents have the highest rates of mental disorder, greater than in marriages where parents are either both native or both foreign born. This suggests that culture conflict that is directly expressed within the family may predispose the offspring to some form of psychopathology.

The studies reviewed to this point have stressed the consequence of cultural isolation and culture conflict in psychiatric impairment. A relationship between social isolation and schizophrenia in particular has been emphasized in the literature. Belknap and Jaco (3) reported a relatively high rate for schizophrenia for those communities in which people reported fewer friends and acquaintances, where there were more rented than owned homes, less organizational membership, less knowledge of neighbors, less visiting, and greater unemployment and job turnover. Confirmatory findings were reported subsequently by Jaco (20). Gerard and Houston (15) have contributed more direct evidence on the relation between schizophrenia and social isolation. In a study of over 300 first-admission male cases of schizophrenia, these authors found that schizophrenic individuals were concentrated among the single, separated, or divorced men who were living alone. Sainsbury (32), similarly, has found a correlation between a high rate of suicide and living alone in a single room in houses broken up into small subdivisions. Thus, suicide, like other forms of social pathology, appears associated with disrupted social relationships.

Kohn and Clausen (21) set out to test the specific hypothesis that social isolation plays a casual role in schizophrenia. They chose a sample of 45 schizophrenic and 13 manic-depressive first-admission patients, and established a group of control subjects individually matched for age, sex, and occupation. On the basis of interviews with the experimental and control subjects these authors found that approximately one third of the schizophrenic and manic-depressive patients and none of the controls showed evidence of social isolation at 13–14 years. Further, there was no evidence that this isolation was based on a lack of available playmates, parental restrictions, or severe illness. Kohn and Clausen concluded that early social isolation is indicative of already existing difficulties in interpersonal relationships.

*Isolation, Antisocial Behavior, and Addiction*

Slums produce a disproportionately high number of persons given to crime, delinquency, and drug addiction. The slums of the largest American cities are populated largely by minority groups, including Negroes, Puerto Ricans, and Mexicans. Wage-earners typically work in low-skill occupations, are underpaid, and yet pay excessively high rents. Life under this set of destructive social conditions sets the stage for an extreme expression of those antisocial behaviors that are a more frequent occurrence in the slums than elsewhere. Thus, Negroes, who constitute approximately 10% of the population, have an arrest record of 30% of the offenses booked by the police. Further, Negroes are charged with nearly two thirds of the most violent crimes—murder, nonnegligent manslaughter, and aggravated assault.

A number of investigators (14, 37, 39) have explored the origins of delinquent behavior. They suggest that the key factor in delinquency is an unstable social setting and the consequent alienation of young people:

a broken home; a migration, such as that of many Puerto Ricans to New York, or of Deep South Negroes northward; a style of life that may have shifted with rising incomes; or working parents who leave children unattended. The causes are several but the outcome is the same. This conceptualization reconciles the seemingly paradoxical observation that delinquency appears at all rungs of the socioeconomic ladder, although disproportionately among the economically deprived. While different in many respects, young law violators from the suburbs and from the slums appear to share one essential characteristic: a disruption of the network of familial and neighborhood ties.

The problem of teen-age use of narcotics typifies the relation between deviant behavior patterns and slum conditions. As reported by Clausen (6), teen-age narcotics users live in areas marked by low income, a high proportion of minority populations, instability of family life, and a high prevalence of other social problems. In Chicago, for example, nearly all narcotic addicts reside in the poorest neighborhoods in the city, which contain one fourth of its population. This same pattern of concentration among drug addicts is found in New York City.

*Isolation and Somatic Disease*

Wittkower and Fried (38) have reviewed a number of reports that indicate that somatic reactions multiply to the extent that the traditional bonds that hold families and communities together are disrupted. For example, Iraquian immigrants who entered Israel as solitary individuals often developed bronchial asthma. These authors also note that persons from primitive inland communities in Peru who are drawn to the urban coastal culture frequently develop psychosomatic symptoms, as did mainland Chinese when they emigrated to Formosa.

A study carried out in Durban, South Africa, on the relation of culture conflict to physical illness has been reported by Abrahamson (1). Degree of ill health in girls was found to be associated with a discrepancy between the degree of modernism or traditionalism of the girl and that of the mother. The greater the discrepancy in style of life between mother and daughter, the higher the incidence of physical symptoms among the offspring.

On the American scene, a relation between the loosening or absence of close personal ties and physical disease has been observed. Thus, physically ill patients suffer a recurrence of symptoms if they become estranged or isolated from those with whom they have had emotionally significant interpersonal relationships (30). Again, in a study of peptic ulcer patients, it was found that in nearly all of them symptoms started with isolation from a community that had been experienced as a protective one (29). In a comparison of cancer patients and experimental controls, an important discriminator was the loss of an important close personal relationship among the cancer patients (23). A relationship between a loss of personal ties, consequent depression, and the onset of a variety of physical diseases has also been reported (33). In this study nearly half the medical patients examined had suffered the loss of a person close to them with an accompanying feeling of helplessness and hopelessness immediately preceding the onset of their symptoms.

### LIMITATIONS OF THE SOCIOLOGICAL FRAMEWORK

In this chapter we have reviewed the influence of broad cultural and social groupings on individual behavior. Their effects are based on such qualities as ethnic identification or, in contrast, conflict over ethnic identity. Also of significance are those styles of life, associated with the various social classes, that mold and modulate individual values, attitudes, and aspirations. We noted, too, that the emotionally close experiences that suffuse family and peer relationships also have an impact on individual behavior. The larger social system and the more intimate relationships of family and peer groups may, of course, influence a person's behavior in quite different ways. Thus, Merton has suggested that isolation and alienation from society generally tend to initiate deviant behavior patterns. Alternatively, many of the studies reviewed have concerned isolation from or breakdown in close interpersonal relationships as a factor associated with the onset of psychopathology. It is a moot point, however, whether the breakup of personal relationships corresponds to social alienation as interpreted by Merton. The disruption of close personal ties would seem to represent more a direct threat to a person's emotional well-being, whereas alienation from the life of the community would appear to imply a lack of identity and purpose. This question remains unresolved, for we have not attempted to distinguish possible differences in the way large and small social systems influence either individual adaptation or the onset and course of pathology. We shall return to this question in the next chapter.

Inherent in the sociological orientation is a focus on group determinants of adaptive and nonadaptive behavior and a corresponding lack of concern with the influence of intrapsychic factors. The consequence is that sociological theorizing can deal only with differences in group rates of adaptive and nonadaptive behavior. Individual susceptibility to disorder is ignored, and deviance is taken to be the consequence of unusual societal pressures. The sociological framework cannot contribute to our understanding of why, under given environmental conditions, some persons (and usually only a small proportion) respond in a deviant manner while others continue to behave appropriately. Nevertheless, a sociological approch to normal adaptation and pathology has much to commend it. It gives needed emphasis to the role that community and interpersonal relations play in insuring or defeating the individual's attempts at social survival.

### REFERENCES

1. Abramson, J. H. Observations of the health of adolescent girls in relation to cultural change. *Psychosomatic Medicine.* 1961, **23**, 156–166.
2. Arieti, S. Manic-depressive psychosis. In S. Arieti (Ed.), *American handbook of psychiatry.* New York: Basic Books, 1959. Pp. 419–454.
3. Belknap, I., & Jaco, E. G. The epidemiology of mental disorders in a political-type city. (Based on 1949 population of 129,500.) In *Interrelations between the social environment and psychiatric disorders.* New York: Milbank Memorial Fund, 1953. P. 237.
4. Berlyne, D. E. *Conflict, arousal, and curiosity.* New York: McGraw-Hill, 1960.
5. Chance, N. A. A crosscultural study of social cohesion and depression. *Transcultural Psychiatric Research Review and Newsletter,* 1964, **1**, 19–24.
6. Clausen, J. A. Social patterns, personality and adolescent drug use. In A. Leighton, J. A. Clausen, & R. N. Wilson, (Eds.), *Explanations in social psychiatry.* New York: Basic Books, 1957.
7. Cohen, A. K. The study of social disorganization and deviant behavior. In R. K. Merton, L. Broom, and L. S. Cottrell, Jr. (Eds.), *Sociology today.* New York: Basic Books, 1959. Pp. 461–484.
8. Dayton, M. A. *New facts on mental disorders.* Springfield, Ill.: Charles C. Thomas, 1940.
9. DeVos, G. A. A comparison of the personality differences in two generations of Japanese Americans by means of the Rorschach test. *Nagoya Journal of Medical Science,* 1954, **17**, 153–265.
10. DeVos, G., & Miner, H. Oasis and casbah—a study in acculturative stress. In M. K. Opler (Ed.), *Culture and mental health.* New York: Macmillan, 1959. Pp. 333–350.
11. Dunham, H. W. The social personality of the catatonic-schizophrene. *American Journal of Sociology,* 1944, **49**, 508–518.
12. Dunham, H. W. Social structures and mental disorder: Competency hypothesis of explanation. *Milbank Memorial Fund Quarterly,* 1961, **39**, 257–311.
13. Eaton, J. W., & Weil, R. J. The mental health of the Hutterites. In A. M. Rose (Ed.), *Mental health and mental disorder.* New York: Norton, 1955. Pp. 223–240.
14. Fyvel, T. R. *Troublemakers: Rebellious youth in an affluent society.* New York: Schocken Books, 1962.
15. Gerard, D. L., & Houston, L. G. Family setting and the social ecology of schizophrenia. *Psychiatric Quarterly,* 1953, **27**, 90–101.
16. Hartmann, H. *Ego psychology and the problem of adaptation.* New York: International University Press, 1958.
17. Harvey, O. J., Hunt, D. E., & Schroder, H. M. *Conceptual systems and personality organization.* New York: Wiley, 1961.
18. Holt, R. R. Forcible indoctrination and personality change. In P. Worchel and D. Byrne (Eds.), *Personality change.* New York: Wiley, 1964. Pp. 289–318.
19. Hunt, J. McV. Motivation inherent in information processing and action. In O. J. Harvey (Ed.), *Motivation and social interaction: Cognitive determinants.* New York: Ronald Press, 1963. Pp. 35–94.

20.   Jaco, E. G. Social factors in mental disorders in Texas. *Social Problems*, 1957, **4**, 322–328.
21.   Kohn, M. L., & Clausen, J. A. Social isolation and schizophrenia. *American Sociological Review*, 1955, **20**, 265–273.
22.   Lemert, E. M. Exploratory study of mental disorders in a rural problem area. *Rural Sociology*, 1948, **13**, No. 48.
23.   LeShan, L., and Worthington, R. Some psychologic correlates of neoplastic disease: A preliminary report. *Journal of Clinical and Experimental Psychopathology*, 1955, **16**, 281–288
24.   Lewin, K. *Field theory in social science*. New York: Harper, 1951.
25.   Lifton, R. J. *Thought reform and the psychology of totalism*. New York: Norton, 1961.
26.   Malzberg, B. *Social and biological aspects of disease*. New York: State Hospital Press, 1940.
27.   McReynolds, P. Anxiety, perception, and schizophrenia. In D. D. Jackson (Ed.), *The etiology of schizophrenia*. New York: Basic Books, 1960. Pp. 248–292.
28.   Merton, R. K. *Social theory and social structure*. Glencoe, Ill.: Free Press, 1957.
29.   Minski, L., and Desai, M. M. Aspects of personality in peptic ulcer patients. *British Journal of Medical Psychology*, 1955, **28**, 113–134.
30.   Pflanz, M., Rosenstein, E., & Uexküll, T. Socio-psychological aspects of peptic ulcer. *Journal of Psychosomatic Research*. 1956, **1**, 68–74.
31.   Sackett, G. P. Some effects of social and sensory deprivation during rearing on behavioral development of monkeys. *Interamerican Journal of Psychology*, 1967, **1**, 55–80.
32.   Sainsbury, P. *Suicide in London: An ecological study*. New York: Basic Books, 1956.
33.   Schmale, A. H., Jr. Relationship of separation and depression to disease. *Psychosomatic Medicine*, 1958, **20**, 259–275.
34.   Srole, L., Langner, T. S., Michael, S. T., Opler, M. K., & Rennie, T. A. C. *Mental health in the metropolis: The midtown study*. Vol. 1. New York: McGraw-Hill, 1962.
35.   Stonequist, E. V. *The marginal man*. New York: Charles Scribner, 1937.
36.   Thomas, W. I., and Zaniecki, F. *The Polish peasant in Europe and America*. New York: Knopf, 1958.
37.   Tunley, R. *Kids, crime and chaos*. New York: Harper, 1962.
38.   Wittkower, E. D., & Fried, J. Some problems of transcultural psychiatry. In M. K. Opler (Ed.), *Culture and mental health*. New York: Macmillan, 1959. Pp. 489–500.
39.   Yablonsky, L. *The violent gang*. New York: Macmillan, 1962.

# 13/THE INTERACTIONIST VIEW

# ON ADAPTATION AND FAILURE

It is not easy to explain why some individuals become deviants and others do not. *Something* associated with the workings of the socioeconomic system undoubtedly plays a role, for mental disorder and other forms of pathology concentrate heavily at the lowest income levels (5). Yet this statement can be accepted only with reservation. Although substantial evidence has been advanced that mental disorder is associated with poverty, this finding applies only to large cities and does not appear to hold for small towns or rural areas (2). Further, mental disorder appears about as prevalent in a socialist economy, in which slum conditions as we know them in Western capitalist society presumably has been eliminated (13), as it is in the United States. Apparently something more than sheer economic deprivation is responsible for differences in the prevalence of pathology across income levels. It is important, therefore, to consider what precise meaning is to be attached to the relationship observed repeatedly between socioeconomic level and pathology.

It should be noted that there is no simple linear relation between either socioeconomic status (SES) or social class, on the one hand, and prevalence of disorder on the other. The correspondence between SES and impairment appears in large part dependent on a disproportionately high number of impaired individuals among the lowest SES. Thus, Hollingshead and Redlich (8) report a high rate of psychopathology within their lowest social class, with little correspondence between class and disorder across their four other social class levels. Similarly, Srole *et al.* (20) found the proportion of psychiatrically well to impaired virtually unchanged from the highest to nearly the lowest rung of the SES hierarchy. Only at the very lowest levels did a marked increment in the rate of psychiatric impairment appear. Those living in dire poverty who are exposed to the stresses of slum living do respond in significant numbers in a pathological fashion. Even so, only a relatively small minority of persons who live under slum conditions actually manifest socially disruptive and severe psychiatric disorder. Less than one half of those living under conditions of extreme poverty have been judged as psychiatrically impaired even when intensively interviewed and only about one in eight have had institutional contact (20).

Therefore, an additional question arises: What are the factors that, even in the presence of social marginality and economic privation, steer a person toward coping or toward maladaptations? To answer this question, we can make use of the fact that cases of mental disorder and other forms of pathology are not randomly distributed within low-income neighborhoods. The various types of disturbances are likely to cluster within a restricted number of the families that reside in these areas. Indeed, a family member with one kind of difficulty tends to have others. In a study (1) conducted in Stamford, Connecticut, investigators traced the appearance of 560 families during a 20-year period within six categories of social breakdown: crime, delinquency, child neglect, divorce, mental disorder, and intellectual retardation. In the span of less than a generation, constellations of these different forms of maladjustment appeared in the same families with extraordinary frequency and variety.

A similar survey (1) was conducted in St. Paul, Minnesota, focused on a group of nearly 6500 families (6% of all the families in the community) whose lives were complicated by major problems of ill health, maladjustment, and dependency. In over 2000 of these families chronic disease or physical handicap appeared, and in nearly 5000 there were other serious problems of ill health. Mental disorder or intellectual retardation occurred in nearly 2000 of these families. In approximately 1800 there was a record of some type of antisocial behavior—crime, delinquency, or child neglect. In 3600 there were chronically unemployable individuals and over 5000 families were dependent on the community for financial assistance.

It has been shown that certain of these constellations of problems also hold for populations in other urban areas. For example, a study (3) that reported on the amount of psychoneurotic disorder in 90 families found that these displayed a high incidence of chronic physical disease. It was discovered, too, that their rates of accidents and attacks of acute illness were considerably higher than in the general population. The occurrence of other forms of pathology was also excessively high, including mental retardation, psychosis, heart disease, and rheumatic fever.

Why are some individuals and some families among the poor particularly prone to manifestations of disorder? A number of investigators (5, 12, 18), have suggested that it is those economically deprived persons subjected to an unusual degree of life stress who are likely to respond in a deviant fashion. In the absence of personal and family difficulties socioeconomic deprivation does not appear to impair mental health (12). That is, there is very little distinction between the average mental health ratings of low and high SES persons when they are suffering from a less than average degree of life stress.

A study of the specific personal and family difficulties that antedate the onset of schizophrenic reactions has been reported by Rogler and Hollingshead (18). This investigation was carried out in a slum of San Juan, Puerto Rico, with 20 married couples in which at least one of the partners had been diagnosed as schizophrenic, and 20 married couples where neither partner was so diagnosed. It was found that in this slum population the schizophrenic couples differed little from the control group in terms of their childhood and even early adult experiences. The factors that distinguished them appeared in the 5-year period that immediately preceded the onset of disorder. During these years a disproportionately high occurrence was noted in the incidence of physical disease in either the patient or his spouse. There occurred also in this period a strikingly high number of deaths of children linked to the subsequent onset of schizophrenic disorder in their mothers. The year immediately preceding the onset of schizophrenia was particularly noteworthy for its high rate of trauma. At this time there often occurred physical sickness in the patient or spouse, a complicated pregnancy, or the illness or death of a child. Unemployment was a frequent precursor of schizophrenia, with an attendant accumulation of debts, as well as economic dependence on relatives or neighbors. Quarrels and threats between the spouses became unusually frequent, and quarrels with neighbors also appeared. These arguments were often over the sexual adventures in which the husband became involved during this period of stress.

Similar trauma have been noted as preceding the onset of physical sickness. In a study of American workingmen and -women, Hinkle and Wolff (6) found that a high proportion of the most severely physically ill had experienced various kinds of social trauma, divorce, separation, conflicts with spouse, parents, or siblings, and unhappy living or working arrangements. In contrast, few of a sample of healthy subjects had suffered such experiences. Holmes, Hawkins, Bowerman, Clarke, and Joffe (9) have reviewed a number of studies on the onset and course of tuberculosis and made a similar observation. In many ways tuberculous subjects appeared as "marginal people." Their precarious social adjustment typically disintegrated in the 2-year period preceding onset of or relapse in the disease, during which there was a high frequency of broken marriages and changes in occupation and residence.

Is the generally harsher life led by the poor (12) sufficient explanation for the high prevalence of disorder among the deprived? Some investigators believe that this is at least a partial answer for the observed relation between poverty and pathology (5, 15). Indeed, Dohrenwend and Dohrenwend propose that much of what is commonly labeled as psychiatric disorder is no more than the transient and to-be-expected reaction of normal individuals who face the unusually severe stresses associated with slum living.

Yet this explanation is not sufficient to account totally for the excessive level of psychiatric impairment to be found among the poor. Under severely stressful life situations individuals who are deficient in education and occupational achievement tend to show a greater degree of psychiatric impairment than do those of higher socioeconomic accomplishment. Parenthetically it should be noted that this finding suggests an asymmetrical relationship between SES and the impact of stress on adaptation. It was noted earlier (in this section) that, at low levels of stress, no difference appears in degree of pathological reactions across SES lines. In the face of intense stress, however, low SES individuals are differentially more impaired. Lower-status persons are more prone to display psychotic-like reactions, while those of higher economic achievement tend to respond with the less severe reactions of neurosis (12).

Why are the poor more vulnerable than the well-to-do? What is there about their personalities that gives them less psychological stamina, and how does this vulnerability come into being? Two possible explanations have been advanced to account for the emergence of the less adaptive personalities of the poor. One emphasizes a disproportionate occurrence among the poor of traumatic experiences early in childhood, including neglect, parental absence, and emotional deprivation. The presumed consequence is the immature or deviant motive states that psychoanalytic theory posit as associated with neurotic or psychotic behavior patterns in adulthood. In turn, this immaturity tends to stultify the development of the person's means for coping with the complexities of adult life. The alternative explanation emphasizes the insufficient opportunity for the children of the poor to master the complex intellectual, occupational, social, and psychosexual skills necessary for effective performance in adult society. These contrasting theoretical positions are illustrated by the work of Hollingshead and Redlich (8) on the one hand, and that of Davis and Havighurst (4) on the other. Thus, Hollingshead and Redlich were guided, in their classic work on *Social Class and Mental Illness*, by the observation that "the psychodynamic concept of unconscious conflict between instinctual forces and the demands of the environment is crucial for many attempts at explanation of most neurotic and psychotic illnesses. Knowing that the different social classes exhibit different ways of life, we conjectured that emotional problems of individuals might be related to the patterns of life characteristic of their class positions." In contrast, Davis and Havighurst see the influence of class on individual development as serving to define and systematize different learning environments for the children of different classes. These environments influence what children will subsequently achieve in life.

The ultimate concern of both these theoretical positions is the indiviual's potential pattern of behavior during adulthood. Their specific centers of interest, however, are quite different. The psychodynamic position posits a latent potential for deviant reactions in adulthood as a consequence of early disturbance in child experience. The appropriate criterion of class affiliation in studies based on this hypothesis is that of the family of origin. This follows because it is presumed that the various social classes are marked by differences in styles of life that, in turn, influence the psychodynamic development of their children. Those studies that have held to the psychodynamic hypothesis, and yet that have made use of the respondent's own class standing in adulthood (and this includes the Hollingshead and Redlich study), appear to have erred in their experimental test of this hypothesis. On the other hand, if we assume the opportunity-for-learning or own-achievement hypothesis, we are more interested in what the person has learned and accomplished within the span of his own lifetime. In that case, our concern is with how well the person has fulfilled himself, including his educational and occupational achievements. Our interest is not so much in the person's social class level, but in his real-life accomplishments. Educational and occupational measures provide the most objective and precise indices of the social class level that the person has achieved through his own efforts. In psychopathology, therefore, an appropriate test of the own-achievement hypothesis is the relation between respondents' own social class level in adulthood and the prevalence, severity, and outcome of psychiatric states.

The distinction between parental and own social class is a meaningful one. In contemporary American society, a person's occupational status is only modestly related to that of the parent, with this relationship accounting for only some 10% or 15% of the common variance.[1] In studies on mental disorder, comparisons have been made of the relative predictive power associated with parental and own occupational or SES level. Results clearly favor the person's own level as the more significant variable. Thus, Srole et al. observed a considerably higher correspondence between own SES and degree of psychiatric impairment among the general population than with parental SES. Similarly, Nuttall and Solomon (17) found a considerably higher relationship between the patient's own occupational standing and outcome in schizophrenia than was obtained with father's occupational level.

[1]Computed from data provided by Kahl (10) and Morgan et al. (16).

The degree to which the occupational achievement of a son surpasses that of his father would appear to provide a relatively direct test of the own-achievement hypothesis. Srole *et al.*, have examined the relation between occupational mobility and mental health. The American-born males in their sample of the general population were divided according to whether the respondents placed above, below, or at the same occupational level as their father. Occupational mobility, upward, downward, or absent, was then compared to mental health rating. A clear and striking relationship between mobility and psychiatric status was obtained. The upwardly mobile scored as psychiatrically most sound, the no-change group at an intermediate level, and the downwardly mobile as seriously impaired. The evidence, then, clearly favors the own-achievement hypothesis.

A person's achievements are not, of course, restricted to the socioeconomic sphere. Throughout this book we have indicated the role played by a person's more general competence in the sphere of interpersonal relations as well as in the world of work as influencing his potential for both constructive adaptation and pathology. Nevertheless, these studies on social competence represent an incomplete analysis of the conditions under which pathological reactions are likely to appear. We have to consider factors beyond the individual if we are to explain fluctuations in adaptive state when coping potential remains fixed. That is, individuals who manifest disorder at one time may fail to do so at another. Again, at any one time and at any given level of coping potential, some persons will be reacting in a pathological fashion, others will not. Thus, we cannot predict an act solely on the basis of knowledge of a person, no matter how complete or theoretically precise this information may be. Behavior is not simply an expression of individuality, but a transaction between the subject and his environment. Prediction requires equally a congruent insight into those determinants of behavior that reside in the environment. Any attempt to predict normal or pathological behavior requires that we adopt what may be termed an "interactionist" position. This proposes that normal social adaptation, that is, a rational and appropriate pattern of behavior, appears to depend on at least two major sets of factors: (1) availability within the person of those psychological resources and skills necessary for participation in community life; and (2) support from the immediate social context within which the person lives, including his family as well as peer and work groups.

Pathology eventuates when a deficiency in personal resources combines with stressful circumstances to create a situation in which the person lacks the adaptive skills for a successful resolution of his difficulties. Suggested is the complementary nature of internal resources and environmental support. Each can substitute for a deficiency in the other. The ineffectual person requires a higher degree of social support in order to adapt constructively in society. Correspondingly, the person gifted with more in the way of coping potential and skills is able to withstand a relatively stressful environment.

## TYPES OF ENVIRONMENT

With this statement we come full circle to the position advanced in Chapter 1. Intervening chapters have attempted to provide the empirical underpinning for this formulation. In particular, the concept of coping potential and its behavioral expression in social competence have been elaborated in considerable detail. An equivalent amount of data is not available on the nature of the social environment nor on just what aspects of environment are of consequence in adaptation and failure. It is possible, however, to delineate in somewhat more precise terms those characteristics of the social environment that are relevant to social survival and the conditions under which deviant reactions are likely to appear. The issue of the environmental context of adaptation and failure arose in the last chapter, but discussion was deferred until the material on multireferral families could be presented. The specific question is the relative contribution to success or failure in coping of the general social system to that of disturbed relationships within a person's immediate family, in peer groups, or at work. We have seen that only a minority of families, even under dire circumstances in life, contribute to the level of social pathology rampant in the community, at least in terms recognized in some form of institutional or help-seeking contact. It appears that it is those experiences in life that touch the person most directly that guide his steps toward either adaptation or failure.

The influence of the larger social system is relatively indirect. Its operations are relevant only as they have affected in the person's past development his coping potential, and in the present, color his interpersonal relations. The expectations that society imposes on each of its members are transmitted through family and peer groups, which convey the values, aspirations, and myths that characterize a culture. Yet family and peer groups are only a very imperfect lens through which the dominant themes of a society are refracted. Families and small groups are not universally identical, even within narrow ranges of social status and ethnic group. They vary widely in their guiding principles. It is not surprising, therefore, that individual susceptibility to pathology shows considerable range even when the person's place in the larger social context is held constant.

We have spoken of the social system as if it acted on each person as a single network of relationships. In actuality, the social system affects two environments in which the person lives, which are separate in time, and yet which together determine whether or not he will manifest some form of pathological behavior. These are, first, the early family environment in which are molded the individual's coping potential, as well as his values and attitudes toward himself and the world about him. The second is the current environment that confronts him with the tasks and stresses of adult living. In brief, early environment determines a person's predisposition for disorder; the later environment may act as its precipitant. Let us examine a little more closely the influence of these two environments.

### The Early Environment

Families at the lowest economic level are more likely to fail in supporting the development of coping behavior in their offspring than are families identified with other class levels. It is relevant to contrast the experiences that more often beset the child brought up in the slums with those more common to the children of the middle class.

As we noted in Chapter 2, the middle-class child is brought up to be a "somebody," imbued with a sense of self-assurance and competence. The goals transmitted to him usually include advanced education, embarking on a career, and economic achievement. Middle-class parents encourage postponement of immediate satisfactions in the service of long-range goals, acceptance of responsibilities, and the constructive use of one's time. The middle-class way of life structures a verbal and ideational world with planning, punctuality, and self-control emphasized as the means necessary for successful achievement.

In contrast, the child of the slums frequently senses himself as weak and defenseless, the external world as powerful and threatening. As a consequence, he is attuned to an expectancy of failure with its inevitable punishment rather than any hope of effective performance and reward. He is more motivated to avoid failure than to be correct or successful and will settle for a much lower level of success and accomplishment than will the middle-class child, who is encouraged toward self-fulfilling achievement. The deprived child, subject to a chronic sense of failure, manifests a relatively low level of achievement motivation. It may be said that the underprivileged child is controlled by his need to stabilize his personal relationships in order to diminish their threat potential rather than by an interest in the intellectual mastery of the objective world (21, 22). To study and to work hard are, from his point of view, basically unrewarded activities, for the child brought up in the slums is too often convinced that education and economic rewards are not to be his lot. The consequence is an unwillingness and inability to commit himself to the mastery of difficult situations or to work at tasks that demand a long-term commitment.

The early environment sets the assumptions by which a person lives. The most basic lesson he learns is whether or not it pays to try. Those who believe that it does are constantly accumulating new techniques for mastering the ways of the world. Those who come to deny the value of effort learn little. As a consequence each group, those who believe that they have much to say about the direction of their lives and those who spurn this belief, are reinforced in their optimism or pessimism; each lives out a self-fulfilling prophecy.

### The Environment of the Adult

The influence of environment for the adult is of a different nature. It acts less to teach than to either confirm or deny the person's assumptions about his likelihood of success or failure. If a person senses that the means of mastery lie within himself, he has little need to call on the resources or skills of others. If he is convinced that he is bereft of the means for self-fulfillment, he is much in need of whatever help he can muster. Unhappily, those least able to cope and most dependent on the support that others might render have least access to such help.

We have seen that those who live under slum conditions are the people who are least able to cope and most prone to respond in ineffectual and inappropriate ways. These are the individuals who live in what Lewis (13) has called "the culture of poverty," those who sense their lives as futile and their condition as hopeless. Intense feelings of helplessness and in-adequacy, of inferiority and low self-esteem are common (8, 11, 12, 19). At the same time each person feels he is fighting his battles alone. The isolation of one person from another characterizes the culture of poverty, and the objective characteristics of personal relationships mold and rein-force these attitudes. For example, marriages are often transient and husbands are frequently described as lazy, drunken, brutal, or promiscuous. Women may have to become prostitutes in order to support their children (14). Children brought up under such conditions all too often live lives that are chaotic and psychologically destructive. It is not surprising that interpersonal relations of this kind so often precipitate pathological reactions in already predisposed individuals.

IMPLICATIONS FOR CORRECTIVE PROGRAMS

One final consideration is the implication of the interactionist position for treatment approaches in contrast to those that follow from traditional assumptions as to the nature of mental disorder. The traditional psychiatric interpretation of many of the major types of social maladjustment is to view them as forms of mental "illness." To clinicians generally, this implies that these disorders reflect some disequilibrium in the intrapsychic function-ing of the psychologically disturbed individual. Mental illness is the presumed consequence of psychodynamic factors originating in the person's experiences early in childhood, or in some peculiar genetic aberration or constitutional sensitivity that antedates even early childhood trauma. The maintenance of a stable psychological equilibrium is felt to depend primarily on the control of intrapsychic conflict, for which purpose a system of psychological defense mechanisms is operative. This position reflects what Hobbs has called an obsession with the world inside a man's skull (7). It stresses not alone the preeminence of psychological factors as explanation of human behavior but the controlling role of unconscious and irrational forces operating outside the awareness of human actors.

Traditional psychotherapeutic programs operate in conformity with this theoretical formulation. Treatment is carried out within the confines of the therapist's office or in hospital settings isolated from the life of the community. These programs tend to concentrate on unresolved problems in the person's past, on an attempt, through verbal communication between the client and the therapist, to lay to rest disruptive memories and emotions. A close and typically dependent client relation to the therapist is seen as a sine qua non for a successful therapeutic outcome.

A new direction in therapeutic programs is now finding increasingly wide acceptance, one that shows a correspondence with the interactionist position advanced in this book. This position views individual psychological problems as influenced by the nature of the community within which they appear, as arising from disorganized conditions of social life. It assumes that all forms of pathological reaction within a community share a common origin in that they reflect a failure in constructive adaptation. As a consequence, there is a lessened inclination to differentiate between various pathological types in terms of proffered psychological services. A common core of therapeutic effort, directed at the development of social competence, is coming to permeate all intervention programs whether these are concerned with those who respond to social failure with criminality or delinquency, with neurosis or psychosis, or with psychosomatic reactions. Correspondingly, there is a tendency to deemphasize the role of unconscious and irrational factors in the psychology of the individual client and to concentrate on eradicating his deficiencies in the skills necessary for living in society, including those appearing in the spheres of education and occupation, as well as in interpersonal and social relations. That is, newer therapeutic approaches that correspond to the interactionist position emphasize the development of skill and competence, encourage an active program of self-help and the overcoming of concrete and immediate difficulties. They accentuate the present and the unfulfilled potentialities of the future. The attempt is to encourage participation in constructive, fulfilling, and emotionally satisfying real-life experiences. Such programs try to foster the development of closer personal relationships and increased participation in the life of the community. The intent is to help the client see that personal difficulties are typically interpersonal in both their origins and consequences, and that their solution lies in joint action and mutual trust.

## REFERENCES

1. Buell, Bradley and Associates. *Community planning for human services.* New York: Columbia University Press, 1952.
2. Clausen, J. A., & Kohn, M. L. Social relations and schizophrenia: A research report and a perspective. In D. D. Jackson (Ed.), *The etiology of schizophrenia.* New York: Basic Books, 1960. Pp. 295–320.
3. Commission on Chronic Illness. *Chronic illness in a large city. The Baltimore study.* 1957.
4. Davis, A. & Havighurst, R. J. Social class and color differences in child rearing. *American Sociological Review,* 1946, **11**, 698–710.
5. Dohrenwend, B. P., and Dohrenwend, B. S. The problem of validity in field studies of psychological disorder. *Journal of Abnormal Psychology,* 1965, **70**, 52–69.
6. Hinkle, L. E., Jr., and Wolff, H. G. Health and the social environment: Experimental investigations. In A. H. Leighton, J. A. Clausen, & R. N. Wilson, (Eds.), *Explorations in social psychiatry.* New York: Basic Books, 1957. Pp. 105–137.
7. Hobbs, N. Mental health's third revolution. *American Journal of Orthopsychiatry,* 1964, **34**, 822–833.
8. Hollingshead, A. B., & Redlich, F. C. *Social class and mental illness.* New York: Wiley, 1958.
9. Holmes, T. H., Hawkins, N. G., Bowerman, C. E., Clarke, E. R., Jr., and Joffe, J. R. Psychosocial and psychophysiologic studies of tuberculosis. *Psychosomatic Medicine,* 1957, **19**, 134–143.
10. Kahl, J. A. *The American class structure.* New York: Holt, 1957.
11. Kaplan, B., Reed, R. B., & Richardson, W. Comparison of the incidence of hospitalized and non-hospitalized cases of psychosis in two communities. *American Sociological Review,* 1956, **21**, 479.
12. Langner, T. S., & Michael, S. T. *Life stress and mental health: Midtown Manhattan study.* Vol. 2. New York: Free Press of Glencoe, 1963.
13. Lewis, O. The culture of poverty. *Scientific American,* 1966, **215**, 19–25. (a)
14. Lewis, O. *La Vida.* New York: Random House, 1966. (b)
15. Merton, R. K. *Social theory and social structure.* Glencoe, Ill.: Free Press, 1957.
16. Morgan, J. N., David, M. H., Cohen, W. J., & Brazer, H. E. *Income and welfare in the United States.* New York: McGraw-Hill, 1962.
17. Nuttall, R. L., & Solomon, L. F. Prognosis in schizophrenic: The role of premorbid and demographic factors. Unpublished manuscript, Psychology Department Library, Boston College, 1964.
18. Rogler, L. H., & Hollingshead, A. B. *Trapped: Families and schizophrenia.* New York: Wiley, 1965.
19. Spinley, B. M. *The deprived and the privileged* London: Routledge & Kegan Paul, 1953.
20. Srole, L., Langner, T. S., Michael, S. T., Opler, M. K., & Rennie, T. A. C. *Mental health in the metropolis: Midtown Manhattan study.* Vol. 1. New York: McGraw-Hill, 1962.
21. Turnure, J., & Zigler, E. Outerdirectedness in the problem solving of normal and retarded children. *Journal of Abnormal and Social Psychology,* 1964, **69**, 427–436.
22. Zigler, E. Familial mental retardation: A continuing dilemma. *Science* 1967, **155**, 292–298.

# APPENDIX

## SOCIAL COMPETENCE INTERVIEW

Ward _____

Date _____

1. Interviewer _____ 2. Subject's Name _____ 3. Subject's No. _____

4. Subject's Hosp. No. _____ 5. Age _____ 6. Birth date _____ 7. Sex _____

8. Marital Status _____ 9. Date of Admission _____ First Admission? _____

If not, date of first admission _____ 10. Days hospitalized before interview _____

I. <u>EDUCATION</u>

11. Grades of education completed: _____ (insert exact amount)

      00 – none
      01 – first grade

      . . . . . . . . . . .

      08 – eighth grade, completed grammar school

      . . . . . . . . . .

      12 – twelfth grade, completed high school, with or without diploma
      13 – completed freshman year at college

      . . . . . . . . . .

      16 – college graduate
      17 – work beyond college, on graduate level, without degree
      18 – MA, DDS, LLB, BD, DVM; 2 year diplomas
      19 – post-MA work, without Ph D degree
      20 – Ph D, any doctoral degree

11a. Note if ungraded school _____ No. years completed _____

Type of school _____

_____

11b. Age at which formal schooling was completed: grade school (8 grades): _____

                    high school (9-12): _____

                    college + (13 or more): _____

TABLE A–1 (*Continued*)

11c. Note degrees, if any earned: _____

_____

_____

11 d. Vocational or professional training after formal schooling:

| Type | No. weeks, months or years | Diplomas or certificates | Age started |
|------|------|------|------|
|  |  |  |  |
|  |  |  |  |
|  |  |  |  |

### II. OCCUPATION

12. Subject's occupation during last 5 (prehospital) years: (list chronologically, starting with last job held

| | Job Title | Description (What did S do, how many people did he supervise, what they did ) | Duration | Part/full time (specify hrs; days) | Income (hourly, weekly, monthly, or yearly) |
|---|---|---|---|---|---|
| 1. | | | | | |
| 2. | | | | | |
| 3. | | | | | |
| 4. | | | | | |
| 5. | | | | | |
| 6. | | | | | |
| 7. | | | | | |
| 8. | | | | | |
| 9. | | | | | |
| 10. | | | | | |

TABLE A–1 (*Continued*)

13. Employment regularity: _____  (Number of months subject was working full time
during the last five years [60 months] prior to hospitalization). Work includes student,
soldier, on strike, sick leave, but not psychiatric illness.

13a. Number of different employers worked for: _____ (During above five years)

14. Has this subject received any public assistance during the last two years? _____

      From what agencies? _____

15. Medical disability: _____(i.e., impairment to work potential)

      0 – absent
      1 – mild
      2 – moderate
      3 – severe

16. Father's occupation:

| Job | Description | Duration | Part/Full Time |
|---|---|---|---|
| 1. | | | |
| 2. | | | |
| 3. | | | |
| 4. | | | |
| 5. | | | |

What was the most common job held? _____

### III. ORGANIZATION AND LEISURE

17. Organizational activity: (a) Do you belong to any clubs, unions, or other organizations?
(b) What is the purpose of these organizations? (c) How often do you attend organization
meetings? (d) What offices do you hold in these organizations?

| (a) Name of organization | (b) Purpose or activity | (c) How often attend | (d) Offices |
|---|---|---|---|
| 1. | | | |
| 2. | | | |
| 3. | | | |
| 4. | | | |
| 5. | | | |

TABLE A–1 (*Continued*)

17 e.  How often do you attend church (each month): _____

18.  Activity level:

18a.  Number of memberships in formal organizations: _____

18b.  Number of meetings attended each month (total): _____

19.  Leisure time activity: (a) Check those activities in which the subject has shown an active
interest during the last 5 years.  (b) How frequently has the subject participated in
these activities?  (Indicate where possible, daily, weekly, monthly, etc.)

Frequency

| | |
|---|---|
| WATCHING TELEVISION | |
| LISTENING TO RADIO | |
| GOING TO MOVIES | |
| INDOOR GAMES: | |
| card and board games | |
| checkers | |
| chess | |
| other (please specify) | |
| ENTERTAINMENT: | |
| parties | |
| drinking beer with others | |
| dancing | |
| group singing | |
| amateur band | |
| other (please specify) | |
| GOING TO SPORTING EVENTS: | |
| races | |
| football | |
| baseball | |
| boxing | |
| other (please specify) | |
| PARTICIPATING IN SPORTS: | |
| fishing, hunting | |
| bowling | |
| golf | |
| hiking | |
| other (please specify) | |

TABLE A–1 (*Continued*)

Frequency

READING:

   magazines (sports, adventure)
   historical novels
   fiction
   mysteries and crime
   comics
   newspapers
   other (please specify)

HOME MAINTENANCE:

   electrical
   gardening
   carpentry
   other (please specify)

HOUSEHOLD:

   cooking (as a hobby)
   sewing, crocheting, etc.
   teaching own children (piano, etc.)
   other (please specify)

BUILDING:

   boats, planes, railroads
   radio, T.V., electronic equipment
   other (please specify)

MISCELLANEOUS:

   painting
   ceramics
   photography
   collecting (stamps, coins)
   other hobbies (please specify)

OTHER ACTIVITIES



19c.   What is your favorite activity? _____

20.    Has the subject ever voted in a city, state, or federal election? _____

20a.   In the last election? _____

TABLE A–1 (*Continued*)

IV. MARITAL STATUS

21.   a. Present legal status: _____

        1 – Married
        2 – Common-law marriage
        3 – Widowed
        4 – Nonlegal separation
        5 – Legally separated
        6 – Divorced
        7 – Marriage annulled
        8 – Single

        Notes: _____

_____

_____

_____

21.   b. Present heterosexual activity: _____

        1 – One continuous marriage, with children
        2 – One continuous marriage, no children
        3 – Remarriage, with or without children
        4 – Lives with (wo)man, other than legal or common-law wife (husband)
        5 – Engaged to be married
        6 – Goes steady or frequently dates only one (wo)man
        7 – Goes out with several (wo)men, frequently
        8 – Goes out with several (wo)men, infrequently
        9 – Does not go out socially with (wo)men

        Notes: _____

_____

_____

_____

TABLE A–1 (*Continued*)

21.    c.  Psychosexual history: _____ (score largest number applicable to
                                                        past experience)

      1 – Uneventful marital and/or premarital course
      2 – Spouse died
      3 – Unhappily married
      4 – Temporarily separated, but reunited
      5 – Went steady but broke up
      6 – Broken an engagement or had an engagement broken
      7 – Separated from spouse, not on legal basis (indicate if religious or choice) _____
      8 – Been divorced, separated, or had a marriage annulled
      9 – Deserted a spouse or been deserted

        Notes: _____


21.    d.  (1) Age at first marriage: _____    (2) Spouse's age of first marriage: _____

        (3) Subsequent marriages: _____    (4) Spouse's age of present marriage: _____
                                                        (if different)

21.    e.  If subject has children, give sex and age of each child: (note:  Own child (O),
                                                        Step-child (S))

                  Sex          Age

          1. _____    _____    O   S

          2. _____    _____    O   S

          3. _____    _____    O   S

          4. _____    _____    O   S

          5. _____    _____    O   S

          6. _____    _____    O   S

          7. _____    _____    O   S

          8. _____    _____    O   S

          9. _____    _____    O   S

         10. _____    _____    O   S

TABLE A–1 (*Continued*)

21.   f.   If subject is female, any miscarriages: _____

22.   Subject's type of residence: _____

      1 – Parental
      2 – Grandparents
      3 – Siblings
      4 – Other relatives, (specify): _____
      5 – Friend
      6 – Spouse
      7 – By him (her) self
      8 – Institutional
      9 – Supported by, or in care of, adult children
     10 – Living alone with, and supporting, young children
     11 – Dormitory or barrack-type arrangements
     12 – Other (specify): _____

## V. ANCILLARY INFORMATION

23.   (a) Subject's religion: _____   (b) Spouse's religion: _____

      1 – Catholic
      2 – Protestant, give denomination: _____
      3 – Jewish
      4 – None
      5 – Other, specify: _____
      6 – Not established

24.   Sibling rank: Starting with the oldest, list the children living in the same house with subject
              during subject's first 18 years (include the subject), circle subject's position,
              give sex of each child: (Note: Step-sibling (S), Half-sibling (H), circle
              letter if applicable)

      1._____ S   H      6._____ S   H

      2._____ S   H      7._____ S   H

      3._____ S   H      8._____ S   H

      4._____ S   H      9._____ S   H

      5._____ S   H     10._____ S   H

TABLE A–1 (*Continued*)

25.   Nationality:

25a.  Country of birth: _____ 25b.  Mother's birthplace: _____

25c.  Father's birthplace: _____

        1 – American (native born parents)          6 – Scottish
        2 – Armenian                                7 – Swedish
        3 – French–Canadian                         8 – Polish
        4 – Irish                                   9 – Other, specify: _____
        5 – Italian

25d.  General descent, if noteworthy: _____

26.   Parental age:  a. Mother's age:  (or age at, and year of death) _____

                     b. Father's age:  (or age at, and year of death) _____

      VI.   CONTACT

27.   Subject's expected address:  (1) (2) address, (3) phone:

        1. _____

        2. _____

        3. _____

28.   Nearest relative:  (1) relationship, (2) name, (3) (4) address, (5) phone:

        1. _____

        2. _____

        3. _____

        4. _____

        5. _____

29.   We will contact you in several months to see how you are doing.  (Write "1" if subject
      acquiesces, "2" if opposes): _____

Examiner's Remarks

TABLE A–1 (*Continued*)

Derived Scales (See accompanying tables)

1. Occupational Type and Level

A.  Job Type (Warner): _____          Subject          Father

| | Subject | Father |
|---|---|---|
| 1 – Professionals | | |
| 2 – Proprietors and Managers | | |
| 3 – Business Men | | |
| 4 – Clerks and Kindred Workers | | |
| 5 – Manual Workers | | |
| 6 – Protective and Service Workers | | |
| 7 – Farmers | | |
| 8 – Students | | |
| 9 – Housewife, keeps house | | |
| 10 – Not scorable | | |

B.  Job Level (Warner): _____          Subject          Father

| | Subject | Father |
|---|---|---|
| 1. | | |
| 2. | | |
| 3. | | |
| 4. | | |
| 5. | | |
| 6. | | |
| 7. | | |

C.  Job Type (Roe): _____          Subject          Father

| | Subject | Father |
|---|---|---|
| 1 – Service | | |
| 2 – Business Contact | | |
| 3 – Organization | | |
| 4 – Technology | | |
| 5 – Outdoor | | |
| 6 – Science | | |
| 7 – General Cultural | | |
| 8 – Arts and Entertainment | | |
| 9 – Student | | |
| 10 – Housewife, keeps house | | |
| 11 – Not scorable | | |

D.  Job Level (Roe): _____          Subject          Father

| | Subject | Father |
|---|---|---|
| 1. | | |
| 2. | | |
| 3. | | |
| 4. | | |
| 5. | | |
| 6. | | |

TABLE  A–1 (*Continued*)

Derived Scales  (See accompanying tables)

II.  Organizational Activity and Use of Leisure Time

A.  Activity Level                           D.  Inward Orientation

B.  Constructiveness                         E.  Social Participation

C.  Outward Orientation                      F.  Sex Identification

TABLE A-2

REVISED SCALE FOR RATING OCCUPATION$^a$

| Rating Assigned to Occupation | 1 Professionals | 2 Proprietors and Managers | 3 Business Men | 4 Clerks and Kindred Workers, etc. | 5 Manual Workers | 6 Protective and Service Workers | 7 Farmers |
|---|---|---|---|---|---|---|---|
| 1 | Lawyers, doctors, dentists, engineers, judges, high-school superintendents, veterinarians, ministers (graduated from divinity school), chemists, etc. with postgraduate training, architects | Businesses valued at $75,000 and over | Regional and divisional managers of large financial and industrial enterprises | Certified public accountants | | | Gentleman farmers |
| 2 | High-school teachers, trained nurses, chiropodists, chiropractors, undertakers, ministers (some training), newspaper editors, librarians (graduate) | Businesses valued at $20,000 to $75,000 | Assistant managers and office and department managers of large businesses, assistants to executives, etc. | Accountants, salesmen of real estate, of insurance, postmasters | | | Large farm owners, farm owners |
| 3 | Social workers, grade-school teachers, optometrists, librarians (not graduate), undertaker's assistants, ministers (no training) | Businesses valued at $5,000 to $20,000 | All minor officials of businesses | Auto salesmen, bank clerks and cashiers, postal clerks, secretaries to executives, supervisors of railroad, telephone, etc., justices of the peace | Contractors | | |

TABLE A–2 (Continued)

| Rating Assigned to Occupation | 1 Professionals | 2 Proprietors and Managers | 3 Business Men | 4 Clerks and Kindred Workers, etc. | 5 Manual Workers | 6 Protective and Service Workers | 7 Farmers |
|---|---|---|---|---|---|---|---|
| 4 | | Businesses valued at $2,000 to $5,000 | | Stenographers, bookkeepers, rural mail clerks, railroad ticket agents, sales people in dry goods store, etc. | Factory foremen, electricians * plumbers * carpenters * watchmakers [*own business] | Dry cleaners, butchers, sheriffs, railroad engineers and conductors | |
| 5 | | Businesses valued at $500 to $2,000 | | Dime store clerks, hardware salesmen, beauty operators, telephone operators | Carpenters, plumbers, electricians (apprentice), timekeepers, linemen, telephone or telegraph, radio repairmen, medium-skilled workers | Barbers, firemen butcher's apprentices practical nurses, policemen, seamstresses, cooks in restaurant, bartenders | Tenant farmers |
| 6 | | Businesses valued at less than $500 | | | Moulders, semi-skilled workers, assistants to carpenter, etc. | Baggage men, night policemen and watchmen, taxi and truck drivers, gas station attendants, waitresses in restaurant | Small tenant farmers |
| 7 | | | | | Heavy labor migrant work, odd job men, miners | Janitors, scrubwomen, newsboys | Migrant farm laborers |

a From Warner, W. L. Social class in America. New York: Harper, 1960. Pp. 140–141.

TABLE A–3

TWO-WAY CLASSIFICATION OF OCCUPATIONS[a]

GROUP

| Level | I. Service | II. Business Contact | III. Organization | IV. Technology |
|---|---|---|---|---|
| 1 | Personal therapists<br>Social work supervisors<br>Counselors | Promoters | U.S. President and<br>Cabinet officers<br>Industrial tycoons<br>International bankers | Inventive geniuses<br>Consulting or chief<br>engineers<br>Ships' commanders |
| 2 | Social workers<br>Occupational<br>therapists<br>Probation, truant<br>officers (with<br>training) | Promoters<br>Public relations<br>counselors | Certified public<br>accountants<br>Business and<br>government<br>executives<br>Union official<br>Brokers, average | Applied scientists<br>Factory managers<br>Ships' officers<br>Engineers |
| 3 | YMCA officials<br>Detectives, police<br>sergeants<br>Welfare workers<br>City inspectors | Salesmen: auto,<br>bond, insurance,etc.<br>Dealers, retail<br>and wholesale<br>Confidence men | Accountants,<br>average<br>Employment<br>managers<br>Owners, catering,<br>dry-cleaning, etc. | Aviators<br>Contractors<br>Foremen (DOT I)<br>Radio operators |
| 4 | Barbers<br>Chefs<br>Practical<br>nurses<br>Policemen | Auctioneers<br>Buyers (DOT I)<br>House<br>canvassers<br>Interviewers, poll | Cashiers<br>Clerks, credit<br>express, etc.<br>Foremen, warehouse<br>Salesclerks | Blacksmiths<br>Electricians<br>Foremen (DOT II)<br>Mechanics, average |
| 5 | Taxi drivers<br>General house-<br>workers<br>Waiters<br>City firemen | Peddlers | Clerks, file,<br>stock, etc.<br>Notaries<br>Runners<br>Typists | Bulldozer operators<br>Deliverymen<br>Smelter workers<br>Truck drivers |
| 6 | Chambermaids<br>Hospital<br>attendants<br>Elevator operators<br>Watchmen | | Messenger boys | Helpers<br>Laborers<br>Wrappers<br>Yardmen |

TABLE A–3 (Continued)

GROUP

| Level | V. Outdoor | VI. Science | VII. General Culture | VIII. Arts and Entertainment |
|---|---|---|---|---|
| 1 | Consulting specialists | Research scientists University, college faculties Medical specialists Museum curators | Supreme Court justices University, college faculties Prophets Scholars | Creative artists Performers, great Teachers, university equivalent Museum curators |
| 2 | Applied scientists Landowners and operators, large Landscape architects | Scientists, semi-independent Nurses Pharmacists Veterinarians | Editors Teachers, high school and elementary | Athletes Art critics Designers Music arrangers |
| 3 | County agents Farm owners Forest rangers Fish, game wardens | Technicians, medical, X-ray, museum Weather observers Chiropractors | Justices of the peace Radio announcers Reporters Librarians | Ad writers Designers Interior decorators Showmen |
| 4 | Laboratory testers, dairy products, etc. Miners Oil well drillers | Technical assistants | Law clerks | Advertising artists Decorators window, etc. Photographers Race car drivers |
| 5 | Gardeners Farm tenants Teamsters, cow-punchers Miner's helpers | Veterinary hospital attendants | | Illustrators, greeting cards Showcard writers Stagehands |
| 6 | Dairy hands Farm laborers Lumberjacks | Nontechnical helpers in scientific organization | | |

TABLE A–3 (*Continued*)

We have taken Roe's* occupations in group listings and have classified them in terms of one additional dimension. We have designated the degree to which an occupation is preponderantly manual or ideational in character, and have indicated this by placing an (M), (I), or (O), before each occupational title.

Definitions of these three letters follow:

(M) signifies that performance of the occupation requires a relatively great amount of manual or physical dexterity.

(I) signifies that performance of the occupation is more concerned with non-manual or thought activity.

(O) signifies that the occupation requires both manipulative and ideational activity, and is not clearly characterized by either.

---

\* Roe, Anne. The psychology of occupations. New York: Wiley, 1956. P. 151.

TABLE A–3 (*Continued*)

OCCUPATIONS IN GROUP I: SERVICE[b]

### Level 1

(I) Personal therapists        (I) Social work supervisors

### Level 2

(O)FBI agents        (I) Probation, truant officers        (M) Occupational therapists
                          (with special training)          (I) Social workers
                                                           (I) Vocational, educational
                                                               counselors

### Level 3

(O)Armed forces, rank          (M)Conductors, railroad        (O)Sheriffs
    equivalent to sergeant     (I) Detectives                 (M) Welfare workers,
(I) Astrologists               (I) Employment interviewers        municipal
(I) City inspectors            (I) Police sergeants           (I) YMCA, YWCA officials

### Level 4

(M) Barbers                    (I) Headwaiters                (I) Religious workers
(M) Bartenders                 (M) Lifeguards                 (I) State Policemen
(M) Chefs                      (M) Light housekeepers         (I) Stewards
(M) Conductors, street car     (M) Practical nurses
(M) Hairdressers               (M) Policemen

### Level 5

(M) Bellhops                   (M) Janitors                   (M) Servants, household
(M) Chauffeurs                 (I) Palm-readers               (M) Taxi drivers
(M)Cooks, average              (M) Privates, armed forces     (M)Train porters
(M)Firemen, city               (M) Prison guards              (O) Ushers
(M) General houseworkers       (M) Psychiatric attendants     (M) Waiters

### Level 6

(M) Bootblacks                 (M) Elevator operators         (M) Street sweepers
(M) Chambermaids               (M) Garbage collectors         (M) Watchmen
(M) Charwomen                  (M) Hospital attendants

TABLE A–3 (*Continued*)

## OCCUPATIONS IN GROUP II: BUSINESS CONTACT[c]

### Level 1

(I) Promotors

### Level 2

(I) Promoters
(I) Public relations counselors

### Level 3

(I) Retail and wholesale dealers
(I) Salesmen: auto, bond, insurance,
    real estate
(I) Confidence men

### Level 4

(I) Auctioneers
(I) Buyers (DOT I)
(O) House canvassers and agents
(I) Interviewers, polls

### Level 5

(M) Peddlers

## OCCUPATIONS IN GROUP III: ORGANIZATION[d]

### Level 1

(I) High government officials    (I) Industrial tycoons    (I) International bankers,
    (President, Cabinet,     (I) Top executives, all      merchants
    members, etc.)           organizations

### Level 2

(I) Bankers                (I) Executives, average    (I) Officers, ship and armed
(I) Brokers                (I) Personnel managers      services, administrative
(I) Buyers (large business)    (I) Politicians           (I) Union officials
(I) Certified public         (I) Public officials
    accountants

TABLE A–3 (*Continued*)

OCCUPATIONS IN GROUP III: ORGANIZATION (Continued)

### Level 3

(I) Accountants
(I) Appraisers
(I) Bank tellers
(I) Buyers (small business)
(I) Credit managers
(M) Draftsmen

(I) Employment managers
(I) Executives, minor
(I) Hotel managers
(I) Manufacturers, small
(O) Owners, catering,
    drycleaning, etc.

(I) Postmasters
(I) Private secretaries
(I) Retail, wholesale,
    dealers and owners
(I) Salesmen: specialty,
    technical
(I) Statisticians

### Level 4

(I) Agents, freight
(I) Bookkeepers
(I) Cashiers
(I) Clerk, correspondence,
    credit, express, mail,
    railroad, etc.
(I) Compilers

(I) Dispatchers
(I) Floorwalkers
(I) Foremen, warehouse
(O) Inspectors, telephone
    and telegraph

(I) Sales clerks
(I) Station agents
(I) Stenographers
(O) Inspectors, street car,
    railroad

### Level 5

(I) File clerks
(M) Multigraph operators

(I) Notaries
(M) Runners

(I) Stock clerks
(M) Typists

### Level 6

(M) Messenger boys

## OCCUPATIONS IN GROUP IV: TECHNOLOGY[e]

### Level 1

(I) Applied scientists,
    consulting, chief
(I) Commanders, large ship

(I) Designers, auto, tools, etc.
(I) Engineers, consulting, chief:
    architectural, civil,
    mechanical, etc.

(I) Inventive geniuses

### Level 2

(I) Applied scientists,
    geological, chemical, etc.
(I) Engineers, architectural,
    civil, etc.

(I) Factory managers (requiring
    technical knowledge)

(I) Ship and armed services
    officers, technical

TABLE A–3 (*Continued*)

OCCUPATIONS IN GROUP IV:  TECHNOLOGY (Continued)

### Level 3

(M) Aviators
　　Contractors, building
　　　carpentry, plumbing
(M) Draftsmen

(I) Engineers, marine, chief
(I) Factory foremen (DOT I)
(I) Radio operators

(I) Small factory managers

### Level 4

(M) Blacksmiths
(M) Bookbinders
(M) Brakemen
(M) Bricklayers
(M) Cabinet makers
(M) Carpenters
(M) Electricians
(M) Electrotypers
(M) Engineers, locomotive,
　　　stationery
(M) Engravers
(M) Factory foremen (DOTII)
(M) Glass-blowers
(M) Gunsmiths
(M) Inspectors, factory

(M) Jewelers
(M) Linotypers
(M) Lithographers
(M) Machinists
(M) Mechanics, plane, auto
(M) Millers, grain
(M) Millwrights
(M) Motormen, electric railroad
(M) Movie operators
(M) Ornamental ironworkers
(M) Painters, house, sign, etc.
(M) Paperhangers
(M) Patternmakers
(M) Photoengravers
(M) Piano tuners

(M) Plasterers
(M) Plumbers
(M) Printers
(M) Repairmen, most varieties
(M) Steeplejacks
(M) Stonemasons
(M) Structural steel workers
(M) Tailors
(M) Telegraph operators
(M) Tinsmiths
(M) Toolmakers
(M) Typesetters, compositors
(M) Upholsterers
(M) Wood-carvers

### Level 5

(M) Annealers
(M) Auto assembly workers
(M) Bakers
(M) Boilermakers
(M) Bulldozer operators
(M) Butchers
(M) Car motormen
(M) Cobblers
(M) Concrete workers
(M) Coopers
(M) Deliverymen

(M) Dry-cleaner hands
(M) Dyers, factory
(M) Finishers
(M) Lathe operators,
　　　automatic
(M) Laundry workers
(M) Leather workers
(M) Linemen, telephone and
　　　telegraph
(M) Motor deliverymen
(M) Riveters
(M) Roofers

(M) Sawmill workers
(M) Sheetmetal workers
(M) Smelter workers
(M) Stonecutters, machine
(M) Switchmen
(M) Tire repairmen
(M) Truckdrivers
(M) Vulcanizers
(M) Waterworks tenders
(M) Wheelwrights

### Level 6

(M) Foundrymen
(M) Helpers, carpenter,
　　　plumber, etc.
(M) Laborers, construction,
　　　process, etc.

(M) Longshoremen
(M) Munitions handlers
(M) Packers
(M) Section hands

(M) Trackmen
(M) Wrappers
(M) Yardmen

TABLE A–3 (*Continued*)

## OCCUPATIONS IN GROUP V: OUTDOOR[f]

### Level 1

(I) Consulting specialists

### Level 2

| | | |
|---|---|---|
| (I) Applied scientists, agronomists, etc. | (I) Landowners and operators, large | (I) Range management specialists |
| (I) Horticulturists | (I) Landscape architects | (I) Wildlife specialists |

### Level 3

| | | |
|---|---|---|
| (M) Apiarists | (M) Floriculturists | (M) Poultrymen |
| (I) County agents | (M) Forest rangers | (M) Tree surgeons |
| (M) Farmers, individual owner | (M) Lumber camp managers | (M) Truckgardeners |
| (M) Fish culturists | (M) Nurserymen (owner) | (M) Surveyors |

### Level 4

| | | |
|---|---|---|
| (M) Fishermen (owner) | (M) Landscape gardeners | (M) Ore graders |
| (M) Laboratory testers (dairy products, etc.) | (M) Miners | (M) Shaftmen |
| | (M) Oil well drillers | |

### Level 5

| | | |
|---|---|---|
| (M) Farm tenants | (M) Irrigators | (M) Oil pumpers |
| (M) Cowpunchers | (M) Lumber inspectors | (M) Teamsters |
| (M) Crusher operators | (M) Miner helpers | (M) Trappers |
| (M) Gardeners | (M) Nursery employees | (M) Tractor drivers |
| (M) Hostlers | | |

### Level 6

| | | |
|---|---|---|
| (M) Dairy hands | (M) Farm laborers | (M) Hoboes |
| (M) Ditch hands | (M) Fishermen | (M) Lumberjacks |

## OCCUPATIONS IN GROUP VI: THE SCIENCES[g]

### Level 1

| | |
|---|---|
| (I) Independent research scientists, all fields | (I) Museum curators |
| (I) Mathematicians | (I) University and college faculties in science |
| (I) Medical specialists, all types | |

TABLE A–3 (*Continued*)

OCCUPATIONS IN GROUP VI:  THE SCIENCES (Continued)

Level 2

(M) Dentists
( M) Nurses
(I) Pharmacists

(I) Scientists, semi–independent
(M) Veterinarians

Level 3

(M) Chiropodists
(M) Chiropractors
(M) Laboratory technicians (trained)

(M) Medical technicians
( I ) Weather observers
(M) X–ray technicians

Level 4

(M) Embalmers

(M) Technical assistants

Level 5

(M) Veterinary hospital attendants

OCCUPATIONS IN GROUP VII: GENERAL CULTURAL[h]

Level 1

(I) Editors (e.g., N.Y. Times)
(I) Educational administrators
(I) Clergymen, high ranking
(I) Judges, federal
(I) Justices, U.S. Supreme Court

(I) Lawyers, high ranking
(I) Prophets
(I) Scholars (creative interpretation)
(I) University and college faculties

Level 2

(I) Clergymen, priests, etc.
(I) Columnists
(I) Educational administrators

(I) Editors, average
(I) News commentators
(I) Teachers, high school and elementary

Level 3

(I) Judges, municipal
(I) Justices of the peace
(I) Law clerks

(I) Librarians
(I) Radio announcers
(I) Repo: ters

TABLE A–3 (*Continued*)

OCCUPATIONS IN GROUP VIII: ARTS AND ENTERTAINMENT[i]

Level 1

Creative artists:
(M) painters
(M) sculptors
(I) writers
(I) composers
(I) choreographers
(M) Museum curators, fine arts

Performers, at highest levels:
(M) actors
(M) singers
(M) dancers
(M) concert artists
(M) conductors
(I) directors
(M) athletic champions
(I) Teachers, at highest levels

Level 2

(M) Athletes, professional
(M) Athletic coaches
(I) Architects
(I) Art critics
(M) Circus performers

(I) Designers, stage, jewelry
(I) Music arrangers, orchestral
(I) Music critics
(M) Performers, average
(I) Teachers, lower levels

Level 3

(I) Advertising writers
(I) Designers, clothes, millinery,
      textiles, tapestries, rugs, etc.
(I) Interior decorators
(M) Magicians

(I) Music arrangers, popular
(I) Showmen
(M) Stage designers, lower level
(M) Vaudeville performers

Level 4

(I) Advertising artists
(M) Decorators, window drapers
(M) Illustrators

(M) Monument makers
(I) Photographers
(M) Racing car drivers

Level 5

(M) Animator artists
(M) Illustrators, greeting cards
(M) Photographic technicians

(M) Show card writers, letter cards
(M) Stagehands

[a] Roe, Anne. The psychology of occupations. New York: Wiley, 1956, P. 51.   [b] *Ibid.*, P. 170.
[c] *Ibid.*, P. 178.   [d] *Ibid.*, P. 183.   [e] *Ibid.*, Pp. 197–198.   [f] *Ibid.*, P. 211.   [g] *Ibid.*, P. 213.   [h] *Ibid.*,
P. 226.   [i] *Ibid.*, P. 236.

TABLE A–4

TYPES OF ORGANIZATIONS

FOR MEN

A. Contributions to Community or Institutions

### 1. Associations

| | |
|---|---|
| Committee on Alcoholism | Red Cross |
| Mental Health | Muscular Dystrophy |
| Retardation | Health |
| Heart | |

### 2. Service Organizations

| | |
|---|---|
| YMCA | Power Squadron (teaching safety at sea) |
| Babe Ruth League (boy's baseball) | Church charitable associations (e.g., |
| Boy Scouts | St. Vincent DePaul) |
| Boy's club | |

### 3. Civic-Oriented Groups

| | |
|---|---|
| Citizens Plan E | Town Water District |
| Community Chest | Civil Defense |
| Exchange Club | Auxiliary Fire Department |
| Community (neighborhood) improvement | Republican Club |

### 4. Fraternal-Civic

| | |
|---|---|
| Kiwanis | Rotary |

### 5. Service to Non-Sectarian Institutions

| | |
|---|---|
| Alumni association (other than social) | Museum board or committee |

### 6. Service to Religious Institutions

| | |
|---|---|
| Council of Churches | Church-supporting group (e.g., Delta Beta Gamma, Temple Brotherhood, Roger Williams Men's Club) |

TABLE A–4 (*Continued*)

B. Professional, Business Associations and Unions

### 1. Professional Societies

Dental                              Mathematicians
Orthodontists                       Auditors
Teachers                            Advertising club
Personnel directors                 Photographers
Accountants

### 2. Non-Professional Associations

Lifeguard                           Trade unions
Letter Carriers                     Army (Navy) Reserves
YMCA Secretaries                    Fire wardens
Machinists

### 3. Business Men's Associations

Chamber of Commerce                 Traffic club
Warehousemen

C. Fraternal-Social

### 1. Fraternal or Ethnic

Masons                              Knights of Columbus
Grange                              Althea Grotto
Odd Fellows                         Ethnic (Polish, Lithuanian, Sons of
Elks                                    Italy)

### 2. Social

Couple's club                       Frohsinn Club
(YMCA) Co-wed                       Bohemian Club
Gay Nineties                        Fraternity
Country club

### 3. Service, Employment or Religious-Affiliated Organizations

Religious (Holy Name)               Employment or academic-affiliated
Veterans (American Legion,              (Foreman's club, University club)
    National Guard, Third Army
    Division)

TABLE A–4 (*Continued*)

## 4. Activity-Oriented

Rowing club                                    Explorer Scouts
Hunting

## D. Educational, Cultural, Musical

Players' guild                                 Education groups (engineering
Musical groups (choir, chorus,                    education)
   orchestra)                                  Scientific hobbies (amateur radio club)
Discussion groups (economics club,
   men's forum)

## TYPES OF ORGANIZATIONS

## FOR WOMEN

## A. Contributions to Community or Institutions

### 1. Associations

Mental Health                                  Guild of St. Agnes (work with
Retardation                                       underprivileged children)

### 2. Service Organizations

Welcome guild                                  Red Cross
Girl Scouts                                    Service Men's club
Camp Fire Girls                                Girl's club
Women's club (scholarships)                    Newcomer's club
YWCA (camp committee)

### 3. Civic-Oriented Groups

League of Women Voters                         Community Fund Campaign
Council of Jewish Women (social                Republican Club
   and legislative action in Israel)

### 4. Fraternal-Civic

Junior League

TABLE A–4 *(Continued)*

5. Service to Non–Sectarian
Institutions

College alumnae                          PTA (Mother's Club for school)
Hospital auxiliary                       Hadassah (medical service in Israel)
Scientific foundation auxiliary          Educational sororities (Pi Lambda Theta,
                                             Delta Kappa Gamma)

6. Service to Religious
Institutions

Church circle or guild                   Church board of education
Missionary or religious education        Church youth group

B. Professional, Business Associations and Unions

American Association of University       Unions
    Women (AAUW)

C. Fraternal–Social

1. Fraternal or Ethnic

Lodges                                   Grange
D.A.R.                                   Eastern Star
Ethnic clubs (Lithuanian,
    Portuguese)

2. Social

Couples                                  Gay Nineties
Women's club                             Card playing

3. Service, Employment, or Religious–Affiliated
Organizations

Religious (Altar Guild, Rosary           Employment–affiliated (college
    Sodality, Dorcas Society,                faculty wives, dental auxiliary)
    Catholic Daughters of America
    Yeshiva Aihe Tominium
    Catholic youth club

4. Activity–Oriented

Ski club

TABLE A–4 (*Continued*)

D.  Educational, Cultural, Musical

Reading club  
Educational or study groups  
Literary club  
Art museum, Craft center  

Musical groups (chorus, choir,  
Oratorio Society)  
Home planners  
Dramatic club

TABLE A–5

REVISED TABLE FOR SOCIAL COMPETENCE DERIVED SCALES

(Organizational Activity and Use of Leisure Time)


A subject's score on a particular scale is equal to the total sum of his scores in the various categories of leisure-time activities (items preceded by Roman numerals) relevant to each scale.

The latter scores are arrived at by scoring "1" for each activity in which the individual participates within each category, and finding the sums of these.

TABLE A–5 (*Continued*)

ACTIVITY LEVEL

I. Participation in sports:

1. Doing:

archery
auto racing
bicycling
boating
bowling
boxing
fishing
hiking
horse racing
horseback riding
hunting
ice skating
motorcycle riding

mountain climbing
road running
roller skating
rowing
skiing
skin diving
sledding
swimming
tobogganing
track
water skiing
weight lifting
wrestling

2. Participating:

baseball
basketball
football
golf

hockey
ping pong
tennis

CONSTRUCTIVENESS

I. Building:

1. Creating:

boats, planes, railroads
model and stock cars

radio, T.V., and electrical
    equipment
tables, shelves, cabinets

II. Reading:

biographies
handyman magazines
magazines
newspapers
nonfiction

philosophy and psychology
poetry
scientific magazines
textbooks

TABLE A–5 (*Continued*)

CONSTRUCTIVENESS (contd)

III.  Miscellaneous:

1.  Doing:

bird watching
car repairs
carving
floral arrangements
ham radio

printing by hand
training dogs
visiting museums
remodel and/or refinish
    antique furniture

2.  Collecting:

antiques
antique guns
coins
plants

stamps
art
photographs
sketches

3.  Creating:

designing clothes
engraving
make (own) fishing tackle

painting
  a) oil painting
  b) number painting
writing (poetry, novels,
    plays, etc.)

4.  Leading:

teaching piano

teaching own children (piano,
    school work)

5.  Participating: (in
      various organizations)

Boy Scouts, YMCA,
  women's clubs, etc.

6.  Listening:

tapes

symphonies

TABLE A–5 (*Continued*)

CONSTRUCTIVENESS (contd)

IV.  Home Maintenance:

    1.  Doing:

| | |
|---|---|
| electrical maintenance | plant raising |
| gardening | tool sharpening |
| handyman at home | carpentry |

V.  Household:

    1.  Doing:

| | |
|---|---|
| baking | cooking |

    2.  Creating:

| | |
|---|---|
| basket weaving | rug braiding |
| dressmaking | sewing, crocheting |
| embroidery | tatting |
| knitting | |

OUTWARD ORIENTATION

I.  Building:

    1.  Creating:

| | |
|---|---|
| radio, T.V., and<br>  electrical equipment | science apparatus |

II.  Home Maintenance:

    1.  Doing:

| | |
|---|---|
| car repairs | handyman at home |
| electrical maintenance | tool sharpening |
| furniture refinishing | yard work |
| gardening | |

TABLE A–5 (*Continued*)

OUTWARD ORIENTATION (contd)

III.  Household:

1.  Doing:

baking                                        cooking

2.  Creating:

designing clothes                             rug braiding
dressmaking                                   sewing, crocheting
embroidery                                    tatting
knitting

IV.  Entertainment:

1.  Doing:

dancing                                       visiting
dating                                           a) children
picnicking                                       b) neighbors
                                                 c) relatives

2.  Participating:

folk and/or group singing                     mothers' clubs
hanging around and/or drinking                union outings
  with friends                                parties

V.  Going to sports:

1.  Attending:

archery                                       horse races
baseball games                                motorcycle races
basketball games                              ping pong games
auto races                                    road running meets
boxing matches                                roller skating derby
drag races                                    sport car rallies
football games                                tennis match
golf tournaments                              track meet
hockey games                                  wrestling match

TABLE A–5 (*Continued*)

OUTWARD ORIENTATION (contd)

VI. Participation in sports:

1. Doing:

| | |
|---|---|
| archery | dog races |
| auto races | fishing (deep sea, etc.) |
| bicycling | hiking |
| boating | horse races |
| bowling | horseback riding |
| boxing | ice skating |
| camping | motorcycle riding and/or races |

2. Participating:

| | |
|---|---|
| baseball | swimming |
| basketball | target practices |
| football | tennis |
| golf | tobogganing |
| hockey | track |
| mountain climbing | trapping |
| ping pong | walking |
| road running | water skiing |
| roller skating | weight lifting |
| rowing | wrestling |
| skiing | |

VII. Reading:

| | |
|---|---|
| magazines | nonfiction |
| newspapers | |

INWARD ORIENTATION

I. Watching TV

II. Listening to radio

III. Going to movies

TABLE A–5 (*Continued*)

<u>INWARD ORIENTATION</u> (contd)

IV.  <u>Indoor games:</u>

          1.  <u>Playing:</u>

| | |
|---|---|
| bingo | checkers |
| card games | chess |
| a) bridge | pool |
| b) canasta | |
| c) mahjong | |
| d) solitaire | |
| e) whist | |

          2.  <u>Doing:</u>

| | |
|---|---|
| crossword puzzles | word games |

V.  <u>Reading:</u>

| | |
|---|---|
| beauty magazines | mystery and crime books |
| comics | sports and adventure magazines |
| love stories | western novels |
| movie magazines | |

<u>SOCIAL PARTICIPATION</u>

I.  <u>Indoor games:</u>

          1.  <u>Playing:</u>

| | |
|---|---|
| card games | checkers |
| a) bridge | chess |
| b) canasta | pingpong |
| c) mahjong | pool |
| d) whist | |

II.  <u>Entertainment:</u>

          1.  <u>Doing:</u>

| | |
|---|---|
| dancing | dating |

TABLE A–5 (*Continued*)

SOCIAL PARTICIPATION (contd)

II. Entertainment (contd):

    2. Participating:

dramatics                                mothers' clubs
folk and/or group singing                parties
amateur band                             picnics
hanging around and/or
   drinking with friends

    3. Attending:

square dances                            union outings

III. Going to sports:

    1. Attending:

airplane shows                           golf tournaments
archery                                  hockey games
baseball games                           horse races
basketball games                         motorcycle races
auto races                               road running meets
boxing matches                           roller skating derby
cat shows                                sport car rallies
dog shows                                tennis match
drag races                               track meet
football games                           wrestling match

SEX IDENTIFICATION

(Degree of positive identification with own sex)

Male

I. Miscellaneous:

    1. Participating: (in
       men's organizations)

YMCA                                     Professional societies (AMA, etc.)
Babe Ruth League                         Trade unions
Boy Scouts                               Army (Navy) Reserves
Kiwanis                                  Chamber of Commerce
Rotary                                   Masons

TABLE A–5 (*Continued*)

SEX   IDENTIFICATION (contd)

2.  Collecting:

antique guns                          stamps
coins                                 sketches
photographs

3.  Creating:

making fishing tackle                 painting and/or drawing
photography                           writing (novels, plays, etc.)

4.  Doing:

bird watching                         sightseeing
correspondence (pen                   training dogs
  pals, etc.)                         travel
ham radio

II.  Home Maintenance:

1.  Doing:

car repairs                           tool sharpening
carpentry                             handy man at home
electrical maintenance

III.  Going to sports events:

1.  Attending:

airplane shows                        horse races
baseball games                        motorcycle races
basketball games                      road running meets
auto races                            sport car rallies
boxing matches                        track meet
drag races                            wrestling match
football games

TABLE A–5 (*Continued*)

SEX  IDENTIFICATION (contd)

Female

I.  Miscellaneous:

    1.  Participating: (in
       women's organizations)

| | |
|---|---|
| Welcome Guild | Eastern Star |
| Girl Scouts | Religious groups (Altar Guild, |
| Women's Clubs |    Catholic Daughters of |
| YWCA |    America, etc.) |
| League of Women Voters | American Association of |
| Hadassah |    University Women |
| | Reading Clubs |

    2.  Collecting:

| | |
|---|---|
| antiques | souvenirs |
| knickknacks | art |
| plants | shells |

    3.  Attending:

| | |
|---|---|
| cat shows | flower shows |

    4.  Creating:

| | |
|---|---|
| ceramics | writing poetry |
| floral arrangements | number painting |
| furniture refinishing | |

    5.  Doing:

| | |
|---|---|
| plant raising | sightseeing |
| correspondence | travel |

    6.  Leading:

| | |
|---|---|
| teaching piano | teaching own children |

TABLE A–5 (*Continued*)

<u>SEX IDENTIFICATION</u> (contd)

II. <u>Home Maintenance:</u>

        1. <u>Doing:</u>

gardening                              yard work

III. <u>Household:</u>

        1. <u>Creating:</u>

baking                            embroidery
basket weaving                knitting
cooking                         rug braiding
designing clothes            sewing, crocheting
dressmaking                   tatting

IV. <u>Entertainment:</u>

        1. <u>Doing:</u>

ballet                              visiting
modern dance                  a) children
                                      b) museums
                                      c) neighbors
                                      d) relatives

        2. <u>Participating:</u>

dramatics                          mothers' clubs

TABLE A–6

SOCIAL COMPETENCE INTERVIEW

**SCORING FORM**

Date _____

Subject's Name _____    Subject's No. _____

| Interview Item No. | Item Description | Score |
|---|---|---|
| 1. — | Intelligence | 1. _____ |
| 2. 11 | Education | 2. _____ |
| 3. Derived Scale IA | Job Type (Warner) | 3. _____ |
| 4. Derived Scale IB | Job Level (Warner) | 4. _____ |
| 5. Derived Scale IC | Job Type (Roe) | 5. _____ |
| 6. Derived Scale ID | Job Level (Roe) | 6. _____ |
| 7. Derived Scale IA | Father's Job Type (Warner) | 7. _____ |
| 8. Derived Scale IB | Father's Job Level (Warner) | 8. _____ |
| 9. Derived Scale IC | Father's Job Type (Roe) | 9. _____ |
| 10. Derived Scale ID | Father's Job Level (Roe) | 10. _____ |
| 11. 13 | Employment Regularity | 11. _____ |
| 12. 13a | Number of Employers | 12. _____ |
| 13. 12 | Maximum No. People Supervised | 13. _____ |
| 14. 18a | Number of Organizations | 14. _____ |
| 15. 18b | Number of Meetings/Month | 15. _____ |
| 16. - | Number of Offices Held | 16. _____ |
| 17. - | Number of Community Associations | 17. _____ |
| 18. - | No. Professional/Business Assns. & Unions | 18. _____ |
| 19. - | No. Fraternal or Social Associations | 19. _____ |
| 20. - | No. Educational, Cultural, Musical Assns. | 20. _____ |

TABLE A–6 (*Continued*)

| | Interview Item No. | Item Description | Score |
|---|---|---|---|
| 21. | — | Number Kinds of Associations | 21. _____ |
| 22. | 21a | Present Marital Status | 22. _____ |
| 23. | 21b | Present Heterosexual Activity | 23. _____ |
| 24. | 21c | Psychosexual History | 24. _____ |
| 25. | 5 | Age | 25. _____ |
| 26. | 7 | Sex | 26. _____ |
| 27. | 20 | Ever Voted? | 27. _____ |
| 28. | 20a | Last Election? | 28. _____ |
| 29. | 21d (1) | Age at First Marriage | 29. _____ |
| 30. | 21d (2) | Spouse's Age at First Marriage | 30. _____ |
| 31. | 21d (3) | Age at 2nd Marriage | 31. _____ |
| 32. | 21d (4) | Spouse's Age at 2nd Marriage | 32. _____ |
| 33. | 21e | Number of Children | 33. _____ |
| 34. | 23 | Type of Residence | 34. _____ |
| 35. | 22a | Religion | 35. _____ |
| 36. | 22b | Spouse's Religion | 36. _____ |
| 37. | 24 | Number of Siblings | 37. _____ |
| 38. | 24 | Sibling Rank | 38. _____ |
| 39. | 24 | Number of Brothers | 39. _____ |
| 40. | 24 | Number of Sisters | 40. _____ |
| 41. | 25a | Country of Birth | 41. _____ |
| 42. | 25b | Mother's Country of Birth | 42. _____ |

TABLE A–6 (*Continued*)

| | Interview Item No. | Item Description | Score |
|---|---|---|---|
| 43. | 25c | Father's Country of Birth | 43. _____ |
| 44. | 26a | Mother's Age at Subject's Birth | 44. _____ |
| 45. | 26b | Father's Age at Subject's Birth | 45. _____ |
| 46. | Derived Scale IIA | Activity Level | 46. _____ |
| 47. | Derived Scale IIB | Constructiveness | 47. _____ |
| 48. | Derived Scale IIC | Outward Orientation | 48. _____ |
| 49. | Derived Scale IID | Inward Orientation | 49. _____ |
| 50. | Derived Scale IIE | Social Participation | 50. _____ |
| 51. | Derived Scale IIF | Sex Identification | 51. _____ |

# AUTHOR INDEX

Numbers in parentheses are reference numbers and indicate that an author's work is mentioned although his name is not cited in the text. Numbers in italics refer to the page on which the complete reference is listed.

## A

# SUBJECT INDEX